The Camargue Area 111

Getting Your Bearings ✦ **In Three Days**
✦ **Don't Miss** ✦ The Camargue ✦ Arles
✦ Nîmes and the Pont du Guard ✦ Stes-Maries-de-la-Mer
At Your Leisure ✦ 5 more places to explore
Where to... ✦ Stay ✦ Eat and Drink ✦ Shop ✦ Be Entertained

The Vaucluse 135

Getting Your Bearings ✦ **In Four Days**
✦ **Don't Miss** ✦ Avignon ✦ Châteauneuf-du-Pape ✦ Orange
✦ Vaison-la-Romaine ✦ Gordes and the Abbaye de Sénanque
✦ The Lubéron
At Your Leisure ✦ 5 more places to explore
Where to... ✦ Stay ✦ Eat and Drink ✦ Shop ✦ Be Entertained

Walks and Tours 165

✦ The Heart of Provence
✦ The Camargue
✦ Vaison-la-Romaine
✦ Gorges du Verdon

Practicalities 175

✦ Before You Go ✦ When To Go
✦ When You Are There
✦ Useful Words and Phrases

Atlas 183

Streetplans 195

Index 187

Compiled by Pam Stagg
Magazine section and contributions by Teresa Fisher

Page layout by Liz Baldin at Bookwork Creative Associates Ltd.
Copy edited by Ann F Stonehouse
Verified by David Halford, Laurence Phillips
Indexed by Marie Lorimer

Published by AA Publishing, a trading name of Automobile Association Developments Limited, whose registered office is Fanum House, Basing View, Basingstoke, Hampshire, RG21 4EA. Registered number 1878835.

ISBN-10: 0-7495-4997-1
ISBN-13: 978-0-7495-4997-8

The contents of this publication are believed correct at the time of printing. Nevertheless, AA Publishing accepts no responsibility for errors, omissions or changes in the details given, or for the consequences of readers' reliance on this information. This does not affect your statutory rights. Assessments of the attractions, hotels and restaurants are based upon the authors' own experiences and contain subjective opinions that may not reflect the publisher's opinion or a reader's experience. We have tried to ensure accuracy, but things do change, so please let us know if you have any comments or corrections.

A CIP catalogue record for this book is available from the British Library.

Colour separation by Keenes, Andover
Printed and bound in China by Leo Paper Products

Find out more about AA Publishing and the wide range of services the AA provides by visiting our website at www.theAA.com/travel

A02724

PROVENCE

SPIRAL GUIDE

AA Publishing

Contents

the magazine 5
✦ Provençal culture ✦ Painters in Provence
✦ Scenic Provence ✦ The Local Tipple
✦ At Home in Provence ✦ How to Play Pétanque
✦ Gourmet Provence ✦ Some of the Best...

Finding Your Feet 23
✦ First Two Hours ✦ Getting Around
✦ Accommodation ✦ Food and Drink
✦ Shopping ✦ Entertainment

The Alpes-Maritimes 35
Getting Your Bearings ✦ **In Three Days**
✦ **Don't Miss** ✦ Nice ✦ The Corniches ✦ Monaco
✦ Fondation Maeght ✦ Parc National du Mercantour
At Your Leisure ✦ 8 more places to explore
Where to... ✦ Stay ✦ Eat and Drink ✦ Shop ✦ Be Entertained

The Var and Haute-Provence 63
Getting Your Bearings ✦ **In Three Days**
✦ **Don't Miss** ✦ St-Tropez ✦ Hyères and the Îles d'Hyères
✦ Gorges du Verdon ✦ Corniche de l'Esterel
At Your Leisure ✦ 7 more places to explore
Where to... ✦ Stay ✦ Eat and Drink ✦ Shop ✦ Be Entertained

The Marseille Area 89
Getting Your Bearings ✦ **In Two Days**
✦ **Don't Miss** ✦ Marseille ✦ The Calanques
✦ Montagne Ste-Victoire ✦ Aix-en-Provence
At Your Leisure ✦ 8 more places to explore
Where to... ✦ Stay ✦ Eat and Drink ✦ Shop ✦ Be Entertained

the magazine

Provençal Culture

Provence is rich in tradition. Not only noted for its landscapes and its climate, its cuisine and its perfumes, it is also celebrated for its very own regional language, literature, customs and costumes.

France was once divided linguistically into the *Langue d'Oil*, spoken in the north, and the *Langue d'Oc* (or Provençal), spoken in the south. This Latin-based language flourished during the Middle Ages, as this was the home of the troubadours who sang of courtly love in Provençal. The language gradually evolved and in 1854 a literary society called the *Félibrige*, founded by local poet Frédéric Mistral, was formed to preserve the language and the identity of Provençal customs and traditions – a group which still exist today. You are most likely to hear Provençal spoken in the

Above: Shopping at the market in Aix-en-Provence

Page 5: Fragrant lavender fields scent the air in Provence

Right: *Jean de Florette*, starring Daniel Auteuil and Yves Montand

Bouches-du-Rhône *département*, around Arles, Glanum and Baux, with regional variants (Monégasque, Mentonnais and Nissart) in Monaco, Menton and Nice.

Provenco?”

Provence has also made a significant contribution to French literature, through such local luminaries as Marcel Pagnol, Alphonse Daudet, Henri Bosco, Jean Giono and Frédéric Mistral, whose best-known work, the epic poem *Mirèio*, written in Provençal, won him the Nobel Prize for Literature in 1904. Pagnol is best known to English speakers following the successful films of his novels *Jean de Florette* and *Manon des Sources*. Admirers of his work can visit Manon's fountain and Pagnol's grave by following clearly signed tours of the countryside surrounding his home town, Aubagne. Jean Giono is the most popular Provençal author in France: his former home in Manosque, where he wrote *Horseman on the Roof*, can be visited. In Aubagne, the Little World of Marcel Pagnol (open Fridays, by appointment) is a re-creation

Above: Franco Zeffirelli's handprints at Cannes

of settings and characters in his works, produced by local *santon* makers. In Fontvieille, you can visit the mill in which Daudet wrote *Les Lettres de mon Moulin* (tel: 04 90 54 60 78, summer only).

Customs and Costumes

Other aspects of Provençal life remain deep rooted in ancient regional rites and customs, especially during December, with its Christmas markets, *santon* fairs (➤ 105, 129), *pastorales* (theatrical representations of the nativity, sung and spoken in Provençal), folk dancing and *Noëls* (Provençal carols). Throughout the year, numerous villages host markets and arts and craft events, and traditional dress is often worn at such festivities.

The costumes of Arlesiénne women are most elaborate, with intricate lace overblouses, distinctive embroidered *fichus* (caps) and flamboyant jewellery. Brightly coloured Provençal prints feature strongly (➤ 16). Muséon Arlaten (➤ 121) in Arles – an ethnographic museum founded by Mistral in 1896 – has an impressive range of traditional clothing and jewellery, and the Costume Festival here (first weekend in July) is one of the region's most colourful affairs.

Musicians in traditional costume form part of a Provençal procession

21st-century Provençal

Provençal culture is making a comeback: certain regions insist on the daily use of the language; it is taught in schools, and it is now an option for the *Baccalauréat* (the French high school graduation exam). In Nice, the local television news is presented in Nissart (with French subtitles); street signs in the old town are written in dialect, and students study it at the university. Local culinary traditions remain alive and well, with such regional staples as bouillabaisse, tapenade and ratatouille as popular as ever on menus of modern Provençal chefs, and there is even a rekindled passion for Provençal bullfighting (*Cours Camarguais*) in Arles and the Camargue – a sport popular here since antiquity.

Even Provençal fashion makes its mark on the catwalks of the world, thanks to local designer, Christian Lacroix – born in Arles, under the star sign of Taurus, the symbol of the Camargue. His daring, boldly Mediterranean clothes are often inspired by the traditional Arlésian costumes.

Right: Renoir's *Terrace in Cagnes*

PAINTERS IN PROVENCE

Provence's rich palette of landscapes and almost magical, incandescent light has inspired artists for centuries, but never more so than in the late 19th and early 20th centuries, when painters, both native and adopted, were drawn to the region, with its stunning sun-drenched scenery.

Pierre Auguste Renoir (1841–1919)

"If you would like to see the most beautiful land in the world, here it is."

The crisp Provençal light fascinated Impressionist painter Renoir, who lived in Haut-de-Cagnes from 1903. In 1907, he fell in love with a small piece of land planted with 100-year-old olive trees, and built a large house there in which he remained until his death. In the Mediterranean sunshine, his work took on a new lease of life, and the warmth soothed his rheumatic joints. He would sit in his wheelchair at his easel beneath his olive trees for hours on end, his brushes strapped to his rheumatic fingers. His house (Musée Renoir, ➤ 56) has remained as it was at his death, and his palette and other mementoes have been preserved, together with several of his paintings, drawings, sculptures and bronzes.

Paul Cézanne (1839–1906)

"I spend every day in this landscape, with its beautiful shapes. Indeed I cannot imagine a more pleasant way or place to pass my time."

Cézanne spent much of his life in and around Aix-en-Provence, painting the limestone hills of the surrounding countryside. His "studio" was the great outdoors, and he was so fascinated by Mont Ste-Victoire (► 98–99) that he painted it over 65 times, from all angles and at all hours. Hardly surprising that some of his greatest canvases include *La Montagne Sainte-Victoire* and *Le Paysage d'Aix*. The city today honours its most famous citizen with a special circuit Cézanne, marked by bronze pavement plaques. It concludes at the studio (9 avenue Paul-Cézanne, tel: 04 42 21 06 53) where he spent the last seven years of his life – still exactly as he left it, with unfinished canvases, palettes and his old black hat.

THE NICE SCHOOL

Art has always thrived in Nice. Examples of today's Nice School of painters – a contemporary group of New Realists, including Raysse, César, Arman, Ben, Tinguely and Yves Klein – can be seen at MAMAC (► 43). Many of their works involve smashing, burning or distorting objects of everyday life as a spoof on society and the highbrow art world.

Vincent Van Gogh (1835–1890)

"In short, I think life here is a happier thing than in countless other spots on earth."

Dutch artist Vincent Van Gogh moved to Arles in 1888, believing "the entire future of the new art is in the Midi." Here he lived with Gauguin in the yellow house which he immortalised on canvas in *La Maison Jaune*. He was so inspired by the brilliant light and intensity of colour in the region that he created over 200 paintings in Arles (including his celebrated *Sunflowers* and *Café de Nuit*) and 150 in St-Rémy-de-Provence. It was here, too, that he cut off his ear and gave it to a surprised prostitute. The city was outraged, and greatly relieved when he voluntarily entered the local hospital in 1889. Ironically, no original Van Gogh paintings remain in Arles today.

Above: Look for the official logo of the local crafts' organisation

***La Montagne Sainte-Victoire*, Paul Cézanne**

Right: *Woman in a Landscape*, Renoir

AN A–Z OF ARTISTS INSPIRED BY PROVENCE

Arman	Cocteau	Léger	Signac
Ben	Derain	Maillol	Toulouse-Lautrec
Bonnard	Dufy	Matisse	Utrillo
Brea	Ernst	Picasso	Vasarely
Camoin	Fragonard	Raysse	Vuillard
Chagall	Klein	Renoir	

Henri Matisse (1869–1954)

"A picture must possess a real power to generate light and for a long time now I've been conscious of expressing myself through light, or rather, in light."

Matisse moved to Nice in 1917. Shortly before his death in 1954, he bequeathed his entire personal collection to the city – today on view at the Musée Matisse (➤ 43) – an ensemble of canvases spanning his working life, from early Old-Master copies through Impressionism and Fauvism to the bright colours and simple shapes of his maturity. This final phase of creativity reached its pinnacle with the Chapelle du Rosaire in Vence, with its compellingly simple interior and sublime stained-glass windows. Matisse considered this masterpiece his "ultimate goal, the culmination of an intense, sincere and difficult endeavour."

Pablo Ruiz y Picasso (1881–1973)

"Some painters transform the sun into a yellow spot, others transform a yellow spot into the sun."

Following the war years in Paris, Spanish artist and sculptor Picasso returned to his beloved Mediterranean in 1946, where the mayor of Antibes lent him a room in the Château Grimaldi to use as a studio. In gratitude, Picasso left his entire output of that period on permanent loan to the castle museum (Musée Picasso, ➤ 55) – 25 paintings, 44 drawings and 150 ceramics designed in the nearby village of Vallauris. Although Picasso only spent three months here, it was one of his most prolific periods. After the melancholy of war, he was hypnotised by the brilliant sunshine and the sparkling air and his work reflected the *joie de vivre* of the Mediterranean through bold and innovative use of line and sunny colours. From 1961 until his death, he lived in Mougins.

SCENIC PROVENCE

Nature has been abundantly kind to Provence, providing it with a rich diversity of landscape, from the untamed marshes of the Camargue and the beautiful beaches of the Riviera to the snow-clad mountains of the Alps. When it comes to exploring, most visitors are at a loss to know where to start. Here is an easy guide to some of its most unforgettable scenery.

It is the beaches of the Riviera that have made the region what it is today, and the main reason for many to visit the south of France. From the shimmering heat of the Côte d'Azur beaches, with their bars and restaurants, to the secret sun-baked coves of the Esterel shoreline, with its ragged red cliffs set against a bright green backdrop of spruce, pine and scrub, there are beaches to suit all tastes. The tortuous Corniche de l'Esterel (➤ 77) between St-Raphaël and Théoule-sur-Mer is still largely untouched by development and embraces some of the Riviera's most grandiose scenery.

Further west, the dazzling white cliffs of the Calanques (➤ 97) are a breathtaking sight, plunging into sparkling

THE COAST...

Relaxing on the beach at Cannes

turquoise fjord-like inlets – best seen by boat trip from Cassis (➤ 97) or on foot along a clearly signed cliff-top path. The Camargue (➤ 116–118) counts among Europe's most important wetlands – a wild, disparate region of brackish lagoons, flat rice fields, sand dunes and salty marshes famous for its white horses, black bulls, pink flamingos and exotic water birds.

With such diversity, some holidaymakers seldom leave the coast. Those who do explore the *arrière pays* (hinterland) are rewarded with lush hills, forests, gorges and mountains. Head off the beaten track and you will find tiny sun-kissed vineyards splashed with poppies, olive groves and scented stripes of lavender, stretching like mauve corduroy across the countryside – the very essence of Provence.

A special treat is to ramble through the scrubland habitats known as *garrigue*, where the air is fragrant with the wild *herbes de Provence* so prominent in regional cuisine – basil, rosemary, marjoram, tarragon and thyme. The white limestone crags of the Chaîne des Alpilles, with their sun-bleached *garrigue*, is a walker's paradise.

The verdant Parc Naturel Régional du Lubéron (➤ 152–154) is one of Provence's most visited areas: a protected park of cedar and pine countryside draped across small mountains between Cavaillon and Manosque, with quaint hill-top villages, almond and olive groves, vineyards and lavender fields. For even more dramatic scenery, head east to the Gorges du Verdon (➤ 74–76), the deepest, longest, wildest canyon in Europe and one of the great natural wonders of Provence.

Anywhere in this area, the snow-capped peaks of the Provençal Alps are never far away. The Parc National du Mercantour (➤ 52–53) is one of the country's most beautiful alpine reserves, spreading over into Italy, while the Parc Régional de Quayras is a wild, forgotten corner of Provence bordering Italy, its hillsides ignited by rare wild flowers summer.

...VERSUS THE COUNTRYSIDE

Below: The peaks of Val d'Allos in the Parc National du Mercantour

THE LOCAL TIPPLE

Provence is one of France's largest and oldest wine-growing regions, first introduced by the Greeks 2,600 years ago. The main wine-producing areas, on the rocky hillsides (*côtes*) in southwest Provence, use a number of traditional grape varieties including Grenache, Cinsault, Carignan, Syrah and Sémillon. The resulting wines range from the intense, heady reds and rich, buttery whites of the Rhône valley to light, fresh, fruity whites and rosés in the south.

THE ART OF DRINKING PASTIS

Ice cubes first, then pastis, then water...a hallowed trio for a great Provençal custom, the aperitif. Although consumed throughout France, this pale yellow anise-flavoured liqueur (with 40–45 per cent alcohol content) is typically associated with Provence, especially Marseille. It was created by the main absinthe producers Pernod and Ricard as a substitute drink when absinthe was originally banned in 1915. Usually served diluted (five parts water to one part pastis), it is an acquired taste, but undeniably evocative of the south of France. *Santé!*

A glass of pastis – the local aperitif

Popular *appellations* include Côtes-de-Provence, Côtes-du-Ventoux, Les Coteaux d'Aix-en-Provence and Les Coteaux-des-Baux. About 75 per cent of all Provençal wine is rosé. Indeed 50 per cent of all French rosés come from here, and the Bandol *appellation* is generally considered the best. Also of special note are the delicious, little-known wines of Bellet, a stamp-sized wine-pocket just behind Nice; the prestigious white wines of Cassis, the oldest appellation in Provence; and the world-class wines of Châteauneuf-du-Pape, Vacquerays, Gigondas and Beaume-de-Venise (famous for its sweet muscat) in the Rhône valley. Many vineyards and cellars are open for *dégustations* (tastings). But beware – you will usually be expected to buy at least one bottle!

Provence's array of historic buildings stands as testimony to its rich past. Perhaps the most unusual style of accommodation is the collection of *bories* near Gordes – extraordinary beehive-shaped, dry-stone huts, which sheltered the earliest farmers and semi-nomadic shepherds as early as the 3rd century BC.

AT HOME IN PROVENCE

The architectural legacy of Roman Provincia is also remarkable, from the magnificent Théâtre Antique at Orange (➤ 146–147) to the extensive remains at Glanum (➤ 128–129) – the oldest classical buildings in France. The city of Arles (➤ 119–121), with its splendid remains including Constantine's public baths, a theatre, arenas and the Alyscamps necropolis, was known as the Rome of the Gauls.

Over the centuries, religious architecture also left its mark on the region, and some of these historic sites are kept alive by various ecclesiastical communities today. Nowhere reflects the calm and contemplation of the countryside more than the Cistercian abbey of Sénanque (➤ 150–151), one of the best remaining examples of 12th-century religious architecture in France, tucked in a secluded valley north of Gordes, amid fields of lavender.

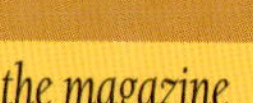

However, it is the *mas* (farmhouse) and *bastide* (country house) which really typify traditional Provençal architecture – picture-postcard rural homes which conjure up glorious images of voguish country interiors and lifestyle. These beautiful, stone houses are cleverly designed to mitigate the effects of the long hot summers and the harsh winters, with thick, rough-cut stone walls, small windows and heavy reinforced wooden doors. Most are built facing south – protected from the rain from the east and the *mistral* wind from the north. For this reason too, the northern wall usually has no windows, and the shutters on the remaining façades keep the houses cool in summer. The terracotta-tiled roofs are gently sloping and influenced by Roman design.

PROVENÇAL PRINTS

In the 17th-century, when Indian printed cottons were all the rage in the court of Louis XIV, local craftsmen fell in love with their bright designs and, using regional inspirations, created the Provençal print, which became the basis for the region's traditional costumes and interiors. Musée Souleïado in Tarascon (tel: 04 90 91 50 11) contains some ancient prints and magnificent costumes. (Souleïado, a Provençal word meaning "a sun-ray piercing through the clouds", is the name of the leading manufacturer of block-printed textiles in Provence).

HOME FURNISHINGS: A SHOPPING LIST

Provençal décor is always in vogue. Here's a guide to the best of the region:

Fabrics: The best Provençal fabrics can be found at branches of Souleïado (Cannes, Aix, Arles, Marseille) and Olivades (Nice, St-Tropez, Arles, Carpentras).

Glass: Biot (➤ 55–56) has long been famous for its hand-blown glassware. Visitors can watch glass-blowers at the Verrerie de Biot demonstrating their unique *verre bullé* (bubble glass).

Ceramics: For terracotta kitchen containers, casseroles, garden pots and oil jars, head to the pottery centre of Vallauris near Antibes. The capital of traditional tiling is Salernes. For tableware, the white decorated earthenware pottery of Moustiers-Ste-Marie – *Faïence de Moustiers* – is famous throughout the world (➤ 80–81).

Tightly-packed rooftops in the small town of Nyons

But it is the interiors of these homes which make them so quintessentially Provençal, with their arched doors, stone-vaulted ceilings and terracotta floor tiles. Add to this waxed ochre walls, Provençal printed calicoes, local ceramics and glassware and you have your dream home. No wonder there are more ex-pats here than in any other part of France.

A fine display of glazed ceramics for sale

OCHRE: THE COLOURS OF PROVENCE

Throughout Provence, ochre is used as a house paint to enliven a dark wall or a dull façade. The ochre industry began here at the end of the 18th-century, centred on the tiny village of Roussillon (► 155–156). The houses here present a full palette of ochre shades – blood red, apricot, pink, gold, orange, mustard, burgundy, russet and brown. The village is surrounded by jagged cliffs and craters of every shade of ochre, and visitors can explore the old open-cast quarries along the Sentier des Ocres (Ochre Trail). Sadly competition from cheap synthetic pigments forced mass-production here to stop in 1958.

WHAT THE EX-PATS SAY

Peter Mayle, in *A Year in Provence*: "Life in Provence is slow, hot and pleasant in the summer; slow, cold and pleasant in the winter. We have lived here for three years now without a day's regret." **Simon Derrick**, yacht broker in Antibes: "I love the crisp days of winter best of all, with clear blue skies and beautiful light, and the snow-topped mountains. In summer months, I escape the crowds and walk in the countryside." **Steve Parker**, pilot in Nice: "Provence has it all – excellent weather, good food, relaxed lifestyle, sailing, skiing...it's the whole 'Alpes-Maritime' thing that I love."

HOW TO PLAY PÉTANQUE

Pétanque (also known as *Jeu de Boules* – "the game of balls") was invented in La Ciotat near Marseille in 1910. It is a team game of great strategy and precision. The aim is to throw heavy metal balls as close as possible to a small wooden ball or *cochonnet* (piglet). The name is derived from the Provençal *pieds tanqués* (fixed feet), as your feet have to remain together within a small circle drawn on the ground when you throw your ball. The game is normally played on hard sand or gravel, and most villages have a special area called the *terrain de pétanque* or Boulodrome – typically outside a local café or in the main square.

Pétanque follows strict rules: everyone takes it in turns to throw their boules, either placing them as near as possible to the *cochonnet*, or shooting them in an attempt to displace your opponent's balls.

When all the balls have been thrown, the team with the ball closest to the *cochonnet* scores a point. Most games are up to 13 points.

Pétanque is currently France's most played sport, enjoyed by about 17 million people, and it is also ranked as a world-class sport, played in over 50 countries. For further information on how and where to play, check the websites www.petanque.org or www.petanque.fr.

VITAL STATISTICS

- **Weight of boules:** 650g–800g (22oz–28oz)
- **Diameter of boules:** 70.5mm–80mm (about 3in)
- **Diameter of *cochonnet*:** 25mm–35mm (about 1in)
- **Minimum playing area:** 15m by 4m (16.5yds by 4.4yds)
- **Playing distance between circle and *cochonnet*:** 6m–10m (6.5yds–11yds)
- **Teams** **triples:** 3 players with 2 boules each
  doubles: 2 players with 3 boules each
  singles: 1 player with 3 boules

GOURMET PROVENCE

La cuisine Provençale is *typified by bold, sun-drenched flavours and hearty Mediterranean dishes full of personality, enriched by olive oil, tomatoes, garlic and aromatic herbes de Provence. As Peter Mayle once remarked: "Everything is full-blooded. The food is full of strong, earthy flavours…there is nothing bland about Provence."* (A Year in Provence).

But there's more to Provençal cuisine than bouillabaisse and the monumental *salade Niçoise* of olives, anchovies, tuna, eggs, potatoes and lettuce. On the coast, fish dishes reign supreme, with such delicacies as *telines Camarguais* (tiny shellfish served with *aïoli*) and *oursins* (sea urchins) alongside such local favourites as *loup* (bass) or *rouget* (mullet). Look for lesser-known dishes such as *beignets de courgettes* (frittered courgette flowers);

TUCK IN AND TUCK UP

What could be better than to enjoy a delicious meal followed by tumbling into bed upstairs afterwards? This is increasingly the trend with new gourmet restaurants in the region – they offer Michelin-starred cuisine with rooms. For instance, two-star Michelin chef Edouard Loubet's farmhouse, La Ferme de Capelongue at Bonnieux, offers 14 apartments and a restaurant serving inventive Lubéron cuisine (www.capelongue.com). Auberge La Fenière (Lourmarin, tel: 04 90 68 11 79, www.reinesammut.com) is managed by Reine Sammut, one of France's top female chefs. Accommodation here consists of seven stylish garden rooms and two gypsy caravans. At the Bastide de Moustiers

farmhouse (Moustiers Ste-Marie, tel: 04 92 70 47 47, www.bastide-moustiers.com), charm and simplicity is the key: the olive oil comes from the neighbouring domaine, the only cheese is local *chèvre* and you can see the vegetable garden from your bedroom window. "The produce alone is the star" is the maxim here, and the food is second to none. After all, this is the country home of that culinary superstar, Alain Ducasse!

BOUILLABAISSE

Few visitors to Provence get to taste an authentic bouillabaisse, although many restaurants offer second-rate versions (*soupes de pecheurs* and *bouillabaisses a notre façon*). This world-famous rust-coloured fish soup originated in Marseille as a nourishing family meal, made with choice fish kept aside by the fishermen especially for their families. It is traditionally made with up to 12 different kinds of fish and cooked in a stock containing saffron, herbs and fennel. In 1980 the *Charte de la Bouillabaisse Marseillaise* was drawn up by half a dozen restaurants to protect their authentic recipe. Try it in Marseillaise at Fonfon (140 rue Vallon des Auffes, tel: 04 91 52 14 38) or Le Miramar (quai du Port, tel: 04 91 91 10 40) by the Old Port. Bon appetit!

pain bagnat (*salad Niçoise* inside a loaf of bread) and *mesclun* (a flavoursome salad of peppery leaves) – try them all at Lou Pilha Leva, a simple "fast-food" hole-in-the-wall at the heart of Old Nice – or piping hot slices of *pissaladière* (onion tart with anchovy and olives) and *socca* (chickpea pancake) from the stalls of nearby cours Saleya market. It is the region's celebrated food markets that have given Provençal cuisine its excellent reputation, together with the intimate local bistros of the hilltop villages, where simple meals are served in hearty portions.

At the opposite end of the spectrum, Provence boasts more than its fair share of gourmet restaurants. Auguste Escoffier, the great French "chef of kings and king of chefs" learned to cook in Nice and, ever since, many of the country's top chefs have flocked to the region to

perfect the art of Provençal haute cuisine. Most famous of all, the legendary chef Alain Ducasse has a restaurant with three Michelin stars – Le Louis XV – in the Hôtel de Paris, Monte Carlo (tel: 0377 98 06 88 64). Just one of the ever-expanding Ducasse restaurant empire, it is conveniently situated beside the Casino, so you can blow your winnings on dinner. Other top chefs in the area include Christian Willer at La Palme d'Or restaurant in Hôtel Martinez, Cannes (tel: 04 92 98 74 14), renowned for his seasonal specialities; and Alain Llorca, who has taken over Le Moulin de Mougins (tel: 04 93 75 78 24). The culinary extravaganzas at these restaurants have come to represent the pinnacle of Provençal cuisine – the experience justifies the expense.

Some of the *Best...*

Hilltop villages

1 Èze (➤ 45)
2 Gordes (➤ 150–151)
3 Grimaud (➤ 78–79)
4 Moustiers-Ste-Marie (➤ 80–81)
5 St-Paul-de-Vence (➤ 51)

Activities

1 Canoe the Verdon Gorge (➤ 74–76)
2 Horse-ride in the Camargue (➤ 116–118)
3 Hang-glide off the top of Mont Ventoux (Association Vaucluse Parapente, Avignon, tel: 04 90 85 67 82)
4 Take a helicopter ride from Nice Airport to Monte-Carlo (Héli Inter Riviera, tel: 04 93 21 46 46)
5 Ski at Serre-Chevalier, Provence's largest ski resort (tourist office, tel: 04 92 24 98 98)

Beaches

1 Cannes – best for star-spotting
2 Cassis (Calanques) – most scenic
3 Îles d'Hyères (Plage de la Palud, Port-Cros) – best island beach
4 Marseille – best watersports
5 St-Tropez (La Voile Rouge) – the trendiest

Children's activities

1 Musée Océanographique, Monaco (➤ 49)
2 Marineland, Antibes(➤ 57) – one of Europe's greatest marine shows
3 Visiobulle, Juan-les-Pins – discover the underwater world of "Millionaire's Bay" in a glass-bottomed boat
4 Grottes de St-Cézaire – fairy-tale world of red caves with "musical" stalactites and stalagmites.
5 Massalia Théâtre, Marseille – France's first marionnette theatre

Cafés

1 Café de la Place (St-Paul-de-Vence), locals' cafe beside the dusty pétanque pitch
2 Café Excelsior (St-Raphaël), France's first *café-chantant* or live-music cafe
3 Sénéquier (St-Tropez), one of the Riviera's top celebrity haunts. Try the nougat!
4 Café de France (Isle-sur-la-Sorgue), historic hot spot for poets, philosophers and artists
5 Les Deux Garçons (Aix-en-Provence), the city's first café and former watering-hole of Cézanne, Piaf, Picasso, Sartre et al

Markets

1 Aix-en-Provence (Tue, Thu, Sat am) – fruit, vegetables, cheese and flowers galore
2 Arles (Sat am) – fruit, vegetables, soaps and fabrics sold by locals in traditional dress
3 Marseille Fish Market (daily am) – boatside stalls
4 Nice's cours Saleya (daily am) – all the colours and fragrances of Provence
5 Grand Marché Truffes et Gastronomie (truffle and gastronomy market), Rognes (December)

Finding Your Feet

First Two Hours

There is ready access to France through the northern coastal ports, such as Calais, and via rail routes, including the Eurotunnel and Eurostar links with the UK. Nice and Marseille are Provence's main international airports. If you are staying in the Vaucluse, the Bouches-du-Rhône or the Var, it is more convenient to fly into Marseille.

Arriving by Road from the UK

Eurotunnel

- The **Eurotunnel** shuttle train (tel: 08705 353 535; www.eurotunnel.com) takes vehicles and their passengers under the English Channel from Folkestone, in the UK, to Calais/Coquelles, in northern France. The journey takes 35 minutes and is the shortest vehicular journey time from the UK to mainland Europe.

Ferries

- Well-equipped **car ferries** link France with the UK (Brittany Ferries tel: 08703 665 333; www.brittanyferries.com. LD Lines tel: 08704 284 335; www.ldlines.com. P&O Ferries tel: 08705 202 020; www.poferries.com. Seafrance tel: 08705 711 711; www.seafrance.com. Speedferries tel: 08702 200 570; www.speedferries.com). The cost varies according to the time, day and month of travel. Book early for the cheapest fares.

In France

- Once in France, a comprehensive system of ***autoroutes* (motorways/ expressways)** fanning out from Paris enables you to cross the country with relative ease. Your motoring organisation can recommend a suitable route to your final destination; or visit www.theAA.com/travel to plan your route online.

Arriving in Nice

By Air

- Most international flights come into **Nice-Côte d'Azur Airport** (tel: 0820 423 333; www.nice.aeroport.fr), in eastern Provence, on the coast 6km (4 miles) west of Nice. The second busiest airport in France, it is well situated for visitors to the Riviera resorts of Antibes, Cannes and Monaco. There are two terminals, with information desks, shops, restaurants, banks, bureaux de change and car-rental firms.
- A **taxi** into Nice will cost around €20–€28 and takes 20 minutes. There's **no rail** link, but buses run to the centre of Nice every 20 minutes (€4). Take bus 23 or 98 to the **bus station** (*gare routière)* near Vieux Nice; or bus 99 to the Nice **train station** (*gare SNCF*).

By Train

- The easiest option is to take the **Eurostar** from **London** to **Lille** (1 hour 40 minutes) and change platforms for the direct **TGV** (*Train à Grande Vitesse*) to **Nice** and all key stations in Provence. Through tickets from the UK are available from Rail Europe (tel: 08708 371 371; www.raileurope.co.uk).

- **Nice Tourist Offices**
  ✉ 5 promenade des Anglais, Nice ☎ 0892 707 407; www.nicetourism.com 🕐 Mon–Sat 8–8, Sun 9–7, Jun–Sep; Mon–Sat 9–6, Oct–May
  ✉ Nice-Côte d'Azur Airport, Terminal 1 🕐 Mon–Sat 8 am–9 pm
  ✉ SNCF Railway Station, Avenue Thiers 🕐 Mon–Sat 8–8, Sun 9–7, Jun–Sep; Mon–Sat 8–7, Sun 10–5, Oct–May

Arriving in Marseille

By Air

- **Marseille-Provence Airport, also called Marseille-Marignane** (tel: 04 42 14 14 14; www.marseille.aeroport.fr), is 30km (19 miles) northwest of Marseille and operates international and regional flights. It has two terminals, both with shops, restaurants and bureaux de change.
- **Taxis** to the city centre take 45 minutes, and cost around €40 by day and €50 by night. **Shuttle buses** to St-Charles train station run about every 20 minutes from 6:10 am to 10:50 pm. After 10:50 they tie in with flights (€8.50, 25 minutes).
- **Marseille Tourist Office**
  ✉ 4 La Canebière, Marseille ☎ 04 91 13 89 00; www.marseille-tourisme.com 🕐 Mon–Sat 9–7, Sun 10–5 (longer hours in peak season)

Arriving in Toulon

By Air

- **Toulon-Hyères** (tel: 04 94 00 83 83; www.toulon-hyeres.aeroport.fr) is 22km (14 miles) east of Toulon and receives daily flights from Paris and weekly flights from London Gatwick. There is one terminal, with a café/bar.
- A **taxi** into Toulon will cost around €40 and take 40 minutes. A **bus** service to the city runs several times during the day, but it does not necessarily coincide with the flight arrivals.
- **Toulon Tourist Office**
  ✉ Place Raimu, Toulon ☎ 04 94 18 53 00; www.toulontourisme.com 🕐 Mon, Wed–Sat 9–6, Tue 10–6, Sun 10–12, Jun–Sep; Wed–Sat 9:30–5:30, Tue 10:30–5:30, Sun 10–12, Oct–May.

Arriving in Nîmes

By Air

- **Nîmes-Arles-Camargue** (tel: 04 66 70 49 49; www.nimes.cci.fr) is a small airport 12km (7.5 miles) southeast of Nîmes, with services from London Stansted, Luton, Liverpool, East Midlands and Dublin by Ryanair. There is a car rental office at the small terminal.
- A **taxi** into Nîmes will cost around €20 and take 25 minutes. A **bus** service meets flights and takes passengers into Nîmes. It costs €5 and the journey time is 25 minutes.
- **Nîmes Tourist Office**
  ✉ 6 rue Auguste, Nîmes ☎ 04 66 58 38 00; www.ot-nimes.fr
  🕐 Mon–Wed, Fri 8:30 am–8 pm, Thu 8:30 am–9 pm, Sat 9–7, Sun 10–6, Jul–Aug; Mon–Fri 8:30–7, Sat 9–7, Sun 10–6, Easter–Jun and Sep; Mon–Fri 8:30–7, Sat 9–7, Sun 10–5, Oct–Easter.

Getting Around

By Car

- **Driving** is a good way to discover the rural areas of Provence. The roads in the region are generally in excellent condition with good signposting. Traffic jams may be a problem on the coast in summer and at weekends.
- If **bringing your own car** to France, you must always carry the following documentation in addition to your passport: a full, valid national driver's licence, a certificate of motor insurance and the vehicle's registration document (plus a letter of authorisation from the owner if it is not registered in your name). Third-party motor insurance is the **minimum requirement**, but fully comprehensive cover is strongly advised. Check that your **insurance** covers you against damage in transit, and that you have adequate **breakdown cover** (for information contact the AA, tel: 0800 444 500; www.theAA.com, or your own national breakdown organisation). You must also display an **international sticker** or distinguishing sign plate on the rear of the car by the registration plate. **Headlights** of right-hand-drive cars must be adjusted for driving on the right.
- **To rent a car** you must be at least 21 years old and have held a full driver's licence for at least a year. You will have to produce your licence and passport or national ID card.
- You'll find most major **car rental** agencies at airports, main rail stations and in the large towns and cities. Book ahead in high season.
- Make sure you have **adequate insurance** and that you are aware of what you are covered for in the event of an accident. Low-cost operators may have a high excess charge for damage to the vehicle.
- Check that your vehicle comes with **roadside assistance**. In the event of a breakdown, refer to your documentation or to the information regarding breakdowns, which is often kept in the glove compartment or under the sun visor.
- If your car **breaks down** on an *autoroute*, phone from the emergency telephones located every 2km (1.25 miles) on the roadside.

Driving Know-How

- Drive on the **right-hand side** of the road (*serrez à droite*).
- Drivers must be **18 or over**, and you'll need to be **21 or over to rent** a car.
- **Speed limits** are 50kph/31mph on urban roads, 90kph/56mph outside built-up areas (80kph/49mph in rain), 110kph/68mph on dual carriageways/divided highways and non-toll motorways (100kph/62mph in rain), and 130kph/80mph on toll motorways (110kph/68mph in rain). Visiting drivers who have held a licence for less than two years must follow the wet-weather limits **at all times**, even when it's dry. Drivers from within the EU who **exceed the speed limit** by more than 25kph/15mph may have their licences confiscated by the police on the spot.
- In **built-up areas** you must **give way** to traffic coming from the right (*priorité à droite*). At roundabouts/traffic circles with signs saying *Cédez le passage* or *Vous n'avez pas la priorité*, traffic already on the roundabout has priority. On roundabouts without signs, traffic entering has priority.
- **Do not overtake** where there is a solid single line in the centre of the road.
- If you have **an accident or break down** you must place a **warning triangle** at a suitable distance from the rear of your car.
- The **blood alcohol limit** is 0.5 per cent (US blood alcohol content 0.05). If you drink, don't drive.

- **Fuel** comes as unleaded (95 and 98 octane), lead replacement petrol (LRP or *supercarburant*), diesel (*gasoil* or *gazole*) and LPG. Many filling stations **close on Sundays** and at 6 pm during the week. Some self-service pumps are operated by debit/credit cards, but cards issued outside France are not always accepted by these pumps.
- Before you take to the road, familiarise yourself with the **French highway code** on www.legifrance.gouv.fr. For information on **road signs**, see www.permisenligne.com.

Trains

- Train services within France are run by the state railway company, the Société Nationale des Chemins de Fer (**SNCF**, tel: 0892 353 535; www.sncf.com), and are generally fast, comfortable and efficient.
- The **TGV** (*Train à Grande Vitesse*) high-speed train links major towns and cities at speeds of up to 300kph/186mph. **TER** (*Transport Express Régional*) provide a local service (*Lignes Régionales*). Reliable services link Nice, Cannes and Fréjus with Marseille. The Rhône valley towns of Avignon, Orange, Arles and Nîmes are also connected by train. Lines from Nice run through the Roya valley and northwest into the pre-Alps. For journey planning try www.ter-sncf.com, and in Provence look for the brochures *Sud-Est* and *TGV-Méditerranée*.
- **Buy tickets** at stations. You must validate your ticket in the designated machine on the platform before you board the train. If there is no ticket office or it is closed, you can pay the conductor on board the train. Some TER platforms do not have validation machines. In this case, the conductor will validate your ticket on the train.
- You can take **bicycles** onto all suitable trains outside the peak hours (Mon–Fri 7 am–9 am and 4:30 pm–6:30 pm).
- Under-26s can get a 25 per cent **discount on travel** (*Découverte 12–25*), and discounts are also available for older people and by booking well ahead (*Découverte J30*). A variety of discount **rail passes** is available for travel within France, or within the whole of Europe, and should be bought before arrival in France from travel agents or Rail Europe (in the UK www.raileurope.co.uk; in the US www.raileurope.com).
- With a minimum of 24 hours notice, the **SNCF luggage service** will pick up your luggage from your hotel and deliver it to your final destination for you. The service operates Mon–Fri, 7 am–9 pm, tel: 0825 845 845.

Long-Distance Buses

- **Long-distance bus routes** within France are generally slightly less expensive than the trains, but much slower. You'll usually find the bus station (*gare routière*) close to the railway station (*gare SNCF*). **Eurolines** (tel: 0892 695 252; www.eurolines.fr) operates services between major towns and cities within France and to other destinations within Europe. **SNCF** (tel: 3635) also runs services as extensions to rail links.

Local Buses

- **Local bus services** link the key towns in Provence. Services are limited on Sundays and official holidays. Buses usually leave from either the **bus station** or the **town square**. You should find timetable details here or at the bus company offices. The **route number** and final **destination** are dispalyed on the front of the bus. You can normally **buy tickets** on the bus or at kiosks/*tabacs* around the town. If you intend to make frequent use of the buses then consider buying a book of ten tickets from the office. You must validate tickets in the machine on the bus.

- In **Aix-en-Provence** a shuttle bus links the town with the TGV station, 15km (9 miles) away. It runs from 4:25 am to 8:45 pm, every 15 minutes at peak times and every 30 minutes at other times. Autobus Aixous (tel: 04 42 26 37 28) operates 20 lines around town and the suburbs. Buses depart from the bus station at avenue de l'Europe. You can buy tickets (1 ticket €1.10, 10 tickets €7.70) from the office at the bus station or on the buses (you must have the exact change).
- In **Arles** and the **Camargue** there are three bus companies (tel: 0810 000 816 for information). Buses depart from the **bus station** at 24 boulevard Clemenceau in Arles. Societé des Transports d'Arles runs four lines. Ceyte Tourisme Méditerranée links Arles with Tarascon, Salon, Marseille and Avignon. Cars de Carmargue runs services to Stes-Maries-de-la-Mer. Tickets for town buses cost €0.80 each, or €7 for 10. Tickets to Aix-en-Provence cost €11.40, and €14.60 to Marseille.
- In **Avignon** Transports en Commun de la Region d'Avignon (TCRA) operates buses from avenue de Lattre de Tassigny (tel: 04 32 74 18 32; www.tcra.fr), and runs 28 routes around Avignon and to surrounding towns such as St-Rémy-de-Provence. Buses do not run within the walls of Avignon. Buses run from 7 am to 8 pm. STDGard runs services linking Nîmes, Avignon and Tarascon. Tickets cost €1.05 and can be purchased on the bus or from the office of the bus company. A two-trip ticket, valid for two people making the same trip at the same time or two trips by one person, is €1.80.
- In **Cannes** Bus Azur runs 20 services in the town and to surrounding towns. You can get information at the bus station at place Cournou Gentille, next to the town hall (tel: 0825 825 599). Buses run from 6 am to 8.30 pm. Sillages runs services from Cannes north into the hills around Grasse (tel: 0800 095 000/04 93 64 88 84; www.sillages-stga.tm.fr). Single tickets cost €1.15 each, 10 tickets cost €10.60 and a pass valid for one week is €11.50. You can buy single tickets on the bus, but the other tickets options can only be purchased from the bus station.
- You can download the **Trans Vaucluse public transport route map** of all bus links through and across the *département* of Vaucluse, from Montelimar to Marseille and Avignon to Digne-les-Bains at www.provenceguide.com.

Taxis

- **Taxis** are a convenient way to get around the major towns and cities, but are generally an expensive option.
- You'll pay a pick-up charge and a charge per kilometre (0.6 miles), plus extra for items of luggage and travel in the evening or on Sundays. All taxis use a **meter** (*compteur*). Make sure that this is reset for your journey. You may be charged for the driver's journey to collect you.
- Some taxi firms provide **chauffeur-driven cars** by the day, if you wish to visit several locations around Provence.
- The best way to find a taxi is to head to a **taxi stand** (indicated by a blue Taxi sign). Phoning for a taxi means the meter starts from the moment it sets off to pick you up.
- Some taxis accept credit cards, but it is best to have **cash** available. It is usual to give a 10 per cent **tip**.

Admission Charges
The cost of admission for museums and places of interest mentioned in the text is indicated by the following price categories:
Inexpensive under €5 **Moderate** €5–€8 **Expensive** over €8

Accommodation

There's a wide variety of accommodation available to visitors to Provence, and you should find something to suit your budget and your taste. Accommodation ranges from the extremely grand hotels on the Riviera to old stone buildings in the country areas. For an authentic experience of France, you may like to try a campsite, stay in a rented *gîte* or perhaps try a family-run *auberge*. The *Bon Weekend en Ville* promotion features a range of hotels in Aix-en-Provence, Avignon and Marseille offering two nights for the price of one from November until the end of March. Your first night must be a Friday or Saturday (www.bon-week-end-en-villes.com).

Types of Accommodation

Hotels

- Hotels are inspected and are **classified into six categories**, from no stars (at the bottom) to four stars and four-star luxury hotels. They must display their rates inside and outside the hotel. Charges are usually **per room** rather than per person, and breakfast is generally charged separately.
- Family-run inns and small hotels, the **Logis de France**, usually offer some of the best accommodation if you're on a budget. All have a basic standard of comfort, and some are in particularly quaint or charming locations. Most have their own restaurant, serving good local food. In remote areas, some hotels offer deals including meals. By prior arrangement, **luggage can be transported** between Logis for you – very useful if you're planning a hiking break. As well as star gradings, Logis also have their own chimney symbol of classification. Find them on the website www.logis-de-france.com, or get a list from the tourist office.
- There are some great **luxury hotels**, if you want to treat yourself. The traditional *belle-époque* hotels of the Riviera, such as Hôtel Négresco ➤ 59, have a cachet which is hard to beat. For something with a more modern twist, look at designer hotels, or for a stay in a luxurious château setting, contact Relais & Château (tel: 08 25 32 32 32; www.relaischateau.com).

Bed-and-Breakfast

- **Chambres d'hôte** offers a taste of life in a real French household, anywhere from a farm to a château. Ask at the tourist offices for local availability. Many of the best are affiliated to the **Gîtes de France** organisation, which grades them with one to four ears of corn (*épis*) according to the level of comfort and facilities. All the establishments listed in the ***AA Bed & Breakfast in France*** are inspected by Gîtes de France.
- For the **top end** of the scale – perhaps a room in a privately owned château – contact Bienvenue au Château (2 rue de la Loire, BP20411, 44204 Nantes; www.bienvenue-au-chateau.com).

Self Catering (Gîtes)

- Self-contained cottages, villas and apartments (**gîtes**) are widely available in towns, villages and country areas, and offer particularly good value for families. They are usually **rented by the week or fortnight**, and may range from simple and basic (bring your own linen) to more elaborate, with swimming pools and other facilities thrown in.
- Many *gîtes* are administered through the **Gîtes de France** organisation, which also inspects and grades them according to comfort and facilities

(www.gites-de-france.fr). Local tourist offices also generally hold this information for their area.

Youth Hostels

- There are around 200 youth hostels (***auberges de jeunesse***) across France, which are open to members from other countries if they have a membership card with photo. For a complete list and details of youth hostels in Provence, contact the Fédération Unie des Auberges de Jeunesse, 27 rue Pajol, 75018 Paris (tel: 01 44 89 87 27; www.fuaj.org).

Camping

- The warm, dry climate in Provence makes camping a very popular choice for visitors both from abroad and from northern France, with a roll-call exceeding **9,000 fully equipped campsites**, plus around 2,300 farm campsites. Sites are **inspected and graded** with a star system like that of the hotels, and range from basic (with electricity, showers and lavatories) to luxurious, with swimming pools and other family sports activities, restaurants and bars, and kids' clubs. You don't even have to take your own tent as many have **pre-pitched tents and mobile homes** on site, complete with cooking equipment, fridge and beds.
- You must **book well ahead**, especially in high season, which runs from April to September. For more information contact the **National Federation of Campsites** (tel: 01 42 72 84 08; www.campingfrance.com). **The *AA Caravan and Camping in France*** gives details of over 450 inspected campsites throughout the country.
- Note that camping or overnight parking of caravans and motorhomes is **not permitted** on the beach or at the roadside. If you get caught out and need to find a campsite, the local tourist office should be able to advise you, and in case of an emergency, police stations can also let you have a list of local campsite addresses. Check with the local town hall if you intend to camp away from official sites, as it is often forbidden, especially in areas at risk from forest fires.

Finding a Room

- If you haven't booked ahead, visit the **local tourist office**, as they will have a list of accommodation with prices. In towns or villages without a tourist office, head for the main square or centre of town, where you're likely to find the greatest concentration of hotels.
- When you **check in**, you may need to complete a registration form and show your passport. Ask to see the room first, especially in cheaper accommodation.
- **Check-out time** is usually around 10 or 11 am.

Seasonal Rates

- Accommodation prices are likely to **vary widely throughout the year**, according to the season. In the resort areas of Provence, higher prices may be charged between April and September.

Prices
Expect to pay per night for a double room:
€ under €100 **€€** €100–€200 **€€€** over €200

Food and Drink

Few nations enjoy their food with quite the pride and relish of the French. Eating out is one of the "must do" experiences on a holiday in Provence, and there's no better way to discover the wealth of local dishes and culinary twists than at a local bistro.

Provençal Cuisine

- Near the **coast**, fish dishes reign supreme – the ultimate fish dish here is, of course, bouillabaisse. *Moules frîtes* (mussels with french fries) are always good value, as are *telines Camarguais*, tiny shellfish served with *aïoli* (garlic mayonnaise). By contrast, meat dishes predominate inland. Try Sisteron lamb with its taste of wild thyme, game dishes or *boeuf gardian* (a spicy beef stew with olives, served with Camarguais rice).
- The **Nice area** has its own distinctive cuisine. Pizzas and pasta taste every bit as good here as they do over the border in Italy. Look out also for *pissaladière* (olive and onion pizza) and *petits farcis* (savoury stuffed artichoke hearts, courgettes and tomatoes).

Vin de Provence

- About 11 per cent of France's **wine** comes from Provence. The chalky soils and warm, dry Mediterranean climate produce the smooth, easy-to-drink wines such as Côtes du Ventoux and Côtes du Lubéron. Some of the more famous labels include Côtes du Rhône.
- Provence is particularly famous for its rosé wines – fresh, crisp and fruity. Côtes de Provence and Côteaux d'Aix are among the best. For white wine try the dry, green-tinged Cassis wines or the fruity Bellet.

Where to Eat

- You'll find a decent **restaurant** or several in every town, where the locals will go for a special occasion. Expect to **reserve your table in advance, dress smartly, and allow plenty of time** for the full gastronomic experience. If the dinner price is beyond your budget, look out for better-value set-menus at lunchtime. The ***menu dégustation*** offers a selection of the restaurant's signature dishes with accompanying wines at a fixed price.
- **Brasseries** are **informal** establishments generally open long hours, where you can sample local dishes alongside staples such as *steak-frîtes* (steak with chips/fries).
- **Bistros** tend to be **small, informal, family-run** restaurants serving traditional and local dishes, with a modest wine list.
- Lunchtime menus tend to offer the **best value**, when a *menu du jour* (daily menu) of two or three courses with wine is likely to cost much less than an evening meal. ***Prix-fixe*** meals of three or four courses also generally offer good value.
- **Service** should be **included in the bill** (*l'addition*) – look for the words *service compris*, or *s.c.* If the service is exceptional, you may like to leave loose change (in a bar) or a tip of 5 per cent (in a restaurant).

Prices
Expect to pay for a three-course meal for one, excluding drinks:
€ under €25 **€€** €25–€50 **€€€** over €50

Shopping

Shopping in Provence can be a real pleasure, whether you're after local produce at the lively markets, looking for chic Riviera fashion in the boutiques or conversing with the small-scale cheese producers in the *marché* (market). Prices may not be cheap, but quality is usually high. Pottery, perfumes, soaps, herbs, olive oil and wine are among the best buys.

Opening Hours

- **Opening times vary** according to the type of shop, the season and the location, and there are no hard-and-fast rules. Some shops close from noon until mid-afternoon (➤ 178).
- **Daily and weekly markets** are a feature of cities and towns, and usually operate from around 7 am to noon. Often the people who produced or grew the food are the people selling it too, and can tell you about their range of cheeses or produce.

Payment

- Shops in towns and major tourist areas usually accept payment by **credit or debit card**. For markets and smaller outlets, carry **euros** in cash.
- Visitors from outside the European Union can reclaim a 12 per cent tax on certain purchases. You'll need a ***détaxe*** form from the shopkeeper, which must be shown with the receipts and stamped at customs, then returned to the shop by post for a refund.

What to Buy

- **Food** is taken very seriously in France. Most small food shops sell only one type of product – you're most likely to see the *boulangerie* (bakery), *pâtisserie* (pastry/cake shop), *fromagerie* (cheese shop), *boucherie* (butcher's shop), *charcuterie* (delicatessen) and *poissonnerie* (fishmonger's). Dried wild herbs and virgin olive oil are the musts for any food shopping trip. For a sweet treat try crystallised fruits in Apt, *berlingots* (stripey boiled sweets) in Carpentras and *marrons glacés* (glazed chestnuts) in Collobrières.
- Visit the local **markets** for the freshest seasonal produce, including fruit, vegetables and cheeses, and products from basketware to pottery. Large cities hold at least one daily market and smaller towns have a weekly one. In autumn and winter look for wild *cèpe* mushrooms and truffles.
- Hypermarkets sell an excellent range of **French wines**. It is also fun to buy from the vineyards (*domaines*) themselves – the Rhône and Lubéron have specialist wine routes. Go for a tasting at a vineyard and you will be expected to buy at least one bottle – and, of course, more if you find something you really like.
- The area around Grasse is world-famous for its **perfumes**, while Marseille is known for its quality **soap**, often made with a base of olive oil. Terracotta pottery is also popular, and you'll find bright ceramics in any market square. For ***faïences*** (fine glazed ceramics) head to Moustiers-Ste-Marie, and for **glassware** try Biot.
- France is known world-wide for its **stylish fashion**, and you'll find designer labels in the chic Riviera resorts and individual boutiques everywhere. You can buy traditional **Provençal cotton** fabrics either by the length or ready-made into scarves, tops and skirts. Souléiado and Les Olivades stores are good places to look.

Entertainment

Epic opera, concerts and drama in the Roman amphitheatres at Arles or Orange and major theatrical performances at the Avignon festival are all part of the arts scene in Provence. For something more intimate, try a fringe show in a café-theatre or jazz in a small, smoke-filled club. Magazines in hotel foyers and tourist offices are a good source of information about all forms of entertainment, including top sporting events.

Live Arts

- All major cities have a **theatre**. The season usually runs from October until late spring, although the fringe scene, specialising in works by local playwrights, has a year-round schedule.
- Avignon's International Theatre Festival in July offers top entertainment and fringe shows in venues ranging from the Palais des Papes to cafés.
- Provence's most famous **operatic and classical music festival** is the Chorégies in Orange. The Roman theatre is the setting for large-scale opera productions such as *Carmen* and *La Traviata*. In Aix-en-Provence, the Festival d'Art Lyrique is held in the courtyard of the Archbishop's Palace, where you are likely to hear performances of works by Mozart and Britten.
- The summer **music festivals** in Aix and Orange have orchestral concerts, as well as the more famous opera. In Nice, you can enjoy sacred music in churches and summer concerts at the Cimiez monastery.
- The world's leading **jazz** musicians are attracted to the Cimiez gardens for the Nice Jazz Festival.
- **Contemporary dance festivals** are held in Aix and Marseille in summer, and the Ballet Preljocaj (www.preljocaj.org) hosts performances throughout the year at the Cité du Livre in Aix. For information on the Ballet National de Marseille, visit www.ballet-de-marseille.com.

Nightlife

- There are **café-bars** all over Provence. In rural areas they are the place for locals to get together for a drink and perhaps enjoy a game of pool. In the cities and resorts they are likely to be more sophisticated places to stop for a drink either before or after dinner. You're likely to find tables outside during the summer, where you can watch the world go by. In cities, bars open at 7 am to serve breakfast and don't close until the early hours of the morning. Out of season and out of the cities, bars may close at 9 pm. Unaccompanied children under 16 are not allowed into bars. The legal age for drinking is 16, although children aged 14 to 16 may drink wine or beer if accompanied by an adult.
- Major cities and resorts have a vibrant **club** scene, and you'll find flyers at tourist offices, music stores and trendy cafés. Clubs may open from 10 pm, but don't expect things to liven up until about midnight. Smart dress is the rule. There is an admission charge at weekends and on some week nights, but this usually includes your first drink.
- **Casinos** are part of the entertainment scene and you should dress up for the ocassion. Tables open around 10 pm and close around 4 am – expect to pay an entrance fee. The place to go is Monte-Carlo's Casino. Only foreigners are allowed to play here, so you'll need your passport and you must be over 18. At the glamorous casino in Nice you can enjoy spectacular dinner cabarets, as well as take your chances at the gaming tables and slot machines.

Sports and Outdoor Activities

- Most tourist offices publish separate booklets detailing their leisure facilities, whether it's a pétanque (boules) pitch, sports hall, swimming pool (*piscine*), tennis court or golf course. Look for details of local sporting facilities amid the tourist publications under *loisirs* (leisure).
- The area around the Lubéron attracts **climbers** from all over the world. Contact the Club Alpin de Français (www.clubalpin.com) for information about climbing lessons or equipment rental for experienced climbers.
- **Cycling** is a popular pastime, as well as a serious sport in France, and you can rent bicycles in towns and at major railway stations. Most tourist offices can offer itineraries for riders with mountain bikes (*vélo tous terrains – VTT*). The **Tour de France** is possibly France's most important sporting event (www.letour.fr). The three-week event crosses the country in July and often includes a stretch in Provence. Arrive early to find a suitable spot along the route, as the roads will be closed well before the race is expected to pass by. You don't need a ticket to watch.
- Many of the rivers in Provence, including the spectacular Grand Canyon du Verdon, are excellent for **kayaking** and **canoeing**. You can rent equipment on site by the hour, the day or longer, or take a guided kayak trip. Fédération Française de Canöe-Kayak: www.ffck.org.
- The waterways of Provence offer plenty of opportunities for **angling** and **fly-fishing**. You will need a licence, available from fishing shops.
- There are plenty of **golf** courses in Provence, especially on the coast. You can get details of special offers on green fees for visitors from tourist offices. They also have details of passes allowing holidaymakers to visit a selection of courses. Fédération Française de Golf: www.ffg.org.
- **Football** is one of the most popular sports in France. Olympique de Marseille and A.S. Monaco are among the region's top teams. A.S. Monaco plays at Stade Louis II (tel: 377 92 05 37 54; www.asm-foot.mc); Olympique de Marseille at Velodrome 3, boulevard Michelet (tel: 04 91 77 56 09; www.olympiquedemarseille.com). The season runs from August to the end of May.
- **Horse racing** is popular in France and there are *hippodromes* (race courses) in some of the coastal towns and resorts in Provence. The main venues are at Cagnes-sur-Mer (www.hippodrome-cotedazur.com) and Marseille (www.hippodrome-borely.com).
- **Horse-back riding** trips into the flat marshes of the Camargue are an ideal way to discover the area's spectacular scenery. You'll also find riding clubs close to major towns and cities, including Les Milles, near Aix. Fédération Française d'Équitation: www.ffe.com.
- **Motor racing** fans will look forward to the most glamorous race in the Formula 1 calendar, when the narrow streets of Monte-Carlo are turned into a race track (www.monte-carlo.mc).
- There are **sailing schools** and boats for rent at most of Provence's ports and marinas (www.voilecotedazur.com). Sailing is also popular in the mountain lakes of the Alpes-de-Haute-Provence, such as Lac de Quinson and Lac du Castillon.
- There are **windsurfing** schools all along the coast. The best places to watch the experts are at Stes-Maries-de-la-Mer and l'Almanarre, near Hyères.
- Provence is criss-crossed by **walking** and **hiking** trails. A series of *Sentiers de Grandes Randonnées* (long-distance trails) and *Petites Randonnées* (shorter walking routes) are marked on maps. Most tourist offices have information about trails and walks in their area, including marked trails around lakes, along river banks or linking historical monuments, and town halls usually have free maps of local walks.

The Alpes-Maritimes

Getting Your Bearings 36 – 37
In Three Days 38 – 39
Don't Miss 40 – 53
At Your Leisure 54 – 57
Where to... 58 – 62

Getting Your Bearings

The name Alpes-Maritimes portrays the very essence of this region – the perfect combination of sea and mountains, attracting millions of visitors annually. After all, the French Riviera is one of the world's most sophisticated holiday playgrounds, with its trio of chic seaside cities – Nice, Monaco and Cannes – each rivalling the other with their luxury hotels, award-winning restaurants, designer boutiques and glitzy marinas brimming with millionaires' yachts.

Despite the Riviera's popularity, it is still possible to escape the bustling tourist-courting coastal resorts and explore the *arrière pays* (hinterland): to ramble through hectares of wild *garrique* landscapes; to hike in the wild hills, forests and mountains of the unspoiled Parc National du Mercantour; and to explore such sleepy hilltop villages as Èze, Biot and St-Paul-de-Vence – all set in countryside painted with the vivid colours of Picasso, Renoir and Matisse.

Art has flourished here for centuries, and today the region boasts more than its fair share of magnificent museums and galleries, including Musée Matisse, Musée Chagall and MAMAC (Musée d'Art Moderne et d'Art Contemporain) in Nice; Musée Picasso in Antibes; Musée Renoir between Cagnes-sur-Mer and Haut-de-Cagnes; and the dazzling Fondation Maeght, one of the world's most distinguished modern art museums, at St-Paul-de-Vence.

From art treasures to sleepy villages, glamorous resorts and dramatic landscapes, the Alpes-Maritimes is a region of great contrasts. No wonder many visitors return here year after year for their annual fix of Mediterranean *joie de vivre*.

Page 35: Resting beside the river in the Parc National du Mercantour

Left: A floral extravaganza, Nice Carnival

★ Don't Miss

1 **Nice** ➤ 40
2 **The Corniches** ➤ 44
3 **Monaco** ➤ 48
4 **Fondation Maeght** ➤ 51
5 **Parc National du Mercantour** ➤ 52

At Your Leisure

6 Vence ➤ 54
7 Grasse ➤ 54
8 Cannes ➤ 55
9 Antibes ➤ 55
10 Biot ➤ 55
11 Cagnes-sur-Mer ➤ 56
12 Villa Ephrussi de Rothschild ➤ 56
13 Menton ➤ 57

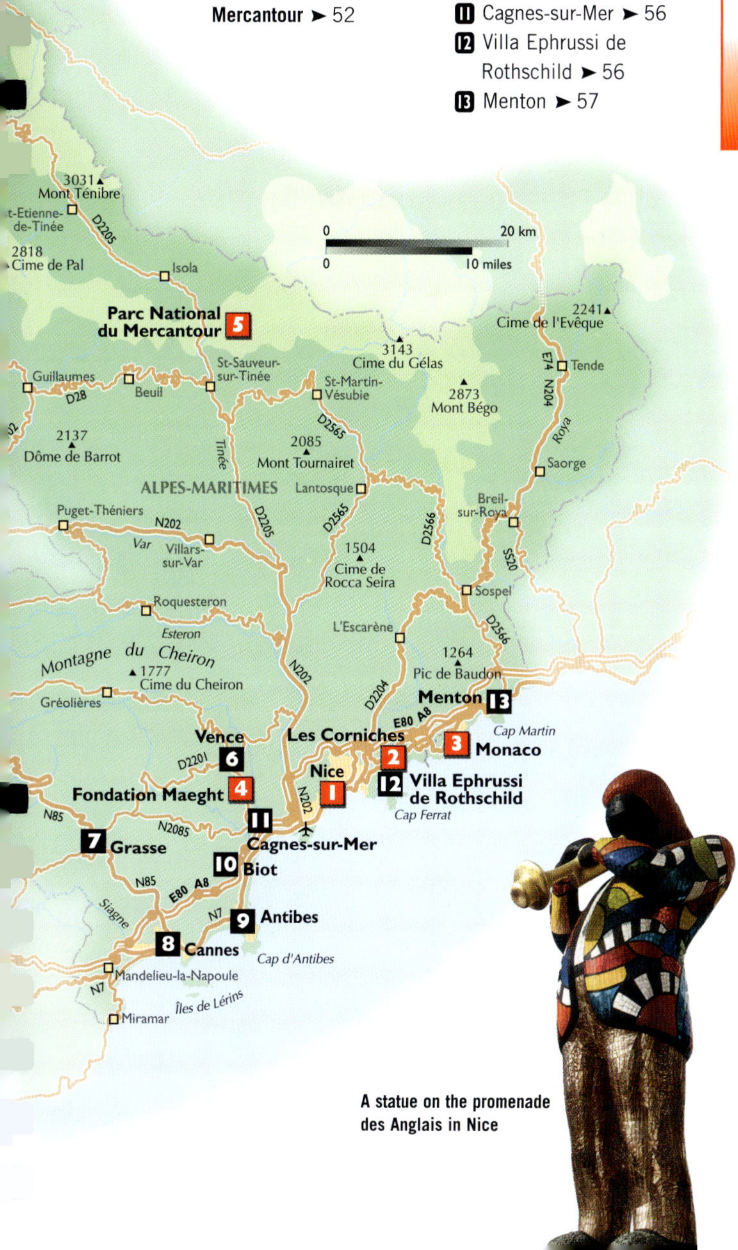

A statue on the promenade des Anglais in Nice

Three days is hardly long enough to explore this region, but it is just enough to get a taste of the glamorous Riviera, by focusing on Nice and Monaco and some of their surrounding sights.

The Alpes-Maritimes in Three Days

Day One

Morning

Start your day in 1 **Nice** (➤ 40–43) at the cours Saleya (➤ 42). This sunny square is home to one of France's best outdoor flower, fruit and vegetable markets (below) and, with all the colours and fragrances of Provence, it is a veritable feast for the senses. Watch the world go by from the pavement terraces of one of the many cafés here, then spend the rest of the morning getting lost in the maze of narrow streets and shaded alleys of Vieux Nice (➤ 42). Here you will find some fascinating specialist boutiques, art galleries and an excellent choice of restaurants for lunch.

Lunch

If you're lucky, you may get a table at La Mérenda (4 rue de la Terrace, no phone), a tiny restaurant near cours Saleya, which specialises in Niçois dishes.

Afternoon

Visit one of Nice's major galleries: the beautiful Musée Matisse (➤ 43) set in olive groves overlooking the city, or the remarkable Musée d'Art Moderne et d'Art Contemporain (MAMAC), which traces the history of French and American avant-garde from the 1960s.

Evening

Stroll the palm-lined waterfront Promenade des Anglais before enjoying a performance at the Opéra de Nice (➤ 62). Dine near by, at elegant La Petite Maison (11 rue St-François-de-Paule, tel: 04 93 92 59 59).

Day Two

Morning

Visit the modern art collection at 4 **Fondation Maeght** (➤ 51), just outside St-Paul-de-Vence. This charming village (left) is also well worth a visit, with its art galleries and sophisticated boutiques which line the steep, cobbled streets.

Lunch

Grab a light lunch on the terrace at Café de la Place (place Général de Gaulle, St-Paul-de-Vence, tel: 04 93 32 80 03), and watch locals playing pétanque.

Afternoon

Drive the snake-like, cliff-hanging 2 **Moyenne Corniche** (➤ 44–47) from Nice to Monaco, for some of the Riviera's most spectacular scenery. En route, stop for refreshment in the picture-postcard hilltop village of Èze (➤ 45).

On arrival in 3 **Monaco** (➤ 48–50), head straight to the world-famous Musée Océanographique (➤ 49), with attractions to fascinate all ages.

Evening

The cobbled streets of Monaco-Ville with their fountain-filled squares and grand Italianate façades are especially atmospheric in the evening light. Experience traditional Monégasque cuisine at Le Castelroc (place du Palais, tel: 0377 93 30 36 68) opposite the Palais Princier (➤ 49), then join bejewelled gamblers to try your luck in the world's most famous Casino (place du Casino, Monte Carlo, ➤ 49, 50, 62).

Day Three

Take a picnic and spend the day exploring the 5 **Parc National du Mercantour** (right, ➤ 52–53). With its high mountains, lakes, forests and verdant meadows, this vast country park is an absolute must for nature-lovers.

1 Nice

Nice, one of the biggest and most vibrant cities along the Mediterranean coast, is the capital of the Riviera. There's an old Italian corner to discover, and if you're here in the two weeks before Lent you're bound to get swept up by the colourful frenzy of the Mardi-Gras carnival, the Riviera's biggest winter event. The entire city is cradled by the vine-clad foothills of the maritime Alps, and this charming setting has attracted many famous artists over the years. As a result, Nice is blessed with more museums and galleries than any French town outside Paris.

Nice's history has been influenced by successive owners, including the Ligurians, the Greeks and the Romans, and only became part of France when the Italians (who called it Nizza) handed it over in the 1860. In the 19th century it became a chic winter resort, with Queen Victoria among its illustrious visitors.

Nice Highlights

The palm-lined **promenade des Anglais**, which graciously sweeps round the Baie des Anges (Bay of Angels), is bordered by a busy highway and the grand façades of luxury *belle-époque* hotels, such as the world-famous **Négresco**. Stretching for several kilometres beside the town's stony beach, on fine days it is full of people taking a leisurely stroll, sitting in the sun or skating. The promenade ends at **Colline du Château**, a high headland which separates the beach and the port. There is no trace of the medieval fortress which once stood here, but you will find shady gardens and fabulous views of the crowded Old Port – busy with all kinds of craft – the sea and town.

The park-like Paillon promenade divides the Old Town from the New and is home to several museums.

Left: Boats in the harbour at Nice
Right: The view from Colline du Château

Hôtel Négresco

The Négresco, one of France's most magnificent hotels, features Churchill, Chaplin, Piaf, Taylor and Burton, Picasso and the Beatles on its guest list. Inside, the décor is inspired by Versailles, while from the outside, its pink-and-white turreted façade looks more like a wedding cake than a hotel. You may have trouble finding the main entrance, which is in a small back street.

Above: Enjoying an meal and a drink on a summer's evening on the cours Saleya
Below: The Cathédrale Orthodoxe Russe St-Nicolas

Around the handsome main square, **place Masséna**, are the broad boulevards and designer shops of the modern city, and a pedestrian-only area of narrow streets lined with specialist shops and inexpensive restaurants. Set back from the sea at the eastern end of the beach is **Vieux Nice** (Old Nice), a maze of dark narrow streets, festooned with flowers and laundry and brimming with cafés, hidden squares and bustling markets. This is the trendiest part of Nice, lively day and night, especially around **cours Saleya**. This spacious square is scene of one of France's top fruit and vegetable markets – the tastes, fragrances and colours of Provence are a feast for the senses. In the evenings, cafés and restaurants fill the square, making it one of Nice's most animated night spots.

On higher ground to the north you'll find **Cimiez**, a district of luxury villas and palatial buildings considered to be the city's smartest residential area. Near by lies the site of a **Roman settlement**, and you can explore Les Arènes (a small oval amphitheatre), paved streets, public baths and a museum of excavated remains. Europe's leading international Jazz Festival is held in Cimiez every July, in the beautiful olive grove beside the **Musée Matisse** (► 43).

The **Cathédrale Orthodoxe Russe St-Nicolas**, in the St-Etiénne district, is a magnificent pink-and-grey Russian Orthodox church, crowned by six gleaming green onion-shaped cupolas. Brimming with precious icons, frescoes and treasures, the church still conducts regular services in Russian.

TAKING A BREAK

Dine on fabulous fresh seafood with a Mediterranean twist at the moderately priced **L'Âne Rouge**, overlooking the harbour (7 quai des Deux-Emmanuel, tel: 04 93 89 49 63).

NICE: INSIDE INFO

Top tips The ***Carte Musées Ville de Nice*** (€6 for 7 days), available from the tourist office, gives unlimited access to many of the galleries and museums.
- Admission to the municipal galleries is **free to all** on the first and third Sundays of every month.

Hidden gems Two of the lesser-known museums, but well worth seeking out, are the **Asian Arts Museum**, at 405 promenade des Anglais, and the **Anatole Jakovsky International Museum of Modern Art**, on avenue de Fabron, which houses naïve art from all over the world.

Top Galleries at a Glance

Musée d'Art Moderne et d'Art Contemporain

196 D2
Promenade des Arts
04 93 62 61 62; www.mamac-nice.org
Tue–Sun 10–6
Inexpensive, free 1st and 3rd Sun of month

This intriguing modern structure of four towers linked by bowed girders and glass holds a great collection of **avant-garde and pop-art** dating from the 1960s. Highlights include works by Lichtenstein, Warhol and Christo, as well as French New Realists (➤ 10). Visit the rooftop terrace for spectacular views of Nice.

Musée Matisse

196, off C3
164 avenue des Arènes de Cimiez
04 93 81 08 08; www.musee-matisse-nice.org
Wed–Mon 10–6
Inexpensive

Matisse (1869–1954), who spearheaded the Fauvist movement in the early 20th century, moved to Nice in 1917, and is buried in the cemetery near by. This gallery, in a handsome 17th-century villa in the gardens at Cimiez, contains the artist's breathtaking collection of his own sinuous sketches and brightly coloured gouache paintings.

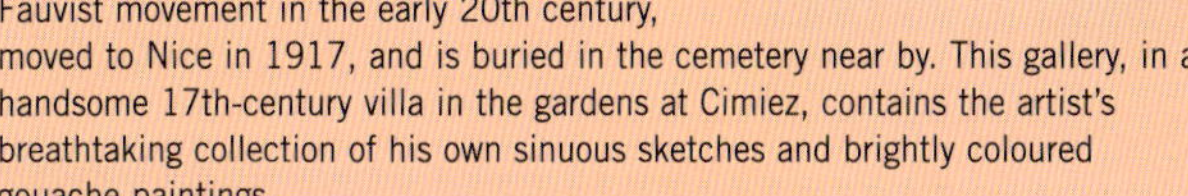

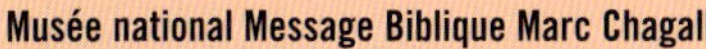

Musée national Message Biblique Marc Chagall

196 C3
Avenue de Dr Ménard, Boulevard du Cimiez
04 93 53 87 20
Wed–Mon 10–5 or 6
Moderate

Located in the heart of a Mediterranean garden at the foot of Cimiez hill, this museum was specially designed to hold the French Surrealist artist's **biblical works**, with fabulous stained-glass panels, mosaics and paintings.

Tourist Information Office

189 D2 5 promenade des Anglais
0892 707 407; www.nicetourism.com
Mon–Sat 8–8, Sun 9–7, summer; Mon–Sat 9–6, winter

Musée Archéologique de Cimiez

196, off C3 160 avenue des Arènes
04 93 81 59 57 Wed–Mon 10–6. Guided tours by appointment Moderate

Cathédrale Orthodoxe Russe St-Nicolas

196 A2 Avenue Nicolas-II 04 93 96 88 02
Mon–Sat 9:15–12, 2:30–6 (5:30 winter), Sun 9:15–12
Inexpensive

A narrow stepped alley in Vieux Nice

2 The Corniches

Three famous corniches (cliff roads) traverse the most dramatic and mountainous stretch of the Riviera between Nice and Menton. The Grande, Moyenne and Inférieure corniches each zigzag their way along vertiginous ledges at three different elevations, overlooking the resorts and beaches.

The Grande Corniche, at the highest level, was built by Napoléon along the route of the old Via Julia Augusta, and passes through picturesque hilltop villages. This is by far the best choice for picnickers and lovers of plants and wildlife. The steep Moyenne Corniche , in the middle, is a wide modern road. This cliff-hanging route, with hair-raising bends, sudden tunnels and astounding views, is frequently used for car commercials and movie car chases. The lowest route, the Corniche Inférieure, was built in the 18th century by the

Prince of Monaco, and follows the coastal contours through all the wealthy coastal resorts and Monaco itself.

There are lots of highlights to explore along this stretch of coastline. The most strikingly situated and best-preserved Provençal hilltop village, **Èze** stands high on a rocky pinnacle ten minutes' drive from Nice and Monaco on the Moyenne Corniche. Known as the *Nid d'Aigle* (Eagle's Nest), it boasts spectacular views over the entire Riviera as far as Corsica. Tall, golden stone houses and a labyrinth of tiny vaulted passages and stairways climb steeply up to the ruins of the once-massive Saracen fortress, 429m (1,407 feet) above sea level, which is surrounded by an exotic garden, bristling with magnificent cacti, succulents and rare palms. Take time to explore the craft shops housed in small caves within the rock – tiny treasure troves of antiques, ceramics, pewter and olive-wood carvings. At the foot of the hill, the two perfume factories of Galimard and Fragonard both contain fascinating museums.

Left: The spectacular view from the Jardin Exotique

Below: The Roman Trophée des Alpes, detail of carving above, rises above La Turbie

To the east, but just as high, is the village of **La Turbie** on the Grande Corniche, easily recognisable due to the huge Roman monument, the Trophée des Alpes, built in honour of Emperor Augustus who captured this Alpine region in the first century BC. In the gardens surrounding the trophy there is a small museum documenting its restoration, and from the terrace behind there is a stunning panorama of Monaco and the coastline from Italy to the Esterel.

On the Corniche Inférieure, or Basse Corniche, **Villefranche-sur-Mer**, close to Nice, remains surprisingly unspoiled and little changed since it was founded in the 14th century as a customs-free port. Its picturesque natural harbour is fringed with old red and orange Italianate houses, tempting waterfront bars, cafés and restaurants. Take time to explore the maze of steep stairways and cavernous vaulted passageways which climb from the harbour through the Vieille Ville (Old Town), and the sturdy 16th-century citadel, with galleries of paintings and sculptures by local artists, including Picasso and Miró.

Jutting out into the Mediterranean, the peninsula of **Cap Ferrat** bristles with luxurious mansions and villas hidden away behind tall gates and impenetrable hedges. These include the peninsula's finest property, Villa Ephrussi de Rothschild, (➤ 56–57). The cape has long been a favourite haunt of the rich and famous, including writer Somerset Maugham, chanteuse Edith Piaf, the Duke and Duchess of Windsor, and movie stars Charlie Chaplin and David Niven. A delightful coast path leads from Villefranche around the cape, past countless tiny azure inlets (ideal for a refreshing dip), and makes a pleasant stroll before lunch in the former fishing village of St-Jean-Cap Ferrat.

On the eastern side of Cap Ferrat is **Beaulieu-sur-Mer**. Sheltered by a natural amphitheatre of hills, this is one of the warmest resorts on the Riviera. Its many attractions include an elegant palm-lined promenade, a glamorous casino, the elegant Edwardian Rotonde, and the extraordinary Villa Grecque Kérylos – a faithful reproduction of an Athenian villa.

Sandwiched between Menton and Monaco, **Roquebrune-Cap Martin** is divided into two areas – Old Roquebrune, an attractive medieval hilltop village, and the smart coastal resort of Cap Martin. Old Roquebrune is a maze

THE CORNICHES: INSIDE INFO

Top tips The **Corniche Inférieure** is very busy in the main tourist season of July and August, so travel early if you want to visit one of the coastal resorts.

- Browse **Roquebrune-Cap Martin's** daily food and flower market.
- Drop into the **local tourist offices** and pick up a map detailing local coastal walks.

Hidden gem In Villefranche-sur-Mer, the tiny 14th-century **Chapelle St-Pierre**, by the quay, was decorated in 1957 with symbolic frescoes by Villefranche's most famous resident: writer and film director Jean Cocteau (tel: 04 93 76 90 70; open Tue–Sun 10–12, 3–7; admission inexpensive).

of ancient flower-filled lanes, steps and vaulted passageways clustered around its 10th-century château, which was built to ward off Saracen attack. A delightful coastal path (promenade Le Corbusier) circles the cape, passing sumptuous villas shrouded in dense foliage.

TAKING A BREAK

Tuck into the *plat du jour* at **La Grotte** in place des Deux-Frères, at the entrance to Roquebrune village. This popular troglodyte restaurant has tables spilling out into the square (tel: 04 93 35 00 04, closed Wed). If you're in Èze then try the tasty crêpes on offer at **Le Cactus** in the old gateway (tel: 04 93 41 19 02, open Feb–Oct).

Tourist Offices

189 E2
Jardin François-Binon, Villefranche-sur-Mer
04 93 01 73 68

189 E2
59 avenue Denis Semeria, Cap Ferrat 04 93 76 08 90

189 E2
Place de Gaulle, Èze
04 93 41 26 00

189 E2
Place Clemenceau, Beaulieu-sur-Mer
04 93 01 02 21

189 E2
218 avenue Aristide Briand, Roquebrune-Cap Martin
04 93 35 62 87

A bird's-eye view of Villefranche-sur-Mer and its harbour

3 Monaco

After the Vatican, Monaco is the world's smallest sovereign state – a spotlessly clean, 2sq km (less than 1sq-mile) strip of skyscraper-covered land squeezed between sea and mountains. It has become an affluent and stylish haven for the world's rich and famous, who are drawn here by its attractive tax-free status.

Monaco is the name of the principality and also the district on the peninsula to the south. This contains the Old Town with its narrow streets and pastel-coloured houses, a startling contrast to the newer high-rise district of **Monte-Carlo**, centred round its glitzy casino and designer shops. With so much evident wealth and glamour, it is hard to imagine Monaco's turbulent past, but at various times it has been occupied by the French, the Spanish and the

Dukes of Savoy. For the last 700 years, the principality has been ruled by the Grimaldi family, the world's oldest reigning monarchy.

The Old Town, **Monaco-Ville**, is reached via a long steep walkway from place d'Armes or by an elevator from parking des Pêcheurs on the seafront. This labyrinth of cool, cobbled streets perched on "the Rock" (a sheer-sided finger of land extending 800m/880 yards into the sea) has been well

High-rise apartments overlook the Mediterranean in the millionaire resort of Monte-Carlo

preserved, with lovely fountain-filled squares and fine Italianate façades.

The **Palais Princier** and surrounding gardens are situated at the western end of Monaco-Ville. In summer, when Prince Albert II is away, guided tours take visitors through the priceless treasures of the State Apartments and the small Musée Napoléon in the south wing of the palace. When he is in residence, the royal colours are flown from the tower and you must be content with the Changing of the Guard ceremony (daily at 11:55 am). Close by is the Cathédrale, built in 1875 and funded by casino profits. Among its treasures are two 16th-century retables by Niçois artist Louis Bréa, and tombs of the former princes of Monaco and the much-loved Princess Grace (1929–82).

The Musée Océanographique is one of France's most popular museums

Monaco's prestigious **Musée Océanographique**, a spectacular aquarium and museum of marine science, is located in a grandiose building on a sheer cliff high above the Mediterranean. Marine explorer Jacques Cousteau set up his research centre here and his remarkable films are regularly screened in the museum's cinema. Superbly lit aquariums hold thousands of rare fish, displays of living corals from all over the world and a state-of-the-art shark lagoon.

The famous Casino

La Condamine, at the foot of the royal palace, is the busy commercial district. It is fun to wander along the quayside and marvel at the size and cost of the yachts, but take time to explore the back streets too, for they hide some superb shops and restaurants. **Fontvieille**, a modern residential and commercial development, built on reclaimed land below the rock of Monaco-Ville, has a marina, sports stadium and excellent shops; it also has the Princess Grace Rose Garden, a peaceful oasis fragrant with the scent of 4,000 rose trees. Just off the Moyenne Corniche, above the residential district of Les Moneghetti, lies one of Monaco's finest attractions, the **Jardin Exotique**, bristling with thousands of cacti and succulents.

The world-famous **Casino**, in glitzy Monte-Carlo, is worth a visit even if you are not a gambler. Its opulent *belle-époque* interior is a riot of pink, green and gold, with marble floors and bronze sculptures. To the left of the casino is the Café de Paris and the casino's Salons Américans, a clattering room of poker machines, with free entry. Ten euros will gain you entry to the Salons Européens in the casino proper, with blackjack, craps and roulette tables; and a further ten will take you into the lavish Salons Privés. Attached to the Casino is a tiny, ornate opera house, which has been graced by the world's most distinguished opera singers. The place du Casino, dazzlingly illuminated by night, is a Monaco must see.

A statue of Princess Grace

TAKING A BREAK

You can rub shoulders with the beautiful people on the sun terrace at **Zebra Square**, a chic restaurant at

10 avenue Princesse-Grace, Monte-Carlo (tel: 377 99 99 25 50), or try **Stars'N'Bars** at 6 quai Antoine I, La Condamine (tel: 377 97 97 95 95, closed Mon in winter), a popular American-style bar-restaurant, perfect for families.

Tourist Information Office
197 C3
2a boulevard des Moulins
377 92 16 61 16;
www.visitmonaco.com;
www.monaco-tourisme.com
Mon–Sat 9–7, Sun 10–12

Palais Princier
197 A2 Place du Palais
377 93 25 18 31 Daily 9:30–6, Jun–Sep; 10–5 Oct. Closed Nov–May Moderate

Musée Océanographique
197 B1 Avenue St-Martin
377 93 15 36 00 Daily 10–6, Oct–Mar; 9:30–7, Apr–Jun, Sep; 9:30–7:30, Jul–Aug Expensive

Casino
197 C3
Place du Casino 377 92 16 20 00 Salons Européens from 2 pm; Salons Privés from 4 pm
Expensive

Jardin Exotique de Moneghetti
197, off A3
Off Moyenne Corniche
Daily 9–7, 15 May–15 Sep (closes 6 or nightfall in winter)
Moderate

Tropical plants thrive in the Jardin Exotique de Moneghetti

MONACO: INSIDE INFO

Top tips The currency in Monaco is the **euro**.
- Don't visit Monaco during the **Grand Prix in May** unless you are a motor racing fan. The principality is crowded and many of the roads are closed.
- You must be over 18 to visit the **Casino**. Don't forget to take your passport and wear a jacket and tie.
- A frequent **bus service** runs the length of Monaco from 7 am to 8 pm.
- For a different perspective of Monaco take one of the **boat trips** from quai des Etats-Unis, Port d'Hercule, tel: 377 92 16 15 15.

Hidden gem Seek out the tranquillity of **Jardin Japonais**, a Shinto garden near the Larvotto beach area.

4 Fondation Maeght

The Fondation Maeght, opened in 1964, is one of the most distinguished modern art museums in the world. It was the brainchild of Aimé and Marguerite Maeght, who were art dealers and close friends of Matisse, Miró, Braque, Bonnard and Chagall, and it was their private collection that formed the basis of the museum.

The gallery is artfully hidden amid umbrella pines above the quaint hilltop village of St-Paul-de-Vence. It is surrounded by a compact park which contains a collection of sculptures, mosaics and murals. The building itself blends into its natural surroundings, with massive windows, light traps in the roof, and extraordinary white cylindrical "sails" atop the building.

Fondation Maeght's remarkable permanent collection consists entirely of 20th-century art and includes works by nearly every major artist of the past 50 years. The star sights include the cour Giacometti – a tiled courtyard peopled with skinny Giacometti figures – Chagall's vast, joyful canvas *La Vie*, and Miró's *Labyrinthe*, a fantastic multi-level maze of fountains, trees, mosaics and sculptures.

The nearby hilltop village of **St-Paul-de-Vence** has strong links with the artistic community. In the 1920s, St-Paul was discovered by a group of young, impoverished artists – Signac, Bonnard, Modigliani and Soutine – who stayed at the modest Auberge de la Colombe d'Or, paying for their lodgings with their paintings. Other artists were also drawn to the village, including Marc Chagall, who is buried in the cemetery here. Today, the village's steep, cobbled streets are full of galleries, and it is one of the most beautiful and well-preserved villages in Provence.

Miró sculpture in the museum's grounds

TAKING A BREAK

The museum's **café** makes a pleasant place to stop for lunch.

---

189 D2
St-Paul-de-Vence
04 93 32 81 63;
www.fondation-maeght.com
Daily 10–12:30, 2:30–6, Oct–Jun; 10–7, Jul–Sep Expensive

FONDATION MAEGHT: INSIDE INFO

Hidden gem Don't miss the **chapel** in the grounds, which contains stained glass by Braque, Ubec and Marq. It was built in memory of the Maeght's son, who died in childhood.

5 Parc National du Mercantour

A short journey inland from the Riviera, on roads climbing through the Tinée, Vésubie and Roya valleys, are the majestic, snow-capped peaks of the Provençal Alps and the Parc National du Mercantour, the only remaining French National State Park. This beautiful mountain region stretches for over 128km (80 miles) along the Italian border and combines superb wildlife with the warm climate of the Mediterranean. It has no permanent inhabitants, but basic refuges on well-marked mountain trails offer shelter or overnight lodgings (these must be reserved in advance).

The small town of **Tende**, on the Roya river, is the main entry point to the park. The highly varied landscapes of the Mercantour range from gentle green pastureland and Alpine forests to glacial lakes, canyons and peaks. The park starts at an altitude of 490m (1,605 feet), and as you climb, the pines and larches of the lower slopes give way to Alpine meadows and rock-strewn scree, before reaching permanent snow on peaks at 3,000m (9,845 feet) high.

Popular with walkers and climbers, the park is carefully managed, with guides, park rangers and facilities. There are 600km (370 miles) of paths in the park and several nature trails, such as those at Lac d'Allos and Col de la Bonette. Two long-distance hiking trails, GR5 and GR52, also cross the area. Most of the park's higher reaches are covered in snow from mid-October to mid-June, limiting accessibility for all but the most experienced climbers.

Trekking the Vallée des Merveilles

PARC NATIONAL DU MERCANTOUR: INSIDE INFO

Top tips **Picking flowers is forbidden** in the park, as are camping, fires, pets and waste disposal.

- For **information about the park** – including walking and ATB (All Terrain Bike) trails, as well as guided tours – call in at the park's main office in Nice, at 23 rue d'Italie, tel: 04 93 16 78 88.
- **Col de la Cayolle refuge** (tel: 04 92 81 24 25) is open from mid-June to mid-September and can provide information on walking and ATB trails, as well as guided tours.

Don't miss The most remarkable excursion into the Parc is the **trek to the Vallée des Merveilles**, a valley on a high tributary of the Roya, where thousands of drawings are etched on the rocks. Many more can be seen in the nearby **Vallée de Fontanalbe**. In a simple style resembling stick men, these images, thought to have been made in the Bronze Age (1800–1500 BC), depict hands, weapons, tools and horns. Guided tours leave Refuge des Merveilles at 7:30, 11 and 3 daily in July and August. On the D91 at Lac des Mesches there is a parking area at the start of the path to the Refuge des Merveilles (a 3-hour walk away).

Flora and Fauna

The park provides sanctuary for most of Europe's mountain animal species, including wild boar, marmot, chamois, ibex and mouflon (wild sheep), as well as bright butterflies. In springtime the meadows are ablaze with bellflowers and blue gentians. There is also the rare big, spiky saxifrage (*Saxifraga florulenta*), the symbol of the park. Soaring overhead are birds such as eagles, kestrels, falcons and vultures. Smaller birds include the ptarmigan, great spotted woodpecker, hoopoe, citril finch, ortolan and rock bunting.

Below: A signpost points the way

TAKING A BREAK

You can have meals at the **refuges** if you make a reservation. Alternatively, take a picnic with you.

---

189 D4

Mercantour Information Office

Parc National du Mercantour, Centre Accueil Valberg, 1 rue St-Jean, 06470 Valberg 04 93 102 58 23; www.parc-mercantour.com Daily 10–1, 3–7, summer; hours vary in winter

Background

In the 19th century, the Mercantour was Italy's royal hunting ground. In 1946, the area was split across national borders, and 68,000ha (168,000 acres) returned to France. Both nations granted the site national park status, and the park has been designated a protected nature reserve since 1979.

At Your Leisure

6 Vence

Vence, only 10km (6 miles) inland from Cannes or Antibes, has long attracted artists. The town's main attraction, **Chapelle du Rosaire**, is in the modern suburbs to the north. The chapel was designed by Henri Matisse (1869–1954) as a thank you to Dominican sisters who nursed him when he was seriously ill. The interior is decorated with powerful black line drawings of the Stations of the Cross, coloured by pools of light from the stained-glass windows.

At the heart of the lovely Old Town are place du Frêne and place du Peyra, where you can drink mineral-rich water from a fountain. From here head down the narrow rue du Marché, lined with mouth-watering food shops, to place Clemenceau, where you'll find Roman tombstones incorporated into the walls of the 10th-century cathedral – the site was formerly a Roman temple. In the baptistery at the back there's a mosaic by Marc Chagall (1887–1985).

188 C2

Tourist Information Office

Place du Grand-Jardin

04 93 58 06 38; www.ville-vence.fr

Chapelle du Rosaire

Avenue Henri-Matisse 04 93 58 03 26 Mon, Wed, Sat 2–5:30, Tue, Thu 10–11:30, 2–5:30 (Fri 2–5:30 during school hols), Sun service at 10 am. Closed mid-Nov to late Dec

Inexpensive

7 Grasse

Lavender fields are one of the memorable sights of Provence, and the flowers they produce are a key ingredient in the modern perfume industry. Molinard, Galimard and Fragonard are the great perfumeries located in Grasse, the **capital of the perfume industry**, which supplies perfumes to all the biggest names, including Chanel and Dior. All three offer factory tours. Roses and jasmine, flowers essential to the industry, are celebrated with their own festivals in May and August. The cathedral on place Godeau is worth a quick look inside for the three early paintings by Rubens, dating from 1601.

188 B1

Tourist Information Office

Palais de Congrès, 22 cours Honoré Cresp 04 93 36 03 56; www.grasse-riviera.com

Mon–Sat 9–7, Sun 9–1, 2–6, Jul–Sep; Mon–Sat 9–12:30, 2–6, Oct–Jun

Top: A shady corner in Vence

8 Cannes

Cannes is a chic resort with excellent shopping, good entertainment, and major international cultural and business events, including the prestigious **film festival** held each May.

The town is divided into two parts. To the west is the Old Port area with its waterside esplanade and narrow lanes which climb to le Suquet, the old hilltop quarter. To the east, modern Cannes is built round la Croisette, the elegant seafront promenade. Floodlit by night and lined with designer shops, this is the place to see and be seen, or perhaps try your own hands in the concrete prints of the stars, set in the pavement outside the Palais des Festivals.

Unfortunately, payment is required for access to many parts of the town's long, sandy beach, but there are public areas at both ends.

188 C1
Tourist Information Office
Palais des Festivals, 1 boulevard de la Croisette 04 92 99 84 22; www.cannes.fr; www.cannes-fest.com
Daily 9–8, Jul–Aug; 9–7, Sep–Jun

9 Antibes

A small thriving resort, Antibes attracts its share of luxury craft in the large yacht harbour, Port Vauban. The most appealing parts of the town are in the central **historic quarter**, where Italianate buildings are crowded into the remains of a 17th-century defensive wall designed by the great military engineer Sébastien le Prestre de Vauban (1633–1707). This area is a maze of cobbled, winding lanes and crowded squares overflowing with shops, restaurants and bars.

The chief reason to visit Antibes is the **Musée Picasso**. Paintings, drawings, ceramics and sculptures, mostly dating to the three months in 1946 that Picasso spent here, are housed in a severe medieval fortress that once belonged to the Grimaldis of Monaco. Closed until January 2008.

189 D1
Tourist Information Office
11 place Général de Gaulle 04 92 90 53 00 Daily 9–7, Jul–Aug; Mon–Fri, 9–12:30, 1:30–6, Sat 9–noon, 2–6, Sep–Jun

Musée Picasso
Château Grimaldi 04 92 90 54 20 Closed until Jan 2008
Moderate

10 Biot

Set back from the sea between Antibes and Nice lies the charming hilltop village of Biot – a mass of steep cobbled lanes leading up to the famous arcaded main square. This little town has been a thriving

Bottom left: Bowls of scents in Grasse
Below: The colourful cours Masséna market, Antibes

pottery centre since Roman times, but today it is famous for its gold- and silverwork, ceramics, olive-wood carving and busy glassworks. Visitors can watch glass-blowers at the **Verrerie de Biot** demonstrating their unique *verre bullé* (bubble glass).

Near by, the striking **Musée national Fernand Léger**, with its huge mosaic façade and stained-glass windows, was founded in 1959 in memory of cubist painter Fernand Léger, who lived at Biot for a short time and inspired the growth of the craft workshops here. The museum contains nearly 400 of his works, including ceramics, tapestries, stained glass and mosaics.

Villa Euphrussi de Rothschild

188 C1

Tourist Information Office
46 rue St-Sébastien
04 93 65 78 00

Musée national Fernand Léger
Chemin du Val de Pôme 04 92 91 50 30 Wed–Mon 10:30–6, Jul–Sep; Wed–Mon 10–12:30, 2–5:30, Oct–Jun Inexpensive, free under 18

11 Cagnes-sur-Mer

Cagnes is divided into three areas: the old fishing quarter and main beach area of Cros-de-Cagnes; Cagnes-Ville, the commercial centre with its smart racecourse beside the sea; and Haut-de-Cagnes. This inviting hilltop village of is crowned by a 14th-century château which houses several exhibitions. The château also hosts the **Festival Internationale de la Peinture** from July to September. Renoir spent the last 11 years of his life near by at Domaine des Collettes, now the **Musée Renoir**. He would sit and paint beneath the olive trees, brushes strapped to his rheumatic fingers.

189 D2

Tourist Information Office
6 boulevard Maréchal-Juin 04 93 20 61 64; www.cagnes-tourisme.com

Musée Renoir
19 chemin des Collettes 04 93 20 61 07 Wed–Mon 10–12, 2–6, May–Sep (5 Oct–Apr). Closed Nov
Moderate

12 Villa Ephrussi de Rothschild

This rose-pink *belle-époque* palace and its gardens belonged to the flamboyant Baroness Béatrice Ephrussi de Rothschild (1864–1934), a woman of seemingly unlimited means. The remarkable interior is lavishly decorated with rare furniture (some pieces once belonged to Marie Antoinette), set off by rich carpets

For Kids

• **Antibes** Treat the whole family to a day at **Marineland**, where you can see dolphins, sea lions, sharks and much more. The complex includes a farm, butterfly jungle, water park and crazy golf (Route N7, opposite Antibes Land, open daily).
• **Grasse** Enjoy **go-karting** for children and adults, just outside Grasse at Fun Kart, Bar-sur-Loup (Route de Gourdon, open daily).
• **Cagnes-sur-Mer** Spend a memorable family night out at the **horse races** at the Hippodrome (Mon, Wed, Fri from 8:30 pm, early Jul–Aug).
• **Monaco** Jacques Cousteau's world-famous **Musée Océanographique** appeals to children of all ages (➤ 49). The **terraces of Fontvieille** were built to house numerous museums, including impressive collections of model boats and vintage cars, and a zoo (naval museum, tel: 0377 92 05 28 48; classic car exhibition, tel: 0377 92 05 28 56; zoo, tel: 0377 93 25 18 31). The **Musée National** is home to a huge collection of dolls dating from the 18th century to Barbie (17 avenue Princesse-Grace; open daily).

and tapestries. Rare *objets d'art* include one of the world's most beautiful collections of Sèvres and Vincennes porcelain. You can wander around the ground floor of the villa and through the stunning gardens at your leisure, but to see the collections on the first floor you must take a guided tour.

189 E2
Chemin du Musée, St-Jean-Cap Ferrat 04 93 01 33 09 Daily 10–6. Closed 25 Dec Expensive

13 Menton

Close to the border, France's most Italianate resort, with its steep jumble of tall, honey-coloured houses, is wedged between a palm-lined bay and a dramatic mountain backdrop. The terraced slopes behind the town are smothered in citrus groves, and every February a spectacular **Lemon Festival** takes place in the Jardins Biovès. The **medieval Old Town** has two magnificent churches – Église St-Michel and the Chapelle de la Conception. Other notable sights include the Musée Jean-Cocteau, the Musée de la Préhistoire Régional, and Palais Carnolès – Menton's main art museum.

189 E2
Tourist Information Office
Palais de l'Europe, avenue Boyer
04 92 41 76 76

Where to... Stay

Prices
Expect to pay per night for a double room
€ under €100 **€€** €100–€200 **€€€** over €200

CANNES

Chalet de l'Isère €
Situated in a quiet part of Cannes, just a 5-minute walk from the centre, this two-star hotel has eight bedrooms which are simply, yet individually decorated. All rooms have air-conditioning, soundproofing and TV. The hotel has its own restaurant, which serves Italian dishes alongside traditional Provençal cuisine, and there is a pretty tiled garden where you can enjoy breakfast. The Palais des Festivals is just a 10-minute walk away.

188 C1 ✉ 42 avenue de Grasse ☎ 04 93 38 50 80

ÈZE

Château Èza €€€
This enchanting hotel is a collection of medieval houses, linked together to form a luxury "eagle's nest". Most rooms and all the suites have private balconies with panoramic views, which can also be enjoyed from the restaurant.

189 E2 ✉ Rue de la Pise ☎ 04 93 41 12 24; www.chateaueza.com

MENTON

Claridge's €
This two-star hotel in the centre of Menton is 5 minutes from the town's casino, the Promenade du Soleil and the beaches. The 39 simply decorated bedrooms are quite small, but they are comfortable and have TV and air-conditioning. Some rooms are suitable for families. Facilities include parking, a bar and a lounge, and there is a terrace which looks onto the street. Breakfast not included.

189 E2 ✉ 39 avenue de Verdun ☎ 04 93 35 72 53; www.claridges-menton.com

MONACO

Hotel Alexandra €€
The Alexandra is a good-value option for its location, less than 500m (550 yards) from the casino, restaurants, nightlife and elegant shops of Monte-Carlo, and with the beaches just a 10-minute walk away. The exterior of this three-star hotel has classic *belle-époque* features, while the 56 modern bedrooms have soundproofing, mini-bar, TV and a safe. Continental breakfast is served in the bedrooms.

197 C3 ✉ 35 boulevard Princesse-Charlotte, Monte-Carlo ☎ 377 93 50 63 13; www.monte-carlo.mc/alexandra

NICE

Hôtel Armenonville €€
A warm welcome awaits at this attractive, two-star hotel in a 20th-century mansion. The 12 bright rooms are tastefully decorated with antique furniture, and have beautiful tiled bathrooms. The hotel is set in flower-filled gardens where breakfast can be served. There is free parking within the hotel grounds.

196 A1 ✉ 20 avenue des Fleurs ☎ 04 93 96 86 00; www.hotel-armenonville.com

Hôtel de la Buffa €€
Set in an early 20th-century building, this unpretentious, two-star hotel, close to the promenade

des Anglais and the sea, makes a comfortable and inexpensive base for exploring the city and the surrounding area. The welcoming hotel has 13 air-conditioned bedrooms which are simply furnished with Provençal fabrics, and all rooms have private shower, hairdryer and TV. The quieter rooms face north, while those facing the street have double glazing. Breakfast not included. Private parking available.

196 B1 56 rue de la Buffa 04 93 88 77 35; www.hotel-buffa.com

Hôtel Négresco €€€

Prominently located on the famous promenade des Anglais, the black dome of the Négresco is a much-loved Nice landmark dating back to 1912 (➤ 41). Inside, it's a luxurious palace of art, with works covering all periods from the Renaissance to the 21st century. Everything here is on a grand scale, and guests staying in the 145 rooms or 24 suites have access to the hotel's own private stretch of Mediterranean beach.

196 A1 37 promenade des Anglais 04 93 16 64 00; www.hotel-negresco-nice.com

ST-JEAN-CAP-FERRAT

Grand Hotel du Cap Ferrat €€€

This is a sumptuous palace in lush, tropical gardens, amid some of the world's most expensive real estate.

189 E2 Boulevard Général-de-Gaulle 04 93 76 50 50; www.grand-hotel-cap-ferrat.com

ST-PAUL-DE-VENCE

La Colombe d'Or €€€

Once a modest 1920s café where Braque, Matisse, Picasso and Léger paid for their drinks with canvases, this is now a deluxe hotel offering all the services you would expect. Advance reservations essential.

188 C2 Place du Général-de-Gaulle 04 93 32 80 02; www.la-colombe-dor.com

Where to... Eat and Drink

Prices
Expect to pay for a three-course meal for one, excluding drinks and service
€ under €25 **€€** €25–€50 **€€€** over €50

ANTIBES

Le Brûlot €

This authentic restaurant, with its antique baker's oven, beamed ceilings and attractive exposed stone walls, is full of character. In the vaulted basement there is a second dining room, which dates from the 12th century. Many of the dishes are prepared on the wood oven, including grilled steak with Provençal herbs, and grilled scampi flambéed with the local aniseed spirit – pastis. A lovely tarte au citron is on the list of desserts. The house specials include couscous and ham on the bone.

189 D1 3 rue Frédéric Isnard 04 93 34 17 76; www.brulot.com Closed Sun and Aug

CANNES

Caffe Roma €

This Italian bar-restaurant with a great atmosphere, is an ideal place for a break and a restorative ice cream or cocktail, or if it's a meal you're after, then try one of the tempting Italian specialities, such as ravioli stuffed with cheese and spinach, or veal with lemon sauce and pine nuts. Desserts include delicious home-made tiramisu. You can choose to eat al fresco on the terrace, or in the elegant dining room. The restaurant, facing the port and the Palais des Festivals, is very popular in both summer and winter.

188 C1 ✉ 1 square Mérimée ☎ 04 93 38 05 04; www.cafferoma.fr ⏲ Daily 7 am–1 am

Claridge €€

There's a pub atmosphere at Claridge, where the international sporting events shown on a large screen in the main room draw a young crowd. The décor here is brasserie style, with marble tables. This is the place to come for a drink, an ice cream, or a more substantial meal of traditional brasserie fare.

188 C1 ✉ 2 place du Général de Gaulle ☎ 04 93 39 05 86 ⏲ Daily 7 am–midnight (2:30 am weekends)

MONACO

Stars'N'Bars €€

The perfect place for families who want a change from formal French restaurants, this popular American-style bar-restaurant offers a predominantly Tex-Mex menu. The bar has lots of games to keep kids amused. In the evenings there's live music or a disco.

197 B1 ✉ 6 quai Antoine I, La Condamine ☎ 377 97 97 95 95; www.starsnbars.com ⏲ Daily (closed Mon in winter), food served 11:30 am–midnight, bar open to 2 am

MOUGINS

Le Moulin de Mougins €€€

This 16th-century former olive mill, surrounded by greenery and decorated with contemporary works of art, is the place to go for a gastronomic treat. The menu is seasonal, with sophisticated Mediterranean dishes, while the excellent wine cellar has more than 5,000 vintages. You can also take cooking classes here.

188 C1 ✉ Quartier Notre-Dame-de-Vie ☎ 04 93 75 78 24; www.moulin-mougins.com ⏲ Tue–Sun 12–2:30, 7:30–9:30

NICE

L'Acchiardo €

One of the few authentic café bar/restaurants remaining in Old Nice, serving simple, nourishing dishes at reasonable prices, and probably the best fish soup in Nice.

196 D1 ✉ 38 rue Droite ☎ 04 93 85 51 16 ⏲ Closed Sat and Sun

Aphrodite €€

The imaginative culinary creations of chef David Faure are a seductive blend of classic French and Niçois cuisine. His delectable desserts would grace any modern art gallery.

196 C2 ✉ 10 boulevard Dubouchage ☎ 04 93 85 63 53 ⏲ Closed Sun and Mon

Chez Simon €€€

Situated just outside the city, this former inn has a traditional dining room with beamed ceilings, wicker chairs and a plough-wheel candelabrum. In fine weather you can choose to eat outdoors on the terrace while watching a game of pétanque. The Provençal cuisine on offer includes stuffed mutton tripe and hake.

189 D2 ✉ St-Antoine-de-Ginestière ☎ 04 93 86 51 62; www.restaurantchezsimon.com ⏲ Daily 12:30–2, 7:30–10. Closed Sun dinner and Mon in low season, 2 weeks Nov and 2 weeks Feb

ST-PAUL-DE-VENCE

Mas d'Artigny €€€

Well known for its regional cuisine, including *fruits de mer* and fish dishes, and local wines.

188 C2 ✉ Route de la Colle ☎ 04 93 32 84 54; www.mas-artigny.com ⏲ Daily

Where to... Shop

There are plenty of shopping opportunities in this area. Cannes and Monaco have a reputation for glamour, Grasse is at the heart of the perfume industry and excellent local markets abound.

MARKETS

Nice holds several markets on the animated cours Saleya, with its many shops and cafés. The **Marché Saleya** offers lots of locally grown produce, including olives, tomatoes and basil (open Tue–Sun 7 am–1 pm); for antiques try the **Marché à la Brocante** (open Mon 8–5), and the **Marché aux Fleurs** for exotic flowers and trees (open Tue–Sat 6:30–5:30, Sun 6:30–1:30). Stroll through the evening arts and crafts market if it is Provençal handicrafts you're interested in (open Tue–Sun 6 pm–midnight, Jun–Sep).

SOUVENIRS AND GIFTS

Grasse, world-renowned as a perfume capital, is home to many perfumeries. **Fragonard**, one of the oldest and most prestigious, has a perfume museum and a shop (20 boulevard Fragonard, factory open 9–6:30, shop 9–6). The tiny, traditional perfumerie **Parfums Poilpot** in Nice (10 rue St-Gaëtan) also has a wide choice of scents from Grasse.

Biot is famous for its traditional bubble-flecked glassware, which is produced and sold at **Verrerie de Biot** (chemin des Combes, Mon–Sat 9:30–6, Sun 10:30–1, 2:30–6). You can buy beautiful hand-blown bottles, jars, dishes and glasses and visit the workshop.

L'Herminette Ezasque in Èze (rue Principale, open summer 10–7, winter 10–6), in the walls of the old gateway, sells wonderful Christmas cribs and *santons*. For beautiful Provençal fabrics, sold by the metre or transformed into finished items, stop at **Les Images de Provence** in Menton (21 rue St-Michel, open daily 9–7).

FASHION

Jacques Loup is an institution for every fashionista in Cannes (21 rue d'Antibes, open Mon–Sat 9:30–8). In addition to its own collection, this shoe shop has the latest designs from international shoemakers. It also stocks clothes from Prada, Marni and Miu Miu.

In Monaco, men will love **Cravatterie Nazionali** for designer ties (7 avenue Spélugues) and **Society Club** (17 avenue Spélugues) for the latest designer labels. Hats for every occasion can be found at **La Chapellerie** in Nice (36 cours Saleya, open Mon–Sat 9:30–12:30, 2–7).

FOOD AND DRINK

In Nice the best place to buy traditional crystallised fruits is at **Maison Auer** (7 rue St-François-de-Paule). For olive oil, visit **Alziari** (14 rue St-François-de-Paule) or **Moulin à Huile Alziari** (318 boulevard de la Madeleine, open Mon–Fri 8–12, 2–6).

The **Caprioglio Wine** store in old Nice has wines to suit all purses, from *vin de table* to the top *crus* (16 rue de la Préfecture). Nice's best ice-cream maker is **Glacier Fenocchio** (2 place Rossetti); here you'll get big servings and truly original tastes.

In St-Paul-de-Vence, visit **La Petite Cave de St-Paul**, a 14th-century cellar containing a choice selection of Provençal wines (47 rue Grande).

Where to... Be Entertained

BARS, CLUBS AND CASINOS

La Siesta in Antibes offers every sort of night-time entertainment, from a casino to dance floors (route du Bord-de-Mer, tel: 04 93 33 31 31, open daily 11 pm–4 am, mid-May to mid-Sep; Fri–Sat 11 pm–4 am, rest of year).

Casino Ruhl, Nice's glamorous casino, offers spectacular dinner cabarets, as well as private gaming rooms (promenade des Anglais, tel: 04 97 03 12 22, open 10 am–5 am). If you want to dance the night away to the latest sounds, from house to R&B, then try Nice's largest indoor nightclub, **L'Odace** (29 rue Alphonse Karr, tel: 04 93 82 37 66, open midnight–4 am); alternatively visit **Le Guest**, an established Niçois nightspot in the Old Port, with tropical guerrilla décor (5 quai des Deux-Emmanuels, tel: 04 93 56 83 83, open 11:30 pm–5 am). **Nocy-Be** is a chic Morrocan café in Vieux Nice, with low lighting, floor cushions, tea, cakes and aperitifs (4–6 rue Jules Gilly, tel: 04 93 85 52 25, open Mon–Fri 5–12:30, Sat–Sun 4–12:30).

While living the high life in Monaco, visit the famous **Café de Paris**, which has a restaurant, as well as a gaming house (place du Casino, tel: 0377 92 16 20 20, open from 10 am). The **Casino de Monte-Carlo** is probably the most famous in the world and has featured in Bond movies (place du Casino, tel: 377 92 16 20 00). If you're still feeling lucky, head for the bright lights of Cannes and **Casino Croisette** (1 esplanade Lucien Barrière, tel: 04 92 98 78 00, open 10 am–5 am, games room from 8 pm), or simply chill out on the terrace of **Le Festival** bar (52 la Croisette, tel: 04 93 38 04 81, open 9 am–midnight).

THEATRE AND MUSIC

Cannes' modern **Palais des Festivals et des Congrès** hosts the annual film festival in May, but is also a year-round venue for international concerts, ballet, theatre and exhibitions (1 boulevard de la Croisette, tel: 04 93 39 01 01).

In Nice, the modern congress, arts and tourism centre **L'Acropolis**, is popular for theatre, films and concerts (1 esplanade Kennedy, tel: 04 93 92 83 00). The **Opéra de Nice** is home of the Nice Opera, the Philharmonic Orchestra and Ballet Corps (4–6 rue St-François-de-Paule, tel: 04 93 13 98 53). The modern **Théâtre de Nice (TDN)** presents world-class shows (promenade des Arts, tel: 04 93 13 90 90).

SPORTS AND ACTIVITIES

There are excellent beaches along the Mediterranean coast, the larger ones offering watersports, and most of the ports and marinas have sailing schools and boats for rent (www.voilecotedazur.com).

You can take to the skies with the **Aéroclub d'Antibes** (Aérodrome de Cannes Mandelieu, 245 avenue Francis Tonner, Cannes La Bocca, tel: 04 93 47 64 43; www.aeroclub-antibes.com) and soar over the bay of St-Tropez, the Alps and the cliffs of Bonifacio in southern Corsica.

Cannes Bowling (189 avenue Francis-Tonner, 06150 Cannes La Bocca, tel: 04 93 47 02 25) has bowling lanes, pool tables and a restaurant.

Palais des Sports Jean Bouin has an Olympic-size skating rink in Nice and welcomes those looking for a little icy adventure (esplanade Maréchal-de-Lattre-de-Tassigny, tel: 04 97 20 20 30).

The Var and Haute-Provence

Getting Your Bearings 64 – 65
In Three Days 66 – 67
Don't Miss 68 – 77
At Your Leisure 78 – 83
Where to... 84 – 88

Getting Your Bearings

The Var and Haute-Provence together boast some of the finest and most dramatic scenery in the south of France, most notably in the two mountainous *départements* of the Alpes-de-Haute-Provence and the Haute-Alpes, where picture-postcard villages and towns, rich in Provençal and Alpine architecture, bear witness to an eventful past. Here, too, is Europe's "Grand Canyon", the Gorges du Verdon, the second deepest gorge in the world after the Grand Canyon, which offers a wealth of sporting activities ranging from climbing and mountain-biking to canoeing and white-water rafting.

★Don't Miss

1 **St-Tropez** ➤ 68
2 **Hyères and the Îles d'Hyères** ➤ 72
3 **Gorges du Verdon** ➤ 74
4 **Corniche de l'Esterel** ➤ 77

At Your Leisure

5 Ramatuelle ➤ 78
6 Grimaud ➤ 78
7 Bormes-les-Mimosas ➤ 79
8 Collobrières ➤ 79
9 Abbaye du Thoronet ➤ 80
10 Moustiers-Ste-Marie ➤ 80
11 Digne-les-Bains ➤ 81
12 Entrevaux ➤ 82

Previous page: The Gorges du Verdon
Below: Riding the rapids

The Var is the most wooded region of France, with its forests of chestnuts, cork oaks and conifers, interrupted only by an occasional hidden village. It also claims Provence's longest coastal strip, far less developed than its famous Riviera neighbour.

The wild, rugged landscape of the blood-red Corniche de l'Esterel, with its jagged creeks and tiny rocky coves, contrasts sharply with the sun-bleached sandy beaches of nearby Fréjus and St-Tropez. The coastal resorts have an air of faded glory, with the exception of St-Tropez, which remains almost as glitzy and hedonistic as it was in its "Swinging" Sixties heyday. The picturesque port here remains a favourite mooring for the ostentatious yachts and gin-palaces of the glitterati, but explore beyond the quayside and you will discover a village of great charm. As French writer Colette remarked: "Once you have visited here, you will never want to leave."

Digne-les-Bains 11
Entrevaux 12
Moustiers-Ste-Marie 10
Gorges du Verdon 3
Abbaye du Thoronet 9
Corniche de l'Esterel 4
St-Tropez 1
Ramatuelle 5
Grimaud 6
Collobrières 8
Bormes-les-Mimosas 7
Hyères 2
Îles d'Hyères 2
ALPES-DE-HTE-PROVENCE
VAR
TOULON
Plateau de Valensole
Parc Naturel Régional du Verdon
Massif des Maures
Montagne de Lure
0 25 km
0 15 miles

From the beaches and nightlife of glitzy St-Tropez to the breathtaking scenery of the Gorges du Verdon and the Alps of Haute-Provence, this itinerary has something to suit all tastes, but is especially suited to lovers of the great outdoors.

The Var and Haute-Provence in Three Days

Day One

Morning

Catch a ferry from 2 **Hyères** to Port-Cros, one of the three **Îles d'Hyères** (➤ 72–73) and France's only offshore national park, with its fantastic woodland walks among holm oak, strawberry trees and myrtle. Bring your snorkel, mask and fins and follow the island's unique underwater path to see octopuses, eels, sea peacocks and black-faced blennies amid colourful sponges and sea anemones.

Lunch

The cafés lining the palm-fringed harbour of Port-Cros are ideal for a light lunch before returning by boat to Hyères.

Afternoon

Drive towards St-Tropez via picturesque 7 **Bormes-les-Mimosas** (above, ➤ 79), a hilly village of ice-cream coloured houses, celebrated for its mimosa festival in February. You may also have time to detour to the equally delightful hilltop village of 6 **Grimaud** (➤ 78–79) or fashionable 5 **Ramatuelle** (➤ 78) en route.

Evening

Soak up the atmosphere of St-Tropez's Old Town at La Citadelle restaurant (➤ 86).

Day Two

Morning
Explore the chic boutiques and galleries of **1 St-Tropez** (➤ 68–71), and the bustling Marché Provençal in place des Lices (Tue and Sat am, ➤ 69), before visiting the Vieux Port (right) to watch the world go by.

Lunch
Sénéquier (➤ 86) on quai Jean Jaurès – one of the top celebrity haunts – serves delicious coffee and light lunches alongside the harbour.

Afternoon
Spend the afternoon on one of St-Tropez's acclaimed sandy beaches (➤ 71), or explore the wild rocky coastline of the blood-red **4 Corniche de l'Esterel** (➤ 77). En route, visit Fréjus, once a busy Roman town and naval base, with its ancient arena and theatre, and one of the oldest baptisteries in France. Walkers will enjoy the two-hour hike (from the Pointe de l'Observatoire) up Cap Roux, the peak of the Massif de l'Esterel (➤ 77), with its spectacular coastal scenery.

Evening
Return for dinner in one of St Tropez's myriad bistros – La Bouillabaisse (➤ 86) is a popular options. Then rub shoulders with the rich and famous at Les Caves du Roy or the VIP Room (➤ 88).

Day Three

Morning
Head north to the **3 Gorges du Verdon** (➤ 74–76), the longest, wildest canyon in Europe and a paradise for sports lovers.

Lunch
Try some regional specialities at Les Santons (place de l'Église, tel: 04 92 74 66 48) in **10 Moustiers-Ste-Marie** (left, ➤ 80–81), a beautiful village renowned for its *faïence de Moustiers*.

Afternoon
Visit the Musée de la Préhistoire des Gorges du Verdon (➤ 76) at Quinson, or drive further north into Haute-Provence to visit the spa town of **11 Digne-les Bains** (➤ 81–82), the lavender-growing capital of Provence. From here, the Train des Pignes runs through breathtaking scenery four times a day to Nice.

1 St-Tropez

This charming fishing port, which reached the height of international fame in the "Swinging" Sixties, continues to be a playground of the rich and famous. Today, most visitors come to rub shoulders with celebrities from the world of pop music, movies and TV in the waterfront cafés on the picturesque old quayside and to admire the yachts, moored before a backdrop of pink and yellow pastel buildings. These are relatively modern, reconstructed from original designs after the destruction that occurred during World War II.

St-Tropez is based around its picturesque **old quayside**, which is very much the place to see and be seen. Despite the large numbers of visitors and huge luxury yachts moored alongside, it still has a villagey charm. At one end of the quay, which curves along the edge of a beautiful bay, are the remnants of the old fortifications, and the jetty called Môle Jean Réveille. Beyond, the tiny, endearing quarter called La Ponche was once a waterside fishermen's district. Another surviving fragment of the fortifications, Tour Jarlier, stands close by.

At the other end of the quay is the **Musee de l'Annonciade**, a stylish art museum in a former 16th-century religious building. Here you'll find one of the finest collections of French late 19th- and early 20th-century paintings and bronzes. Most of the 100 or so canvases belong to the great movements of pointillism, fauvism and nabism, with many of the paintings depicting local scenes. Look for Paul Signac's *L'Orage* (1895), Bonnard's *Le Port de St-Tropez* (1899) and Camoin's *La Place des Lices* (1925), along with works by Dufy, Derain, Vuillard and others.

Turning away from the quay, you'll find the Old Town, or Vieille Ville, with its narrow streets, small old houses and several chic little boutiques. This area, closed to traffic in summer, is relatively uncrowded and a pleasant place to get away from the crowds on the quayside. On the edge of the old quarter is the

ST-TROPEZ: INSIDE INFO

Top tips Don't drive to St-Tropez – traffic is terrible, with a long wait to get into town and nowhere to park. Instead, use the large public parking areas at Port Grimaud and take the passenger ferry across the bay.

- Visit in mid-May or mid-June when the town's *bravades* **festivals** are held.
- In the summer take a **shuttle bus** from the place des Lices to the beaches.

Above: Exploring the Old Town of St-Tropez
Left: Sénéquier on quai Jean-Jaurès is a popular café

town's large main square, **place des Lices** (also known as place Carnot). This is the real heart of St-Tropez, and remains very much as it looked in Camoin's *La Place des Lices* (➤ opposite), lined with ancient plane trees and bohemian cafés. The best time to visit is on Tuesdays or Saturdays for its colourful market, but come anytime for a game of pétanque and a glass of pastis with the locals.

There are good views from the Citadel

From here the town extends into more modern areas.

The **Église St-Tropez** owes its name to a Roman centurion called Torpes, who was martyred for his Christian faith. His head was buried in Pisa and his body put in a boat with a dog and cockerel, who were to devour it. However, when the boat washed up here, his remains were miraculously untouched. For over 400 years the town's most important festival – the Bravade de St-Torpes – has been celebrated in his honour each May. You can see a gilt bust of St Torpes and a model of his boat in the 19th-century baroque-style church, with its distinctive pink and yellow bell-tower.

To the east of town visit the 16th-century hilltop fortress, **La Citadelle**, if only for the view, which embraces the orange curly-tiled roofs of St-Tropez's Old Town, the dark and distant Maures and Esterel hills, and the glittering

History

Founded by Greeks as Athenopolis (City of Athena), the town has long been a popular meeting place for artists. Liszt and Maupassant were its first celebrities in the 1880s, followed by neo-Impressionist painter Signac a decade later. Soon Matisse, Bonnard, Utrillo and Dufy fell under St-Tropez's spell, immortalising the town in paint. Many pictures can be seen in the **Musée de l'Annonciade** (➤ 68 and 71).

blue of the bay, flecked with sails. The Citadel contains a naval museum, illustrating the town's long and glorious history, right up to the 1944 Allied landings that destroyed so much of the town.

TAKING A BREAK

La Table du Marché, a smart bistro-cum-deli, offers excellent meals, light snacks, regional specialities, cakes, pastries and wines. It also serves afternoon tea (38 rue Georges Clemenceau, tel: 04 94 97 85 20, open daily all year).

---

193 E3

Tourist Information Office
Quai Jean-Jaurès
04 94 97 45 21
Daily 9:30–8, Jul–Aug; daily 9:30–12:30, 2–7, Apr–Jun, Sep–Oct; daily 9.30–12.30, 2–6, Nov–Mar

La Citadelle
Montée de la Citadelle
04 94 97 59 43
Daily 10–6:30, Apr–Sep; daily 10–12:30, 1:30–5:30, Oct–Mar
Moderate

Église St-Tropez
Rue de l'Église
Daily

Boats of all sizes fill the harbour at St-Tropez

Beaches

For sandy beaches you'll have to travel out of town onto the **Cap de St-Tropez**, on the peninsula. Here there are over 6km (4 miles) of enticing golden sand, divided into individual beaches, each with a different character. The trendy **Club 55** caters for the Paris set, **Tahiti-Plage** was once the movie stars' favourite, but nowadays star-spotters have more luck at the frivolous **La Voile Rouge**. For water sports head for **Pago Pago** and for seafood try **Bora Bora**.

There are plenty of beaches to choose from in St-Tropez

Musée de l'Annonciade

✉ Place Georges-Grammont
☎ 04 94 17 84 10
🕐 Wed–Mon 10–12, 3–8, Jun–Sep, (closes 10 Wed, Fri Jul–Aug); 10–12, 2–6, Oct–May. Closed Nov, 1 Jan, 1 May, Ascension, 25 Dec
Moderate

Pastel-coloured buildings front the harbour

2 Hyères and the Îles d'Hyères

Exotic plants flourish in the southerly resort of Hyères-les-Palmiers, so-called because of its important palm-growing industry. Hyères' main attraction today lies off the Var coast – the three beautiful islands of the Îles d'Hyères.

The Town

A Gothic gateway in the defensive wall in Hyères' **Old Town** leads into an atmospheric residential district of narrow streets lined with tall buildings, which climb to the ruins of a château in a park with wide views. The main square is the place Massillon marketplace, overlooked by the Tour des Templiers, once commanded by the medieval Knights Templar. Other reminders of the Middle Ages include two Romanesque–early Gothic churches: St-Paul and St-Louis. Modern Hyères, below the Old Town, is laid out with wide, busy boulevards edged with palm trees. The Jardins Olbius-Riquier, to the southeast of the old town, are glorious tropical gardens with a small animal enclosure.

A double sandbar, 4km (2.5 miles) long, connects Hyères to the **Giens Peninsula**. Here you'll find salt pans which attract numerous wading birds, and the small resort village of Giens. La Tour Fondue, at the eastern tip of the peninsula, is the departure point for ferries to the island of Porquerolles.

Above: The tower of St-Paul's Church rises above the town of Hyères

HYÈRES AND THE ÎLES D'HYÈRES: INSIDE INFO

Top tips It is **best to park** in the new town, in avenue A Denis or avenue J Jaurès, as parking in the Old Town is difficult.

- You **can't take your car to the islands**; park at the ferry terminal at Giens or near Hyères port.
- The **best beach** on the islands is Plage de la Palud, at Port-Cros.
- **Check the time** of the last ferry back before setting off for the islands.

Don't miss You can take **guided snorkelling tours** (bring your own snorkel) from La Palud beach.

The Islands

At around 18sq km (7sq miles), **Porquerolles** is the largest of the Îles d'Hyères. Preserved as a nature reserve, its forest paths are popular with walkers and cyclists. The south coast of the island has rocky cliffs, while there are sandy beaches on the north coast. Ferries arrive at the little quay of Porquerolles village on the north coast, overlooked by the 19th-century Fort Sainte-Agathe (now an exhibition venue).

Port-Cros, around 10sq km (4sq miles), lies to the east. It is covered with dense Mediterranean woodland and is protected as a national park. Walkers use a network of pretty paths, including a marked trail which leads up to the Fort de l'Estissac and Fort du Moulin, beside the village. The rocky **Île du Levant**, just 8sq km (3sq miles), is the most easterly of the island group. Much of the island has been taken over by the army and is closed to the public, while the remainder is a nudist resort.

TAKING A BREAK

Call in for a dish of sea bass and a glass of wine in **La Colombe** in Hyères (663 route de Toulon-La Bayorre, tel: 04 94 35 35 16) or take a picnic to the islands.

Tour des Templiers in Hyères

192 B2 (town)
192 C1 (islands)

Tourist Information Office
Forum du Casino, 3 avenue Ambroise Thomas, Hyères-les-Palmiers
04 94 01 84 50; www.ot-hyeres.fr
Daily 8:30–7:30, Jul–Aug; Mon–Fri 9–6, Sat 10–4, Sep–Jun

Île de Porquerolles
Daily from Giens; timetables at www.tlv-tvm.com

Île de Port-Cros and Île du Levant
From Port-St-Pierre; timetable at www.tlv-tvm.com

Getting to the Islands

You reach the Îles d'Hyères by **public ferry** from two harbours: **Port St-Pierre** near the heart of Hyères town or the **harbour** on the Giens peninsula. The direct ferry from Giens to the Île de Porquerolles takes 20 minutes. Ferries from Port St-Pierre go to Port-Cros (1 hour) and Le Levant (90 minutes).

3 Gorges du Verdon

The Gorges du Verdon, the deepest and most dramatic river gorge in mainland Europe, takes in 21km (13 miles) of steep limestone cliffs and vegetation. Winding, narrow roads, dotted with breathtaking viewpoints giving fabulous vistas of the rocky terrain, line each side of the ravine. At the bottom run the clear waters of the river which gives the chasm its name, and which flow into the vast man-made Lac de Ste-Croix, created in 1970.

The gorge, one of the natural wonders of the world, was formed over millions of years by the River Verdon. It was surveyed for the first time in 1905 by the great speleologist Édouard-Alfred Martel. Yet even today, geology dictates that the winding roads are few and modest in scale as the canyon narrows to 198m (650 feet) across. The steep limestone cliffs rise to 700m (2,300 feet) high on each side, make them accessible only to experienced climbers. The southern route from Moustiers-Ste-Marie, the Corniche Sublime (D71), carved out in the 1940s, gives the best views, with the Balcons de Mescla viewpoint the highlight. Loop north via the ancient hilltop village of Trigance to return along the northern side and the Route des Crêtes.

Taking in the magnificent view from the Route des Crêtes

Édouard-Alfred Martel

Martel (1859–1938) is known worldwide as the father of speleology – the science of cave exploration. From an early age, and despite training as a lawyer, Martel began a pioneering exploration of the underground caverns in the limestone landscape of the Causses. His three-day exploration of the Gorges du Verdon, previously believed impenetrable, was undertaken with two companions. Martel's journey was driven partly by curiosity, and partly by the need for research into water supplies, and in the 1950s the government considered blocking the whole valley for a reservoir, but settled instead for the more limited Lac de Ste-Croix.

Exploring in the Gorges

The river powers a hydroelectric plant, and is dammed below Moustiers, offering good opportunities for experienced canoeists and white-water rafters. Short walks lead from many of the viewpoints, such as the zigzag path from the Point Sublime, on the north side. Hardy walkers can tackle the challenging Sentier Martel footpath, which runs along the valley floor between Rougon and Meyreste and takes at least one day.

TAKING A BREAK

There are plenty of cafés to choose from in the cobbled squares of **Moustiers-Ste-Marie**, though parking may be difficult in high summer. There are also lots of good *belvédères*, or viewpoints, where you can stop for a picnic and enjoy the panoramas.

192 B5

Tourist Information Office

Hôtel-Dieu, rue de la Bourgade, Moustiers-Ste-Marie (western edge of canyon)

04 92 74 67 84; www.ville-moustiers-sainte-marie.fr

Daily 10–5:30, 6:30 or 7:30, Mar–Oct; 2–5, Nov–Feb

Musée de la Préhistoire des Gorges du Verdon

Route de Montmeyan, Quinson

04 92 74 09 59; www.museeprehistoire.com

Daily 10–8, Jul–Aug; Wed–Mon 10–6 or 7, Feb–Jun, Sep to mid-Dec Moderate

Scaling the heights above Lac de Ste-Croix

GORGES DU VERDON: INSIDE INFO

Top tips The **narrow roads** which run along each side of the canyon are in places only just wide enough for two cars to pass – so take extra care if you are in a wider vehicle or towing.

- Driving just a short stretch of the **Corniche Sublime** will give you a good taste of this natural phenomenon.
- For a **drive** along the canyon ► 172–174.
- The **Sentier Martel footpath** along the river has collapsed tunnels and is subject to sudden changes in water level. It is best walked with an experienced guide or in a group.
- ***Faïence*** is the local decorative earthenware pottery, and you'll see it on sale on the streets and in the little shops of Moustiers-Ste-Marie.

Don't miss The modern, boat-shaped **Musée de la Préhistoire des Gorges du Verdon**, designed by architect Sir Norman Foster, is at Quinson, just southwest of Lac de Ste-Croix. This fabulous museum, dedicated to the people who inhabited the Gorges area around 400,000 years ago, has a re-created cave, interactive displays, and neolithic tools and other items found in the area.

4 Corniche de l'Esterel

The Corniche de l'Esterel is a winding coastal road between St-Raphaël and Théoule-sur-Mer, flanked on one side by the wild red mountains of the Massif de l'Esterel, and on the other by the sparkling blue sea. The road explores the rugged natural landscape and reveals secret coves and deserted bays.

The Corniche de l'Esterel, also known as the Corniche d'Or (Golden Coast Road) or N98, was carved into the impressive seafront cliffs over a century ago. The Touring Club de France was involved in its development, and the route is popular with cyclists. Just as dramatic by car, bus or train, the tortuous road is punctuated by viewpoints overlooking inviting beaches, sheltered yacht harbours, jagged inlets and deserted coves. A small range of hills known as the Massif de l'Esterel rises behind the coast between the little beach resort of Fréjus, with its Roman remains and medieval buildings, and the glitzy resort of Cannes. The hills provide a perfect backdrop, with their harsh, rugged mountains of brilliant red volcanic rock jutting into the sea.

Covered in green spruce, pine and scrub, and wild flowers in summer, the massif is a protected conservation area, and two valley zones, the Ravin du Mal Infernet and the Ravin du Perthus, have been designated biological reserves. They are both easily reached by road.

TAKING A BREAK

Café Excelsior, on promenade du President René Coty, St-Raphaël (tel: 04 94 95 02 42) offers popular fish dishes.

This stretch of wild coast is a ragged shoreline of red cliffs

193 F4

Tourist Information Office
Rue Waldeck Rousseau, St-Raphaël 04 94 19 52 52
Mon–Sat 9–12:30, 2–6:30

CORNICHE DE L'ESTEREL: INSIDE INFO

Top tips Visit the **tourist office** at Fréjus or St-Raphaël for a walking map of the massif, published by the Office National des Forêts.

- Some paths in the massif may be **closed in summer** because of fire risk.

At Your Leisure

5 Ramatuelle

At the heart of the St-Tropez peninsula, just a short distance inland from the busy, chic resort, lies the pretty village of Ramatuelle. Surrounded by vineyards which produce the local Côtes de Provence wine, this is one of the most fashionable places in the area to own a second home. Every summer the village hosts popular **jazz and theatre festivals**.

On the road (D89) above Ramatuelle, three ancient windmills, **les Moulins de Paillas**, offer magnificent views of the coast and the surrounding countryside. The nearby hilltop village of **Gassin**, built as a look-out point during the time of the Saracen invasions, is today a colourful place with smart boutiques and restaurants.

193 E2
Tourist Information Office
Place de l'Ormeau
04 98 12 64 00

6 Grimaud

The medieval village of Grimaud stands on the eastern slopes of the Massif des Maures, not far from St-Tropez. One of Provence's most photogenic hilltop villages, it is crowned by an **11th-century château** belonging to the Grimaldi family, after whom the village is named. The main street, the rue des Templiers, leads to the beautiful Romanesque **church of St-Michel**, the **Hospice of the Knights Templars** and a restored 12th-century mill.

Photogenic Ramatuelle – a typical Provençal hilltop village

🗺 193 D3
Tourist Information Office
✉ 1 boulevard des Aliziers ☎ 04 94 55 43 83; www.grimaud-provence.com
🕐 Mon–Sat 9–12:30, 3–7, Jul–Aug; Mon–Sat 9–12.30, 2:30–6:15, Apr–Jun, Sep; Mon–Sat 9–12:30, 2:15–5:30, Oct–Mar

7 Bormes-les-Mimosas

The pretty village of Bormes is perched on a hilltop on the Massif des Maures, just inland from the coast. At its heart is a steep medieval village with ice-cream coloured houses, evocative lanes and passageways climbing up towards the ruins of the Château des Seigners de Fos at the top of the hill.

In February, when the mimosa is in full bloom, the village celebrates with a sensational *corso fleuri* – an extravaganza of floral floats made from thousands of tiny yellow mimosa flowers.

Visit the tourist office for a map of the *circuit touristique* that explores Bormes' steep medieval stairways and alleys, a fine 16th-century chapel dedicated to Bormes' patron saint, the **Église St-Trophyme**, and the ruined 13th- to 14th-century **château** at the top of the hill.

🗺 192 C2
Tourist Information Office
✉ 1 place Gambetta ☎ 04 94 01 38 38; www.bormeslesmimosas.com 🕐 Daily 9–12:30, 2:30–6:30, summer; Mon–Sat 9–12:30, 2–6, winter

Fragrant lavender fields, for which Provence is famous, are a feature of the countryside

8 Collobrières

In the centre of the Massif des Maures, this traditional little village, surrounded by a forest of chestnut trees, is well known for the sweet *marrons glacés* (candied chestnuts) made here. Collobrières holds an annual festival at the end of October celebrating the humble chestnut. Buy chestnuts at the local market, on Sundays, and also Thursdays in summer. The village is also known for its cork, which grows in the forests near by.

Further up the road (off the D14), the **Chartreuse de la Verne**, a beautiful Carthusian monastery, sits isolated among the dense Maures forest, 12km (7 miles) from Collobrières. Founded in 1170 and originally inhabited by Carthusian monks, the complex of cloisters, chapels and cells has been home to a group of Sisters of Bethlehem nuns since the 1980s.

🗺 192 C2
Tourist Information Office
✉ Boulevard Charles Caminat
☎ 04 94 48 08 00 🕐 Tue–Sat 10–12, 2–6, also Mon in Jul, Aug

Chartreuse de la Verne
🕐 Wed–Mon 11–6, mid-May to mid-Oct; Wed–Mon 11–5, mid-Oct to mid-May. Closed religious holidays

For Kids

- **Cap de St-Tropez** Take your pick of the best beaches (➤ 71).
- **Luna Park** (at Gassin, Golfe de St-Tropez, open early Apr to mid-Sep) has some of the most exhilarating fairground rides in Europe.
- **Village des Tortues** Take a fascinating one-hour tour of this remarkable "village" with its 1,200 turtles and tortoises (at Gonfaron, off Aix–Cannes autoroute, open Mar–Nov).

9 Abbaye du Thoronet

The 12th-century Abbaye du Thoronet, hidden deep in the forest of La Daboussière to the south of Entrecasteaux, is the purest of the three great Cistercian monasteries in Provence and the first to be established (the other two are Sénanque ➤ 150–151 and Silvacane ➤ 103–104). The austere abbey soon became wealthy through substantial donations, but by the 14th century it had gone into decline and it was finally abandoned in 1791. Restoration began in the 1850s.

Passing through the gatehouse, you see ahead the low church, built in pink stone, with a square bell-tower and a plain, undecorated interior. Beside the church are attractive cloisters, a chapter house and a tithe barn, which originally stored goods given as tithes, but later became an oil mill. Mass is sung by the Sisters of Bethlehem in the church every Sunday at noon.

The plain interior of the Romanesque church of the Abbaye du Thoronet, bathed in golden light

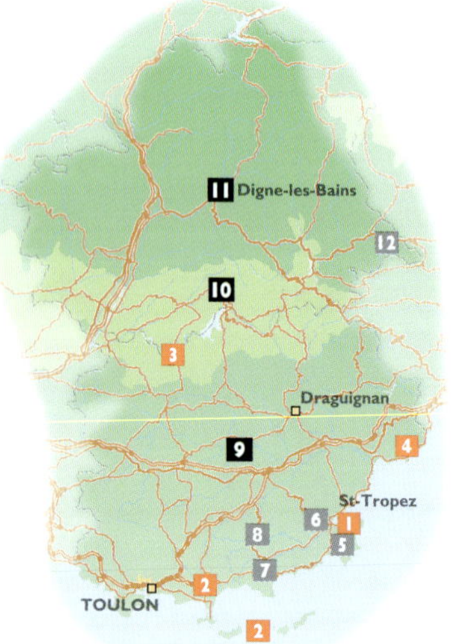

192 C4
04 94 60 43 90
Daily 10–6:30 (closed 12–2 Sun), Apr–Sep; Mon–Sat 10–1, 2–5, Sun 10–12, 2–5, Oct–Mar
Moderate

10 Moustiers-Ste-Marie

Perched high on a ridge surrounded by sheer cliffs, Moustiers is one of the main access points for a drive along the great gorges of the Verdon river (➤ 74–76). In the 5th century,

Smoke drifts from a chimney-pot among the tightly packed rooftops in Moustiers-Ste-Marie

monks settled on a rocky ledge above the village, and the present chapel of **Notre-Dame-de-Beauvour** on the site, just a short walk from the village, dates from the 12th and 16th centuries. There are two annual pilgrimages to the chapel. A long chain strung across the gorge suspends a renowned gold star high above the village. The star was presented to the village by a knight called Blacas to celebrate his release from captivity during a crusade.

In the 17th and 18th centuries, white, decorated earthenware pottery from the village became famous throughout the world. Now *faïence de Moustiers* has been revived and is sold in craft shops in every square.

186 C2

Tourist Information Office

Hôtel-Dieu, rue de la Bourgade

04 92 74 67 84; www.ville-moustiers-sainte-marie.fr

Daily 10–5:30, 6:30 or 7:30, Mar–Oct; 2–5, Nov–Feb

11 Digne-les-Bains

Its sheltered location, mild and sunny climate, invigorating air and the thermal springs to the south of town have made Digne-les-Bains a renowned spa centre. It is an excellent base for touring the hills by foot, by car or on the old narrow-gauge

The spa at Digne-les-Bains is renowned for its therapeutic benefits

"**Pinecone**" line that runs through the beautiful mountain valleys to Nice four times a day.

Digne's other major attraction is lavender. This aromatic plant, renowned since the Middle Ages for its therapeutic qualities, has made Digne the lavender-growing capital of Provence. During the spectacular purple processions of the annual **lavender festival**, for five days in early August, even the streets get doused with lavender water! You can buy lavender products at the market on Wednesdays and Saturdays in place du Général-de-Gaulle, and follow a Route de la Lavande, which passes through Digne and takes in all the main lavender producing places in the area.

186 C3
Tourist Information Office
Rond-Point du 11-Novembre 1918
04 92 36 62 62;
www.ot-dignelesbains.fr

12 Entrevaux

The impressive medieval village of Entrevaux is situated above a narrow gorge in the mountains between Nice and Digne. Once an important border defence between France and Savoy, it was heavily fortified in the 1690s by Vauban, Louis XIV's military architect.

The main access to the town is across a drawbridge, through the Porte Nationale or Porte Royale into a jumble of medieval houses lining the narrow streets. There's plenty to see here, including the fortified cathedral, a restored oil mill and flour mill, a communal bread oven and a collection of historic motorcycles. A remarkable ramp leads up a sheer rock face to Vauban's ruined **Citadel**. There is little to see at the fortress, but it is well worth the climb for the views of the Haut-Var and the mountains beyond. The Porte d'Italie, the town's third

gateway, opens onto to a pleasant riverside walk.

187 F2

The medieval village of Entrevaux seems to tumble down the hillside to the River Var below

Vauban's fortified bridge spans the narrow gorge, providing access to the village of Entrevaux

Tourist Information Office
Porte Royale 04 93 05 46 73
Open summer only Tue–Sat 9:30–12, 1:30–4:30. Access to citadel by automatic turnstile Inexpensive

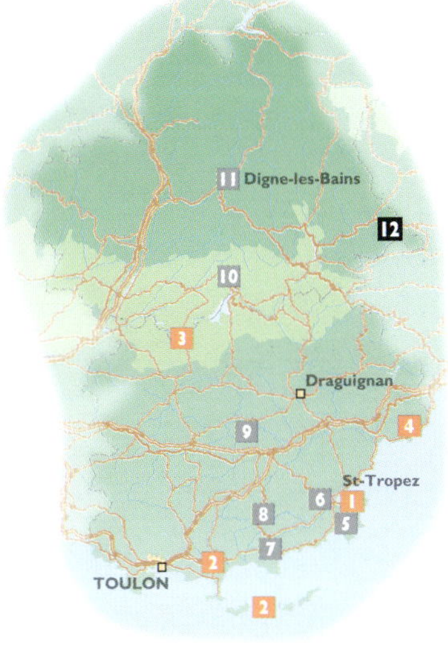

Where to... Stay

Prices
Expect to pay per night for a double room
€ under €100 €€ €100–€200 €€€ over €200

BORMES-LES-MIMOSAS

Le Bellevue €

This simple family-run hotel has spectacular views over red roofs to the sea, and is good value in this often expensive part of the world. The friendly restaurant serves fresh seafood and local Provençal dishes.

192 C2 12 place Gambetta 04 94 71 15 15; www.bellevuebormes.fr.st Closed Oct–Jan

MOUSTIERS-STE-MARIE

La Ferme Rose €–€€

This two-star inn takes its name from its pink (*rose*) façade. Inside you'll find beamed ceilings, a tiled floor and, in the restaurant, bistro furniture and some 1950s-style pieces such as a jukebox. You can enjoy breakfast (extra charge) in the garden in summer.

192 A5 04360 Moustiers-Ste-Marie 04 92 75 75 75; www.lafermerose.fr.fm Apr to mid-Nov, Christmas and New Year

La Bastide de Moustiers €€€

This former cottage, now a four-star inn, houses one of chef Alain Ducasse's restaurants (➤ 86). There are 12 bright bedrooms, each named after local themes and individually decorated. Some rooms are located in a separate building away from the main hotel, and have a private terrace and direct access to the gardens, from where there are far-reaching views over the surrounding countryside. There is an elegant dining room, and in good weather lunch and dinner are served on the terrace. The outdoor pool is surrounded by a terrace.

192 A5 Chemin de Quinson 04 92 70 47 47; www.bastide-moustiers.com

RAMATUELLE

Camping Kon Tiki €

This high-class camping ground, on the edge of the beautiful Pampelonne beach, is very popular, so reserve ahead. The mobile homes come in different styles, but each has two bedrooms, a kitchenette, lounge area and bathroom. Alternatively, bring your own caravan (trailer) or mobile home, and hook up to water and electricity. Extensive facilities here include currency exchange, safety deposit boxes, watersports, a grocery, restaurant, bar, tennis court and hot showers.

193 E2 Route des Plages 04 94 55 96 96; www.campazur.com Closed Nov–Mar

La Ferme d'Augustin
€€–€€€

This three-star hotel, a short walk from Tahiti beach and close to the centre of St-Tropez, combines traditional furnishings with modern amenities – a spa bath in the bathroom and dressing rooms in the suites, which also have a private terrace and garden. The comfortable lounges have beamed ceilings and stone fireplaces. Outside, the *balneo* pool (heated and with hydro massaging jets) is set in well-maintained gardens.

193 E2 Tahiti 04 94 55 97 00; www.fermeaugustin.com Closed mid-Oct to mid-Mar

ST-TROPEZ

Hôtel Le Baron Lodge €–€€
This hotel at the foot of the citadel has 14 peaceful double rooms, and the comfortable atmosphere of a large house. The airy rooms look onto the harbour or towards the citadel. It's an easy walk downhill to the port. This is a lovely place to stay, without being excessively luxurious. The staff are friendly and helpful, and some parking is available. Recommended.
193 E3 23 rue de l'Aïoli 04 94 97 06 57; www.hotel-le-baron.com Closed mid-Nov to mid-Dec

Hôtel Byblos €€€
This luxurious hotel is popular with the jet set. Behind an ochre and blue façade, the sophisticated interior is decorated with local materials. Spacious rooms and suites are furnished with antiques, Provençal fabrics and ceramics.
193 E3 Avenue Paul Signac 04 94 56 68 00; www.byblos.com Closed Nov to mid-Apr

Hôtel Lou Cagnard €–€€
This comfortable budget hotel is an excellent option, with rooms that are airy, clean and simple. Enjoy breakfast in the lovely garden on a sunny morning. Private parking is available.
193 E3 18 avenue Paul Roussel 04 94 97 04 24; www.hotel-lou-cagnard.com Closed Nov–Dec

Mas de Chastelas €€€
Stay with Depardieu, Belmondo and other French film idols at this beautiful 18th-century *mas* (farmhouse) situated just outside St-Tropez. Set in spacious grounds, the hotel's facilities include two swimming pools, an outdoor Jacuzzi and tennis courts.
193 E3 Quartier Bertaud, Gassin 04 94 56 71 71 Closed Nov–Dec, but may vary

Where to... Eat and Drink

Prices
Expect to pay for a three-course meal for one, excluding drinks and service
€ under €25 **€€** €25–€50 **€€€** over €50

BORMES-LES-MIMOSAS

Lou Portaou €€
In a picturesque corner of Bormes, this small restaurant serves a simple menu of fresh Provençal cuisine.
192 C2 1 rue Cubert-des-Poètes 04 94 64 86 37 12–1:30, 7–9:30. Closed Mon eve and Tue mid-Sep to mid-Jun

COLLOBRIÈRES

La Petite Fontaine €
Try some local delicacies of the Massif des Maures, washed down with wine from the local cooperative on a shady terrace. Peaceful surroundings.
192 C2 1 place de la République 04 94 48 00 12 Closed Sun dinner, Mon

DIGNE-LES-BAINS

Le Grand Paris €€
Holds the reputation as Digne's best restaurant, set in a former 17th-century convent. Try the pigeon accompanied by courgette flowers cooked in a *jus* flavoured with truffles.

186 C3 19 boulevard Thiers 04 92 31 11 15 Closed Dec–Feb

GRIMAUD

Les Santons €€

Top cuisine, fresh local ingredients and impeccable service in elegant Provençal surroundings. Les Santons serves classic French and Mediterranean dishes and is one of the region's top restaurants, so make a reservation to ensure a table at weekends or in summer.

193 D3 D558 04 94 43 21 02 Closed Wed, Thu lunch, Nov–Mar

MOUSTIERS-STE-MARIE

La Bastide de Moustiers €€€

Dine in the country home of the world's top chef, Alain Ducasse. The menu changes daily and features sensational dishes that embrace all the flavours and perfumes of the region, using seasonal produce from the local markets. The restaurant is part of a four-star inn (➤ 84).

186 C2 Chemin de Quinson, 04360 la Grisolière 04 92 70 47 47 Closed Mon–Wed, Oct–Feb

ST-TROPEZ

La Bouillabaisse €€

A restaurant that majors on fish, set in a traditional fisherman's cottage on the beach.

193 E3 Plage de la Bouillabaisse 04 94 97 54 00 Closed dinner Sun–Thu, mid-Oct to mid-May

Le Café €€

Formerly known as Le Café des Arts, this cosy bar/stylish restaurant has a long history as a centre for intellectual and artistic debate. The archetypal French bar has brown leather couches, wooden fittings and old leather-bound books on the shelves. The terrace is an ideal place to enjoy a meal or a coffee while watching a game of pétanque. Le Café is situated next to the cinema on the place des Lices, and is not to be confused with the newer Café des Arts on the corner.

193 E3 5 place des Lices 04 94 97 44 69; www.lecafe.fr Food daily 12–2:30, 7:30–11; café 8 am–midnight

Chez Fuchs €€

An unpretentious, family-run bar-*tabac*, serving cigars as well as hearty bistro fare. Traditional dishes and a lively atmosphere make tiny Chez Fuchs hugely popular. Book ahead or be prepared to wait.

193 E3 7 rue des Commerçants 04 94 97 01 25 Closed Sun–Mon

La Citadelle €€

This tiny atmospheric restaurant has tables that spill out on to the street. Don't miss the delicious tarte tatin.

193 E3 1 rue Aire du Chemin 04 94 54 81 19 Daily 12–2, 7–10:30, Apr–Oct

Sénéquier €€

You can't miss the distinctive red awnings and matching tables and chairs on the waterfront, for this is one of the best-known spots in town and a must for breakfast. There's no denying the coffees are on the pricey side, but this is really the place to be on a sunny morning in St-Tropez (➤ 68).

193 E3 Quai Jean-Jaurès 04 94 97 00 90 Daily 8 am–2 am, summer; 8 am–8 pm, winter

La Table du Marché €–€€

This smart bistro-cum-deli, situated in a narrow street close to the harbour, offers excellent meals and an array of light snacks, regional specialities, wines, pastries and cakes (a house speciality is chocolate cake filled with cream) in a relaxed setting. It also serves afternoon tea.

193 E3 38 rue Georges Clemenceau 04 94 97 91 91 Lunch and dinner all year, 8 am–midnight

Where to... Shop

MARKETS

St-Tropez has several markets including the **Marché aux Poissons**, the picturesque fish market (place aux Herbes, open 7–1). This is the best place to get Mediterranean fish such as red mullet, scorpion fish and rainbow wrasse. Even if you are not going to buy, it is worth a visit for the lively atmosphere. At the **Marché Provençal** (place des Lices, open Tue, Sat 8–1) you'll find all the typical food of Provence – there's also an antiques corner and local crafts.

Collobrières is surrounded by chestnut groves and its farmers' market, the **Marché Collobrièrois** (place de la Libération, open Thu, Sun 8–1), sells chestnut products ranging from *marrons glacés* and chestnut jam to chestnut-wood wickerwork. Cork products and other regional specialities such as olives and honey are also on offer.

FOOD AND DRINK

In St-Tropez seek out **Tarte Tropézienne** (36 rue Clemenceau, open 8–8 Feb–Oct) for the cake filled with cream that gives this shop its name. The cake was given its name by Brigitte Bardot in 1955. Nearby, at Gassin, **Petit Village** (Carrefour de la Foux) stocks the wines of the Maîtres Vignerons of St-Tropez.

Delicious mountain produce – fruit, vegetables, cheeses, truffles, pâtés, honey and herbs – are sold in Gap at **Les 4 Saisons** (place aux Herbes).

You can pick up the tastes (*saveurs*) and colours of Provence at **Saveurs et Couleurs** in Digne-Les-Bains (7 boulevard Gassendi, open Tue–Sat 8:30–12:30, 2:30–7:15) which stocks fine oils, vinegars, prepared dishes, alcohol, perfumes, Marseille soap, goods made from Provençal fabrics, and other decorative items made of olive wood and terracotta. Also stocks products from Hédiard, the world-famous Parisian *épicerie*.

SOUVENIRS AND GIFTS

Pierre Basset in St-Tropez (route des Plages) is one of the many shops selling traditional terracotta and enamelled tiles, jars, pots and vases in sunny colours.

Pépinières Cavatore (chemin de Bénat, tel: 04 94 00 40 23; www.pepinierescavatore.com) in Bormes-les-Mimosas is a nursery specialising in mimosa – visit in February to see the trees in full bloom. It's worth a visit, even if you aren't planning on buying anything. Credit cards are not accepted.

Moustiers-Ste-Marie is known for its decorated *faïences*, and you can browse the beautiful collection of vases, plates and pitchers at the studio of **Atelier Soleil** (chemin Marcel Provence, open 10–7).

In Digne-les-Bains, every imaginable lavender product is available from **La Maison de la Lavande** (38 boulevard Gassendi).

FASHION

Head to St-Tropez for trendy boutiques. **Hermès** (place Grammond) offers the ultimate in French chic, while **Blanc Bleu** (3 rue Allard, open 9:30–12, 3–7) is good for stylish, sporty fashion for both sexes. **Rondini** (16 rue Clemenceau) is famous for making the Tropézienne, a Roman-style sandal worn by many celebrities, including Picasso.

Where to... Be Entertained

BARS, CLUBS AND CASINOS

Reputedly the spiciest nightspot in St-Tropez, **Les Caves du Roy** is the haunt of the rich and famous. Admission is free but the drink prices are extortionate (Hôtel Byblos, avenue Paul-Signac, tel: 04 94 97 16 02, open 11 pm–5 am Easter–Oct). The star-studded **VIP Room** (boulevard 11-Novembre 1918, tel: 04 94 97 14 70, open 9 pm to 3 am or 5 am) is *the* place to see and be seen. For a good choice of draught beers try **Bar Anglais** (Hôtel Sube, 15 quai Suffren 83990, tel: 04 94 97 30 04, open 8 am–1 am, closes 3 am May–Oct) on the first floor of the prestigious Hôtel Sube. **La Bodega de Papagayo** (résidences du Nouveau Port, tel: 04 94 79 29 50) is a restaurant-nightclub near the Old Port. It has a terrace with great views, and is a good place for a bit of celebrity-spotting. Clubby music pumping into the small hours makes it popular with the young crowd. Bands perform almost every night during the high season. If clubbing is not your style, **Octave Café** (place de la Garonne, St-Tropez, tel: 04 94 97 22 56) is a stylish café with comfy chairs, low tables, and lounge and live music. You'll find jazz musicians playing in a small back bar area.

Digne-les-Bains' home of culture is **Palais des Expositions** (1 place de la République, tel: 04 92 31 15 21; www.mairie-dignelesbains.fr) This modular auditorium holds up to 3,000 people and hosts concerts, including international singers, and theatre and dance productions.

SPAS

A variety of different treatments are available at the spas at Digne-les-Bains and Gréoux-les-Bains. Options at **Établissement thermal de Digne-les-Bains** include facials, mud wraps and sessions at the aquagym (Eurothermes, Digne-les-Bains, tel: 04 92 32 32 92, open mid-Feb to Nov). If you are here during the first weekend in August, then you can join in the five days of festivities when Digne celebrates its other main industry – lavender.

Hydrotherapy has also been practised at **Etablissement Thermal de Gréoux-les-Bains** for centuries. Apart from the regular spa treatments there are also "Hydrotherapy-plus-golf" deals (quai des Hautes Plaines, tel: 08 26 46 81 81; www.sante-eau.com, open Mon–Sat, Mar to mid-Dec).

SPORT

The 18-hole golf course, **Golf de Digne les Bains**, nestles between mountains and has a restaurant, two-star hotel, swimming pool and tennis court (57 route du Chaffaut, Digne-les-Bains, tel: 04 92 30 58 00; open 9–6 (8–8 during the high season).

In Fréjus, you can discover a variety of dive sites, including wrecks, between Dramont and St-Tropez with **Centre International de Plongée de Fréjus** (Aire de Carénage, Port Fréjus, tel: 04 94 52 34 99; www.cip-frejus.com, open all year by appointment).

To expericence thrills on the water, **Aqua Viva Est** in Castellane offers guided full- and half-day white-water rafting, canoeing and kayaking trips along the Gorges du Verdon and the Vésubie and Tinée rivers (12 boulevard de la République, tel: 04 92 83 75 74, open Apr–late Sep).

The Marseille Area

Getting Your Bearings 90 – 91
In Two Days 92 – 93
Don't Miss 94 – 101
At Your Leisure 102 – 105
Where to... 106 – 110

Getting Your Bearings

There is a surprising amount of diversity in this small region, which embraces Marseille, France's premier port, and Aix-en-Provence, the old capital of Provence.

The city of Marseille has a particularly strong personality – laidback, vibrant and edgy. A world away from the stereotypical cities of the Riviera, this Mediterranean rough diamond lacks the glamorous promenades and glitzy hotels of Nice and Cannes, and the cache of St-Tropez. It is a traditional, hard-working city, famous for its shipping, its soap, its pastis, its bouillabaisse, the world's largest annual pétanque competition and *La Marseillaise* (► 94). Its extraordinary blend of history, race and culture led Alexandre Dumas to describe it as the "meeting place of the entire world."

By contrast, few cities are as quintessentially Provençal as Aix-en-Provence, with its beautiful honey-hued *hôtels particuliers* (mansion residences) adorned with ornamental wrought-iron balconies; its sun-baked squares splashed by nearly 100 fountains; and its lively, colourful locals' markets. Aix is the home of the Post-Impressionist artist, Paul Cézanne. It is easy to see why he was so inspired by the surrounding countryside, especially the great Montagne Ste-Victoire, with its limestone peak which reflects every hue of light and shade.

Other celebrated residents are commemorated in their home towns: Nostradamus in Salon-de-Provence, and writer Marcel Pagnol in Aubagne. Here, too, is the Château de Barben with its magnificent Le Nôtre gardens; the Cistercian Abbaye de Silvacane; and the spectacular fjord-like coastline at the Calanques. And be sure to try the speciality dish of seaside town Cassis – *oursins* (sea urchins), washed down by a glass of the local dry, fruity white wine.

Page 89: Chez Fonfon on the waterfront in Marseille
Left: A fisherman working on his nets

★ Don't Miss

1 Marseille ➤ 94
2 The Calanques ➤ 97
3 Montagne Ste-Victoire ➤ 98
4 Aix-en-Provence ➤ 100

At Your Leisure

5 Martigues ➤ 102
6 Salon-de-Provence ➤ 102
7 Château de la Barben ➤ 103
8 Abbaye de Silvacane ➤ 103
9 Cassis ➤ 104
10 Aubagne ➤ 105
11 Gémenos ➤ 105

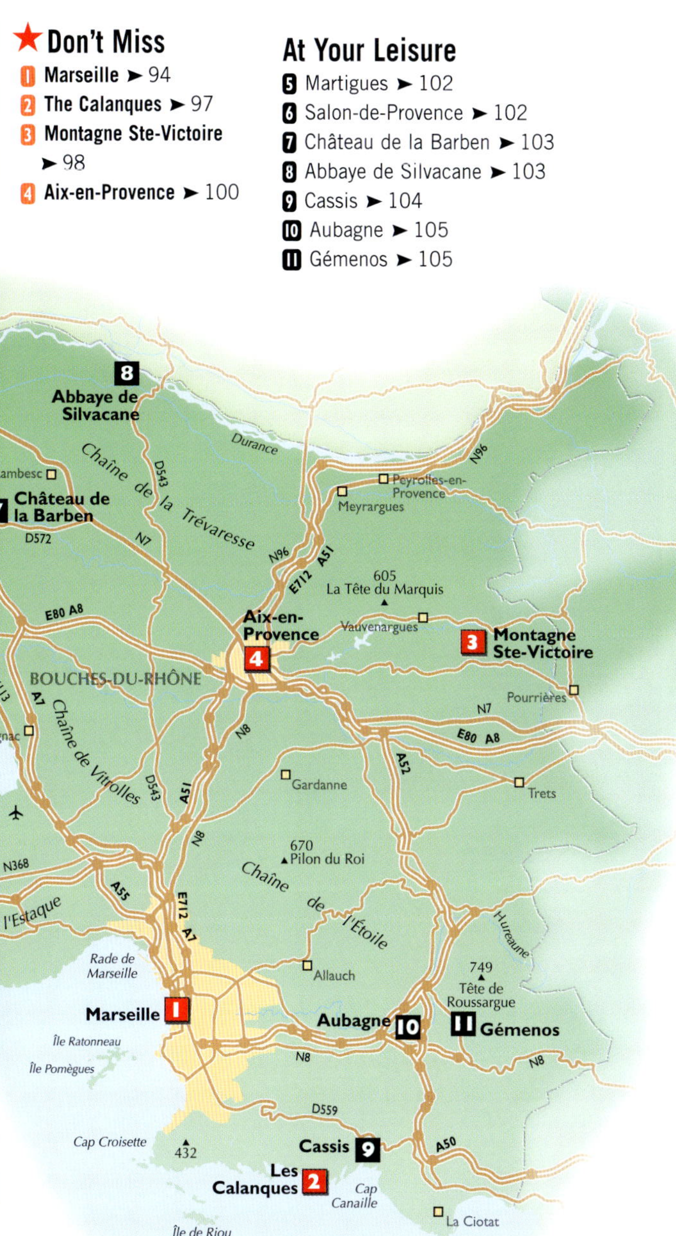

Not only does this tour embrace the exhilarating city of Marseille and the elegant ancient Provençal capital of Aix, but it also includes boat trips, cafés, markets and landscapes, and some excellent eateries too.

The Marseille Area in Two Days

Day One

Morning

Start your tour of **1 Marseille** at the Vieux Port (left, ➤ 94), where the city's heart beats loudest. Try to get up early enough to see the daily fish market on the quai des Belges. Explore the quartier du Panier (➤ 95), the oldest part of the city, where the Greeks built their temples. Today, this atmospheric district is a maze of dark, cobbled, souk-like streets where at times you have to remind yourself which side of the Mediterranean you are on.

Lunch

Le Roi du Couscous (63 rue de la République, tel: 04 91 91 45 46) serves arguably the best couscous in town.

Afternoon

Admire Marseille's striking coastline on a boat trip from the Vieux Port to the plunging white cliffs of the famous fjord-like **2 Calanques** (➤ 97). Or take a boat to the offshore fortress of Château d'If (➤ 94), with its extraordinary blend of fact, fiction and legend.

Evening

Return to the Old Port of Marseille, to enjoy an aperitif and watch the sun set in Le Suffren (quai du Belge), followed by a meal to remember in Le Miramar (quai du Port, tel: 04 91 91 10 40), one of the city's renowned bouillabaisse restaurants. Or catch a performance at the Opéra de Marseille (➤ 110), where Roland Petit's famous National Ballet Company is based.

Day Two

Morning

Spend the morning exploring the beautiful, ancient town of 4 **Aix-en-Provence** (➤ 100–101). Highlights include the cafés of the the main boulevard, cours Mirabeau (below); the Old Town and its ancient cathedral to the north; and the quartier Mazarin, with fancy mansions to the south. And there's always at least one morning market – either for fruit and vegetables, flowers or books.

Lunch

Try the local game dishes at La Brocherie (➤ 107).

Afternoon

Art lovers in particular will enjoy the circuit Cézanne footpath (➤ 101), which leads to the studio (Atelier Paul-Cézanne, ➤ 101) of the city's most celebrated citizen – a poignant memorial to this great Impressionist artist, which remains just as he left it at his death in 1906.

Cézanne spent much of his life painting the limestone hills surrounding Aix and, in particular, his beloved 3 **Montagne Ste-Victoire** (right, ➤ 98–99), which he painted over 65 times. Drive westwards out of Aix along one of the narrow country lanes and you too will see this inspirational landscape.

Evening

Return to Aix for dinner at L'Aixquis (➤ 107).

1 Marseille

Marseille, France's premier port on the west coast of Provence, is a lively place with a long history and a distinctive mix of ethnic and cultural influences. The city has plenty to offer, including museums and art galleries and trips to the offshore islands. Start your visit at the vibrant Vieux Port (Old Port), at the heart of the city, where bright fishing boats unload their catches each morning and the surrounding streets are filled with bars and restaurants.

A boat trip to the forbidding Château d'If

Vieux Port

Tourist boats departing from quai des Belges take visitors to the infamous **Château d'If**, a forbidding fortress castle 3km (2 miles) offshore on a barren, rocky island. Built in 1528 by François I to protect the port, it later became a prison, and today guided tours take you to the cells once occupied by aristocratic prisoners. Alexandre Dumas used the château as the setting for his book *The Count of Monte Cristo* (1844).

Close to the port, behind quai de Rive Neuve, is the quartier de l'Arsenal, the place to go to taste the local fish soup, bouillabaisse (► 21). To the south, perched on a hilltop, is **Notre-Dame de la Garde**, a 19th-century basilica topped with a huge gilded Madonna, which is strikingly lit at night.

La Marseillaise

During the French Revolution 500 volunteers were sent from Marseille to Paris. As they marched northwards, they sang a song, recently composed by Rouget de Lisle in Strasbourg. By the time they reached Paris, it had been adopted as the anthem of the revolution, and was named *La Marseillaise* in honour of the city's "choir".

North of the Old Port is the colourful **le Panier** district, where stepped alleys and rundown tenements climb up from the docks. Although heavily damaged during World War II, the area is scattered with interesting historic buildings. At the foot of the district is the **Musée des Docks Romains**, which displays a collection of first- to third-century AD Roman objects discovered during post-war rebuilding work. Further up is the former 17th-century hospice, La Vieille Charité. These arcaded galleries now house a cultural centre hosting art exhibitions and a museum. The ostentatious 19th-century neo-Byzantine Cathédrale de la Major, with its domes and striped façade, overlooks the modern docks.

Leading up from the Old Port and through the heart of the city is **La Canebière**, the main thoroughfare of Marseille, where you'll find many shopping streets. North of here is the fascinating **Musée d'Histoire de Marseille**, which records the city's history and has a third century Roman merchant ship as its focal point. Alongside is the Jardin des Vestiges, an archaeological site which has been transformed into a pretty garden. A walkway allows an overview of the ruins of the original Greek ramparts, traces of a roadway and parts of the dock as it was in the first century AD. Many of the items excavated here are on display in the museum.

Working and pleasure boats moored side-by-side in the Old Port of Marseille

To the east of the city is **Palais Longchamp**, a grandiose 1860s palace now home to Marseille's main art gallery, the Musée des Beaux-Arts, with masterpieces by Rubens, Brueghel and Corot, and pieces by local Marseille architect, sculptor and painter Pierre Puget. The palace also houses the Musée d'Histoire Naturelle, which has a zoo behind it. Both the Musée des Beaux-Arts and the Musée d'Histoire Naturelle are currently closed for renovation.

TAKING A BREAK

Sample the ultimate bouillabaisse (➤ 21) beside the Old Port at **Le Miramar** (12 quai du Port, tel: 04 91 91 10 40; closed Sun, Mon lunch).

The gilded Madonna and Child atop Notre-Dame de la Garde is one of the city's major landmarks

198 B2
Tourist Information Office
4 La Canebière 04 91 13 89 00; www.marseille-tourisme.com
Mon–Sat 9–7, Sun 10–5
Metro 1: Vieux Port

Château d'If
198, off A2
04 91 59 02 30 Daily 9:30–6:30, May–Sep; Tue–Sun 9:30–5:30, Oct–Apr
Moderate From quai des Belges (04 91 55 50 09, Apr–Oct)

Musée des Docks Romains
198 B2
28 place Vivaux 04 91 91 24 62
Tue–Sun 11–6, Jun–Sep; Tue–Sun 10–5, Oct–May Inexpensive

Musée d'Histoire de Marseille
198 C3
Square Belsunce, Centre Bourse
04 91 90 42 22
Mon–Sat 12–7 Inexpensive

Palais Longchamp
98, off D3
142 boulevard Palais Longchamp
Palais: 04 91 14 59 50; Musée des Beaux-Arts: 04 91 14 59 30
Musée des Beaux-Arts and Musée d'Histoire Naturelle are currently closed for renovation
Metro 1: Longchamp–Cinq-Avenues
Inexpensive

La Canebière runs through the heart of the city from the Old Port

MARSEILLE: INSIDE INFO

Top tips Street parking is difficult so **use the parking areas**. There are five near the Vieux Port.
- The monthly ***Marseille Poche*** and ***Ventilo*** list hundreds of events in the city.
- Beware of **pickpockets** in Le Panier district and avoid the area at night. Keep a close eye on your belongings at markets, in seafront areas and in bars.

Hidden gem The **Musée Cantini**, a modern art gallery with a good Surrealist collection and works by Matisse, Dufy, Miró, Kandinsky and Picasso, was a private home in the 17th century (19 rue Grignan, tel: 04 91 54 77 75; open Tue–Sun 11–6, Jun–Sep; Tue–Sun 10–5, Oct–May; moderate).

2 The Calanques

Just outside Cassis, dazzling white cliffs plunge into the crystal waters of spectacular narrow inlets or *calanques* – creating a dramatic coastline of magnificent mini-fjords. The weathered limestone cliffs are popular with climbers and the clear, deep water is ideal for bathing and scuba-diving, making the area a popular excursion from nearby Marseille.

The Calanques can be reached on foot, taking a waymarked path across the high clifftops, followed by a steep scramble down to the beaches, or by boat from Cassis. Picturesque **Port-Miou**, lined with yachts and pleasure craft, is the first and longest *calanque*. **Port-Pin** is the smallest, with a tiny shingle beach shaded by pines, while **En Vau**, the third inlet, has stark, precipitous cliffs and needle-like rocks rising from the sea. The 1.5-hour walk to reach it, and the steep descent to the sandy beach, keep it free from crowds.

Further west, the Sormiou and Morgiou creeks can be reached by car. When diving at Sormiou in 1991, Henri Cosquer discovered a cave lined with paintings of bison, deer, fish and horses dating from around 25,000 BC. The site was listed as a historical monument in 1992.

Safe moorings in the sheltered inlets of the *calanques*

TAKING A BREAK

Sur les Quais on the Old Port at La Ciotat is the yacht club's bar and restaurant (tel: 04 42 08 14 14).

---

191 E1

Tourist Information Office

Quai des Moulins, Cassis

08 92 25 98 92; www.cassis.fr

➤ 104

THE CALANQUES: INSIDE INFO

Top tip Enjoy a different perspective of the *calanques* on a 45-minute **boat trip** with commentary from the port at Cassis, between 9 and 6 daily.

3 Montagne Ste-Victoire

Artist Paul Cézanne (1839–1906) was fascinated by Mont Ste-Victoire, a huge sunlit wedge of limestone rising in the Provençal countryside east of Aix. He painted it more than 65 times, often portraying it as a blue-grey pyramid rising above red soil and a dense forest of dark green trees, making this great Provençal landmark famous worldwide.

Mont Ste-Victoire lies just east of Aix-en-Provence. Viewed end on, this pale ridge 16km (10 miles) long (running east–west) takes the form of a shapely pyramid. On its lower slopes, the red soil of the Coteaux-d'Aix vineyards give way to thick forest, scrub and fragrant herbs. Above the trees, the limestone peak reflects the light and shadow creating extraordinary designs of blue, grey, white, pink and orange on the landscape.

The mountain was Paul Cézanne's favourite local subject. He would walk from Aix to paint it again and again, from all angles and at all hours, creating some of his greatest canvases, including *La Montagne Sainte-Victoire* (1904) and *Le Paysage d'Aix* (1905). In a letter to his son in 1906, he wrote "I spend every day in this landscape, with its beautiful shapes. Indeed, I cannot imagine a more pleasant way or place to pass my time."

The mountain is encircled by the D10 on the north and the D17 on the south, which give easy access to its viewpoints and trails. Just off the D10, the Barrage de Bimont (7km/4 miles from Aix) dams the River Infernet to form an artificial lake, the **Lac du Bimont**, which provides water to the local towns.

Further along the D10, a marked trail near Les Cabassols farm leads up the steep 3km (2-mile) path to **La Croix de Provence**, the peak (945m/3,100 feet) at the western end of the mountain. Allow several hours for this walk, as the path is difficult in places, requiring sure-footedness. It is worth the effort for the views across the blue and purple hills. **Vauvenargues**, on the D10, is a small, pretty village. The 17th-century château (not open to the public) standing on a rock near by was the home of artist Pablo Picasso.

At the southeastern end of the mountain is the village of **Pourrières**, believed to have been named after a Roman victory over invading Germanic tribes in 102 BC. From here to Puyloubier, south of the mountain on the D17, is vine country, producing rosé wines.

TAKING A BREAK

There are picnic tables and benches by the dam of **Barrage de Bimont**.

---

191 F3

Tourist Information Office

2 place du Général-de-Gaulle, Aix-en-Provence

04 42 16 11 61; www.aixenprovencetourism.com

Left and below: Cézanne's beloved mountain rises up out of the dark green landscape

MONTAGNE STE-VICTOIRE: INSIDE INFO

Top tips Wear **stout shoes or hiking boots** for the climb to La Croix de Provence.
- Paths may be closed between July and September because of the **risk of fire**.
- **Don't smoke** when walking through forest or scrubland as you may risk starting a forest fire.

Hidden gem The area around the **Barrage de Bimont** and **Lac du Bimont** has been turned into a pleasant park with picnic tables and benches.

4 Aix-en-Provence

Aix, the historic capital of Provence, is a city of fountains and fine mansions, art and culture. The shaded main street, cours Mirabeau, is lined with pavement cafés and leafy plane trees, and within a short walk is the attractive medieval and Renaissance Old Town with its narrow lanes, markets and pretty squares.

The city started life as Aquae Sextiae, a Roman spa dating from 123 BC. Aix thrived culturally during the Middle Ages under Good King René, an ardent patron of the arts, and prospered during the 17th and 18th centuries when many Renaissance mansions were built.

The **cours Mirabeau** divides Old Aix (Vieil Aix) to the north from the quartier Mazarin, with its elegant mansions to the south. Running down the middle of the cours Mirabeau is a series of fountains, including the moss-covered Fontaine d'Eau Thermale, a natural hot spring. This broad boulevard is the place to stroll or sit at a café table under the trees and watch the sauntering crowds go by. Between here and the **Cathédrale St-Sauveur** are some of the most interesting streets, with markets and restaurants, and shops selling bright Provençal handicrafts and designer clothes. This is also where you'll find the town's main square, **place de l'Hôtel de Ville**, with its Italianate town hall. Rising from one corner of the building is a 16th-century belfry, the Tour de l'Horloge, its tower adorned with an astronomical clock. The cathedral, a mix of styles from Romanesque to baroque, has 16th-century Flemish tapestries in the chancel and superb medieval art, noteably Nicolas Froment's famous triptych *Le Buisson Ardent* (1475–56), depicting a vision of the Virgin and Child surrounded by the eternal burning bush of Moses.

Above: An outdoor restaurant on cours Mirabeau

Below: La Rotunde Fountain in place du Général-de-Gaulle

Paul Cézanne was born and spent much of his life here, painting in the limestone hills of the surrounding countryside (► 98–99). A themed walk around Aix, marked by bronze pavement plaques, leads to his preserved studio, **Atélier Paul-Cézanne**, where he spent the last seven years of his life. Here you can see his unfinished canvases, palettes and his old black hat. To view some of his paintings, visit **Musée Granet**, the city's main museum, which has a small collection of his early works. Located in the Gothic priory of the Knights of Malta, the museum displays European paintings collected by 19th-century artist François Granet, along with extensive archaeological finds dating to Roman Aix. The museum has been refurbished and is currently only partially open to the public.

Top left: A plaque of Cézanne
Above: The artist's studio

191 E3

Tourist Information Office

2 place du Général-de-Gaulle
04 42 16 11 61; www.aixenprovencetourism.com

Atélier Paul-Cézanne

9 avenue Paul-Cézanne
04 42 21 06 53; www.atelier-cezanne.com
Daily 10–12, 2–6, Oct–May; 10–7, Jun–Sep
Moderate

Musée Granet

Place St-Jean-de-Malte
04 42 52 88 32
Partially open, phone for details
Free

TAKING A BREAK

Treat yourself at one of Aix's most elegant cafés – **Des Deux-Garçons** (► 108), popular for its brasserie-style menu.

AIX-EN-PROVENCE: INSIDE INFO

Top tips The **Visa for Aix and its Region** card gives reductions on the entry price to various museums, as well as discounts on bus tickets. Buy it from the tourist office and museums.

- Visit the **flower market** (Tuesday, Thursday and Saturday morning) at place de l'Hôtel de Ville.
- Aix has seven annual festivals, including France's élite opera festival, the **Festival International d'Art Lyrique et de la Musique**, lasting for three weeks in July.

At Your Leisure

Pastel-coloured houses line the quai in Martigues

5 Martigues

Martigues, an excellent base for exploring the Étang de Berre, has picturesque canals that run through its centre between its three separate "villages".

Jonquières, on the southern side of the main canal, Canal de Caronte, is the busiest and best place to go for a meal or a drink. In the middle is **L'Île**, which has several restored 17th- and 18th-century houses, as well as the splendid Église Ste-Madeleine-de-l'Île. Stand on the bridge at quai Brescon, next to the church, to admire the celebrated view of fishing boats moored on the canal. The scene, known as the *Miroir des Oiseaux* (the birds' mirror), was painted by Felix Ziem (1821–1911). Works by Ziem and other artists are on display in the **Musée Ziem**, in the third village of **Ferrières**.

The Chaîne de l'Estaque, a range of low hills, runs along the coast between Martigues and Marseille. Here you can follow woodland walking trails and enjoy sea views.

190 C3

Tourist Information Centre

Rond Point de l'Hôtel de Ville

04 42 42 31 10; www.martigues-tourisme.com

All year daily from 9 or 10 am

Musée Ziem

Boulevard du 14 Juillet

04 42 41 39 60

Telephone for details

6 Salon-de-Provence

This large industrial town sits between the Crau plain and the hills of western Provence at a junction of roads linking Arles, Avignon, Aix and Marseille.

The Porte de l'Horloge in Salon-de-Provence

The astrologer Michel de Nostradame moved here from St-Rémy in 1547 and remained until his death in 1566. It was here he wrote the prophetic tome *Centuries*. His former home, **Maison de Nostradamus**, is today a museum of his life. Near by is the lovely 17th-century gateway, **Porte de l'Horloge**, with a beautiful 18th-century fountain, called the Grand Fontaine, opposite. Nostradamus's tomb is in the Église St-Laurent, in the north of the town.

The Château de l'Empéri, in place des Centuries, dates from the 10th century and is home to the **Musée d'Armes et d'Histoire Militaire**

190 C4

Tourist Information Office
Cours Gimon 04 90 56 27 60
Mon–Sat 9:30–6:30, Sun 10–12, Jul–Aug; Mon–Sat 9:30–12:30, 2–6, Sep–Jun

Maison de Nostradamus
11 rue Nostradamus
04 90 56 64 31
Mon–Fri 9–12, 2–6, Sat–Sun 2–6
40-minute audioguide in English

Musée d'Armes et d'Histoire Militaire
Place des Centuries 04 90 56 22 36 Wed–Mon 10–12, 2–6

7 Château de la Barben

A magnificent fortified castle on the top of a rocky hill, La Barben was originally a medieval fortress, but it was rebuilt many times over the centuries and today's pile is more like a stately home.

La Barben was acquired by King René in the 15th century. He sold it to the de Fortins, who eventually turned it into a luxurious home. Inside, there are lavish period furnishings and fine craftsmanship, including striking 16th- and 17th-century Flemish and Aubusson tapestries and elegant 18th-century painted ceilings.

The imposing towers of the Château de la Barben seem to be part of the living rock

The highlight is a spectacular **terraced garden** in formal French style, created by André Le Nôtre, the landscape designer of Versailles. The formality of the flower borders, statuary and basins is emphasised by the surrounding untamed woodland. Other attractions include a reptile collection and a zoo.

190 C4
13330 La Barben 04 90 55 25 41
Daily 10–12, 2–6, Jun–Aug
Moderate

8 Abbaye de Silvacane

Nestling in a peaceful setting close to the south banks of the Durance, the Abbaye de Silvacane was the last of the three great Cistercian abbeys to be built in Provence, known as the Three Cistercian Sisters (the other two are Sénanque

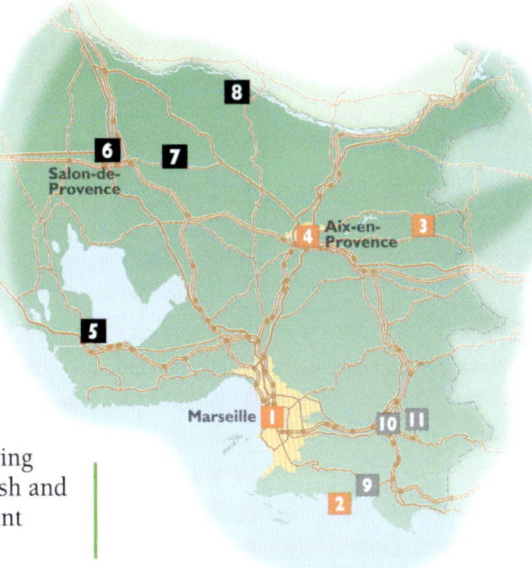

The Abbaye de Silvacane – one of Provence's great Cistercian abbeys

➤ 150–151 and du Thoronet ➤ 80). Silvacane, considered the loveliest of the three, is a perfect example of the simple, austere elegance promoted by the Cistercians. The name, from Silva Cana, is Latin for Forest of Reeds, which was all that was here before the monks drained the marshes to create farmland. Founded in the 12th century, the abbey prospered until raids and crop failure in the 14th century ruined it. It was turned into farm buildings before restoration began in the 19th century. The stark beauty of the clean-lined, pale stone church is echoed in a charming cloister with an old fountain. The most striking part of the abbey is the refectory, rebuilt in 1423 in Gothic style. It has a rose window and is less austere than other parts.

191 D4
La Roque d'Anthéron
04 42 50 41 69
Daily 10–6, Jun–Sep; Wed–Mon 10–1, 2–5, Oct–May Moderate

9 Cassis

This busy little fishing port and modern beach resort basks in a sheltered bay between the white cliffs of the Cap Canaille and the breathtaking *calanques* (fjord-like inlets) to the west (➤ 97). The surrounding hills are cloaked with olives, almonds, figs and the famous terraced vineyards of the region's prestigious *vin de Cassis*. In the village centre, *boccia* players meet in dusty squares, while fishermen spread their nets along the quayside, beside waterfront cafés.

There's a small beach of sand and pebbles, and an old castle perched on a hill. An easy clifftop path, linking Cassis with Marseille, gives magnificent views out to sea, but to fully appreciate the dazzling white cliffs and narrow creeks, take a **boat trip** from the quay.

191 E2
Tourist Information Office
Quai des Moulins
08 92 25 98 92; www.cassis.fr
Mon–Fri 9–7, Sat, Sun 9:30–12:30, 3–6, Jul–Aug; Mon–Fri 9–12.30, 2–6, Sat 9:30–12:30, 2–5:30, Sun 10–12:30, Mar–Jun, Sep–Oct; Mon–Fri 9:30–12:30, 2–5:30, Sat 10–12:30, 2–5, Sun 10–12:30, Nov–Feb

For Kids

- **Château de la Barben** The château (➤ 103) has a vivarium (reptile collection) in the castle's vaulted sheep pen, and a zoo with bears, lions and hippos (daily 10–6).
- **Cassis** Spend time on the small pebble and sand beach (➤ above).

Relaxing on the small beach at Cassis

10 Aubagne

Aubagne is a major production centre for traditional Provençal ceramics, which have been made here since the 16th century. Local potters specialise in *santons* (traditional clay figurines) and beautiful decorative items, which can be bought from artisans' shops in the Old Town and at the town's pottery markets and fairs. Aubagne is also the birthplace of playwright and film director Marcel Pagnol (1895–1974), who set many of his works in the town and surrounding countryside. Signed tours take in locations from the films of his novels *Jean de Florette* and *Manon des Sources*.

191 E2

Tourist Information Office

Avenue Antide-Boyer

04 42 03 49 98

The elegant town hall at Gémenos

11 Gémenos

Gémenos, close to the *autoroute* and Marseille, is a typical Provençal village, with narrow streets, steps and old houses. While you're in the main square look inside the courtyard of the 17th- to 18th-century Granges du Marquis d'Albertas, a huge building that once housed agricultural workers. Another building of interest is the beautiful 17th-century château, now the town hall.

Outside the village on the D2 are the ruins of the 13th-century **Abbaye de St-Pons**, the setting for religious music concerts in summer.

191 F2

Tourist Information Office

Cours Pasteur 04 42 32 18 44; www.gemenos.fr Daily 10–12, 3–6, Oct–Apr; Mon–Sat 10–12, 2–5, May–Sep

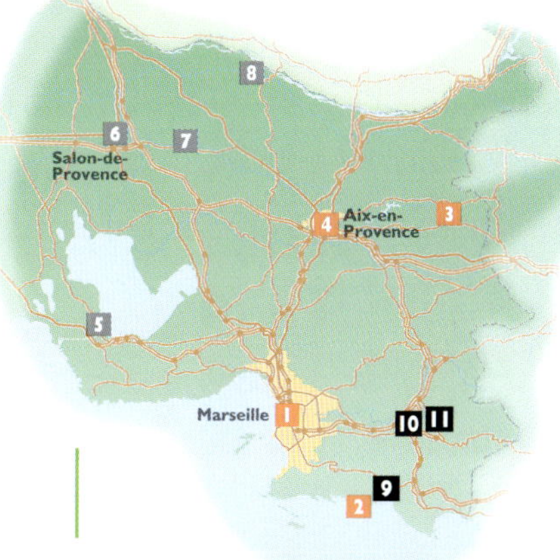

Where to... Stay

Prices
Expect to pay per night for a double room
€ under €100 **€€** €100–€200 **€€€** over €200

AIX-EN-PROVENCE

Des Augustins €€€

This hotel offers a blend of history and modernity within a 15th-century former Augustinian convent, in the centre of Old Aix.

191 E3 3 rue de la Masse 04 42 27 28 59; www.hotel-augustins.com All year

Le Pigonnet €€€

The four-star Le Pigonnet, at the end of a tree-lined street in the heart of town, is a beautiful family-run *bastide* (country house) hotel furnished with local antiques. Many of the elegant bedrooms look out over the flower-filled gardens, and some have terraces with views of Montagne Ste-Victoire, while others overlook the pool.

191 E3 5 avenue du Pigonnet 04 42 59 02 90; www.hotelpigonnet.com

CASSIS

Auberge de Jeunesse de Cassis €

This youth hostel, in the massif of Calanques and one hour on foot from Cassis, is great for those who don't mind roughing it – there are no showers and accommodation is in a 10-bed dormitory. Cooking equipment is available. Waste is recycled and solar energy used.

191 E2 La Fontasse 04 42 01 02 72; www.fuaj.org Closed Jan to mid-Mar

Les Roches Blanches €€

In a commanding clifftop position with gardens leading down to the sea, this four-star hotel has breath-taking views. Most bedrooms have a balcony or terrace, and all have been decorated with fine fabrics. You can enjoy dinner on the terrace or in the dining room. The pool, set on the edge of the terrace, seems to flow into the Mediterranean, which fills the horizon.

191 E2 Route des Calanques 04 42 01 09 30; www.roches-blanches-cassis.com Closed late Nov

GÉMENOS

Le Relais de la Magdeleine €€

This hotel, situated in a pretty garden, has an attractive 18th-century façade. It is decorated with antiques, and the bedrooms have period furniture, tiled floors and spacious bathrooms. The restaurant serves fine Provençal cuisine, which you can eat on the terrace.

191 F2 Route d'Aix-en-Provence 04 42 32 20 16; www.relais-magdeleine.com Closed Dec to mid-Mar

MARSEILLE

Le Corbusier €

The hotel is in a block of 300 apartments designed by Le Corbusier in 1952 as part of a design experiment. It was a prototype for "vertical living", combining living space and recreational facilities under one roof. As such, it comes complete with play areas, shops, a cinema, a bar and a library. The bedrooms look to the sea, or the park and terrace. Private parking is available.

191 D2 280 boulevard Michelet 04 91 16 78 00; www.hotellecorbusier.com Closed Jan

Hôtel Hermès €

Situated in the heart of the city by the Vieux Port, this two-star hotel is in a bustling position surrounded by restaurants and cafés. Although lacking the character of older hotels, the 28 bedrooms are light and airy and have a TV, and some have a balcony.

191 D2 ✉ 2 rue Bonneterie ☎ 04 96 11 63 63; www.hotelmarseille.com All year

Hôtel de Rome et St-Pierre €

This three-star hotel is in a 19th-century building, just a short walk from the Vieux Port. You'll find comfortable armchairs in the reading room and wrought-iron furniture in the breakfast room. There are 43 bedrooms, all with a TV and mini-bar, and there is a safe and laundry service. There is no restaurant, but the hotel does have a bar.

191 D2 ✉ 7 cours St-Louis ☎ 04 91 54 19 52 All year

Hôtel St-Louis €

This two-star hotel has a Napoleonic façade lined with wrought-iron balconies, and is listed as a historic monument. It is in a good position close to lively Le Canebière and the Vieux Port. The 22 comfortable bedrooms are simply decorated, and all have TV. The reception area, with its terra-cotta décor and tiled floor, has more character. Facilities include internet access.

191 D2 ✉ 2 rue des Récollettes ☎ 04 91 54 02 74; www.hotel-st-louis.com All year

Le Petit Nice Passédat €€€

The contemporary interior of this four-star hotel exudes calm and tranquillity. All the bedrooms have air-conditioning, a sea view, satellite TV, mini-bar and safe. The restaurant is excellent.

191 D2 ✉ Anse de Maldormé, Corniche J F Kennedy ☎ 04 91 59 25 92; www.petitnice-passedat.com All year

Where to... Eat and Drink

Prices
Expect to pay for a three-course meal for one, excluding drinks and service
€ under €25 **€€** €25–€50 **€€€** over €50

AIX-EN-PROVENCE

L'Aixquis €€€

In summer the entrance to this delightful restaurant is bedecked with colourful, flower-filled, hanging baskets. Inside, the subdued lighting, beautifully laid tables and fresh flowers make it the ideal place for a romantic dinner. The menu reflects fine Mediterranean cuisine and features dishes such as warm lobster salad with coral vinaigrette.

191 E3 ✉ 22 rue Victor Leydet ☎ 04 42 27 76 16; www.aixquis.com Tue–Sat 12–1:30, 7:30–9:30

Autour d'une Tarte €

You'll be tempted by the generous slices of sweet and savoury tarts on dispay here, which make a perfect snack. There is a takeaway service.

191 E3 ✉ 13 rue Gaston de Saporta ☎ 04 42 96 52 12 7–7. Closed Sun

La Brocherie €€

Try one of the meat dishes, spit-roasted in the large chimney, or the fish, at this rustic restaurant. Delicious game in season.

191 E3 ✉ 5 rue Fernand-Dol ☎ 04 42 38 33 21 12–2, 7:30–10. Closed Sat lunch, Sun

Café des Deux-Garçons €€

"Les 2 G", founded in 1792, was once the haunt of Cézanne, Picasso, Piaf and Zola. Today, it remains one of Aix's most elegant cafés, popular for its brasserie-style menu, which includes simple seafood dishes.

191 E3 53 cours Mirabeau 04 42 26 00 51 Daily 12–3, 7–11

Le P'tit Puits €€

Le P'tit Puits refers to the well in the vaulted basement at this restaurant. The dining room is warm and welcoming, with dark orange tablecloths and soft lighting creating a relaxed atmosphere. The extensive menu includes fondues, stuffed baked potatoes, salads and Provençal fish dishes.

191 E3 14 rue Bernardines 04 42 91 42 77 Mon–Fri 12–2:30, 7:30–10, Sat 7:30–10

Unic Bar €

This is a perfect bar for people-watching as it is opposite Aix's colourful fruit and vegetable market (➤ 109). In summer, fresh fruit juice is the house speciality.

191 E3 40 rue Vauvenargues 04 42 96 38 28 Daily 6 am–2 am

CASSIS

Le Romarin €€

Rosemary (*romarin*) is used in the cuisine here, along with other fresh local produce. On the menu you will find dishes such as goat's cheese salad with pine nuts, grilled lamb on skewers and plenty of fish.

191 E2 5 rue Séverin Icard 04 42 01 09 93; www.leromarin.com Wed–Mon lunch and dinner, Jun–Aug; Thu–Mon lunch and dinner, Sep–Dec, Feb–May. Closed Jan

La Voute €

A heaped pan of *moules frîtes*, washed down with *vin de Cassis*, represents excellent value for money at this restaurant on the waterfront.

191 E3 2 quai des Baux 04 42 01 73 33 12–2:30, 7–10:30. Closed Mon eve, Tue eve and Wed

MARSEILLE

Les Arcenaulx €€

Numerous books line the walls of Marseille's former arsenal. Diners sit at long red banquettes to enjoy the regional cuisine, which includes honey and lemon duck served with citron-scented courgette (zucchini) gratin. In the afternoon, Les Arcenaulx is a tea room.

191 D2 25 cours Estienne d'Orves 04 91 59 80 30; www.les-arcenaulx.com Mon–Sat noon–11 pm

Chez Fonfon €€€

The lively fishing port is the place to try bouillabaisse, the superb fish soup for which Marseille's restaurants are especially famous. Chez Fonfon has been run by the same family for more than 50 years and is an institution in the town.

191 D2 140 rue du Vallon des Auffes 04 91 52 14 38 Mon 7:30–10, Tue–Sat 12–2, 7:30–10

Chez Loury €€

This popular restaurant, close to the Old Port, uses the best of Mediterranean ingredients in dishes such as herb-roasted sea urchin, home-smoked salmon and bouillabaisse.

191 D2 3 rue Fortia 04 91 33 09 73; www.loury.com Mon–Sat 12–2, 7:30–9:30

Toinou €–€€

Not surprisingly, fish and seafood are the specialities here at Toinou – the home of Francis Rouquier, France's champion shellfish opener. The maritime theme extends to the décor, which resembles the inside of a boat, and the waiters, dressed in nautical uniforms.

191 D2 3 cours St-Louis 04 91 33 14 94 Daily 12–10:30

Where to... Shop

MARKETS

Aix-en-Provence has several interesting markets, including the **Marché aux antiquaires**, which is the place to browse for period furniture, old books and decorative items (place du Palais de Justice, open Tue, Thu, Sat 7–1). For fresh produce visit the **Marché des Producteurs**, also in Aix, where local farmers display their cheeses, fruit and vegetables under the shade of plane trees (place Richelme, open daily 7–1). In Marseille, at the **Marché des Capucins**, you'll find spices, fruit and vegetables from all over the world and some household goods (place des Capucins, open Mon–Sat 8–7), and the **Marché aux Poissons** has fresh fish, which is gutted and scaled on the spot (quai del Belges, daily 8–1).

SOUVENIRS AND GIFTS

For traditional *faïence* (high-quality glazed ceramics) and *santons* (traditional clay figurines dressed or painted in regional costumes), visit **L'Atelier d'Art** in Aubagne, the pottery capital of France (2 boulevard Émile-Combes, tel: 04 42 70 12 92). *Santons* are also produced at **Santons Marcel Carbonel**, which sells 700 different figures (6 promenade du Jeune Anacharsis, tel: 04 42 03 17 45, open Tue–Sat 9:30–12:30, 2:30–6:30).

Marseille is known all over the world for its soap. You can buy it enriched with clay, essential oils and honey and attractively packaged at one of the city's few remaining specialist soap stores, **La Compagnie de Provence**, which is situated close to the Old Port (1 rue Caisserie, tel: 04 91 56 20 94, open Mon–Sat 10–7).

FOOD AND DRINK

Confiserie Entrecasteaux, in Aix, is one of the best places to buy *calissons* (a local speciality), glacé fruit, nougat and chocolate (2 rue Entrecasteaux, tel: 04 42 27 15 02, open Mon–Sat 8–12, 2–7). **Maison Béchard** is also well known for its *calissons* (12 cours Mirabeau, tel: 04 42 26 06 78). Puyricard's handmade chocolates are considered the finest in France, and you can visit their factory, **Chocolaterie Puyricard**, in a northern suburb of Aix (420 route du Puy-Ste-Réparade, quartier Beaufort, Puyricard, tel: 04 42 96 11 21).

At **Le Four des Navettes**, Marseille's oldest bakery, try the famous orange-flower *navettes* – boat-shaped biscuits (136 rue Sainte, tel: 04 91 33 32 12). **Torrefaction Noailles** is a sweet-shop-cum-tea salon, and another local favourite (56 La Canebière, tel: 04 91 55 60 66, open Mon–Sat 7 am–8 pm, Sun 9–1, 3–7:30).

FASHION

Madame Zaza of Marseille is the place to go for leading designs which show a distinct Mediterranean influence. Inside the pleasant store you'll find shirts and skirts, which are sometimes embroidered with gold (73 cours Julien, tel: 04 91 48 05 57, open Mon–Fri 10–1:30, 2–7, Sat 10–7).

Petit Boy in Aix sells fashions for children aged from 6 months to 16 years (6 rue Aude, tel: 04 42 93 13 05).

ART, ANTIQUES AND BOOKS

In Aix, you can browse the shelves at **Librairie de Provence**, a large bookshop with an excellent choice of regional travel, literature and culinary titles (31 cours Mirabeau, tel: 04 42 26 07 23). **Yves Ungaro** is an aladdin's cave of pictures and *objets d'art* at the heart of Aix's antiques quarter (1 rue Jaubert, tel: 04 42 63 22 94).

Where to... Be Entertained

BARS, CLUBS AND CASINOS

In Aix-en-Provence, the **Casino de Aix**, housed in a strikingly modern building, has slot machines by the hundreds, a games room, four restaurants and a concert hall (avenue de l'Europe, tel: 04 42 59 69 00, open 10 am–3 am, until 4 am Fri–Sun); you must be over 18 to enter the games room.

Hot Brass, an established haunt for jazz lovers, is the place to go for traditional jazz (quartier Celony, route d'Eguilles, tel: 04 42 21 05 57, open Fri–Sat 11:30 pm–5 am), or try **Le Scat**, a traditional club with live jazz, soul, R&B and reggae (11 rue de la Verrerie, tel: 04 42 23 00 23, open Tue–Sat 11 pm–5 am).

The place to see and be seen for Aix's beautiful young people is **Bistrot Aixois**. It's packed at weekends, but there's more room, and air, upstairs (37 cours Sextius, tel: 04 42 27 50 10, open Mon–Sat 7 pm–2 am). **Happy Days**, on the liveliest square in town, is also popular with the fashionable crowd (place Richelme, tel: 04 42 21 02 35, open Mon–Sat 8 am–2 am, food served 12–4). **Trolleybus**, Marseille's number-one rock venue, also has bars and bowling alleys (24 quai de Rive-Neuve, tel: 04 91 54 30 45, open Tue–Sat 11:30 pm–5 am, until 6 am Sat–Sun; Tue–Wed, bar only, open until midnight).

THEATRE, OPERA AND CINEMA

La Fonderie, in Aix-en-Provence, is the venue for plays and concerts ranging from rock to reggae. There are two auditoriums and a bar (14 cours St-Louis, tel: 04 42 63 10 11). The nine-screen cinema complex **Le Cézanne**, also in Aix, screens the latest Hollywood blockbusters and major French films, although Hollywood films are rarely shown in their original language (1 rue Marcel-Guillaume, tel: 08 36 68 72 70; www.lecezanne.com).

Marseille has several theatre venues. **Théâtre National de Marseille la Criée**, the city's leading theatre, gives widely acclaimed performances (30 quai de Rive-Neuve, tel: 04 96 17 80 00). Language proves no barrier at **Massalia Théâtre**, France's first marionette theatre, when children's favourite fairy tales come alive (41 rue Jobin, tel: 04 95 04 95 70).

Built in 1685, **L'Opéra de Marseille** is the stately home of the Philharmonic Orchestra of Marseille and also hosts operas throughout the year (place Ernest Reyer, tel: 04 91 55 11 10; www.mairie-marseille.fr).

SPORTS AND ACTIVITIES

In Aix, you can test your skills on the indoor karting track at **Kart'In Aix** (Zone d'Activité des Milles, 820 rue André Ampère, tel: 04 42 97 79 99, open Tue–Thu 6 pm–midnight, Fri 6 pm–1 am, Sat 3 pm–1 am, Sun 3 pm–9 pm). There are popular ten-pin bowling alleys at **Bowling du Bras d'Or**, and a large screen showing sport is also on site (23 boulevard Charrier, tel: 04 42 27 69 92, open 2 pm–2:30 am).

The region's top spectator sport is *le foot* (football) and its top team is **Olympique de Marseille** (www.om.net for tickets).

You can go diving with **Centre de Loisirs des Goudes** in the Bay of Marseille, around the Rioux archipelago, and explore caves and wrecks. Some packages include meals, use of kayaks and mountain bikes (2 boulevard Alexandre Delabre, tel: 04 91 25 13 16; www.goudes-plongee.com, open 8 am–10 pm).

The Camargue Area

Getting Your Bearings 112 – 113
In Three Days 114 – 115
Don't Miss 116 – 125
At Your Leisure 126 – 129
Where to... 130 – 134

Getting Your Bearings

The Camargue area is centred round the Bouches-du-Rhône – a beautiful region of timeless medieval villages and honey-coloured farmsteads, smothered in bougainvillaea and oleander, their pink-tiled roofs and trellised vines sharply defined against cloudless blue skies. It is a traditional, romantic region, once home of the troubadours, where courtly love first developed. Before that, it was the most important part of the Roman Empire outside Italy.

Above: The Roman amphitheatre in Nîmes

Ancient monuments abound, including the remarkable ruins of Glanum, a Greco-Roman town; and the Roman arena, theatre, chariot-race course and necropolis of Arles – magnificent ancient treasures which have made this city, the former Roman capital of Provence, a UNESCO site. Arles today is a lively, popular city, which has successfully preserved many local customs, costumes and traditions.

Just beyond the official borders of Provence in the nearby Languedoc region, the medieval ramparted town of Aigues-Mortes, the dazzling Roman bridge – the Pont du Gard – and the extensive Roman remains of Nîmes are worth a visit.

Back in Provence, the Bouches-du-Rhône area boasts some of the region's most beautiful and varied countryside – from the lacy limestone peaks of the Alpilles and the nodding sunflower fields of Arles' resident artist, Vincent Van Gogh, to the sandy marshes of the Camargue. This untamed region is famous for its gypsies and unique nature reserve, where pink flamingos, young bulls and white horses splash through the marshes – surely one of the most evocative images of all Provence.

Page 111: The Pont du Gard

Left: A white spoonbill poised for flight in the Camargue

★ Don't Miss

1. **The Camargue** ➤ 116
2. **Arles** ➤ 119
3. **Nîmes and the Pont du Guard** ➤ 122
4. **Stes-Maries-de-la-Mer** ➤ 124

At Your Leisure

5. Aigues-Mortes ➤ 126
6. Abbaye de Montmajour ➤ 126
7. Les Baux-de-Provence ➤ 127
8. St-Rémy-de-Provence and Glanum ➤ 128
9. Tarascon ➤ 129

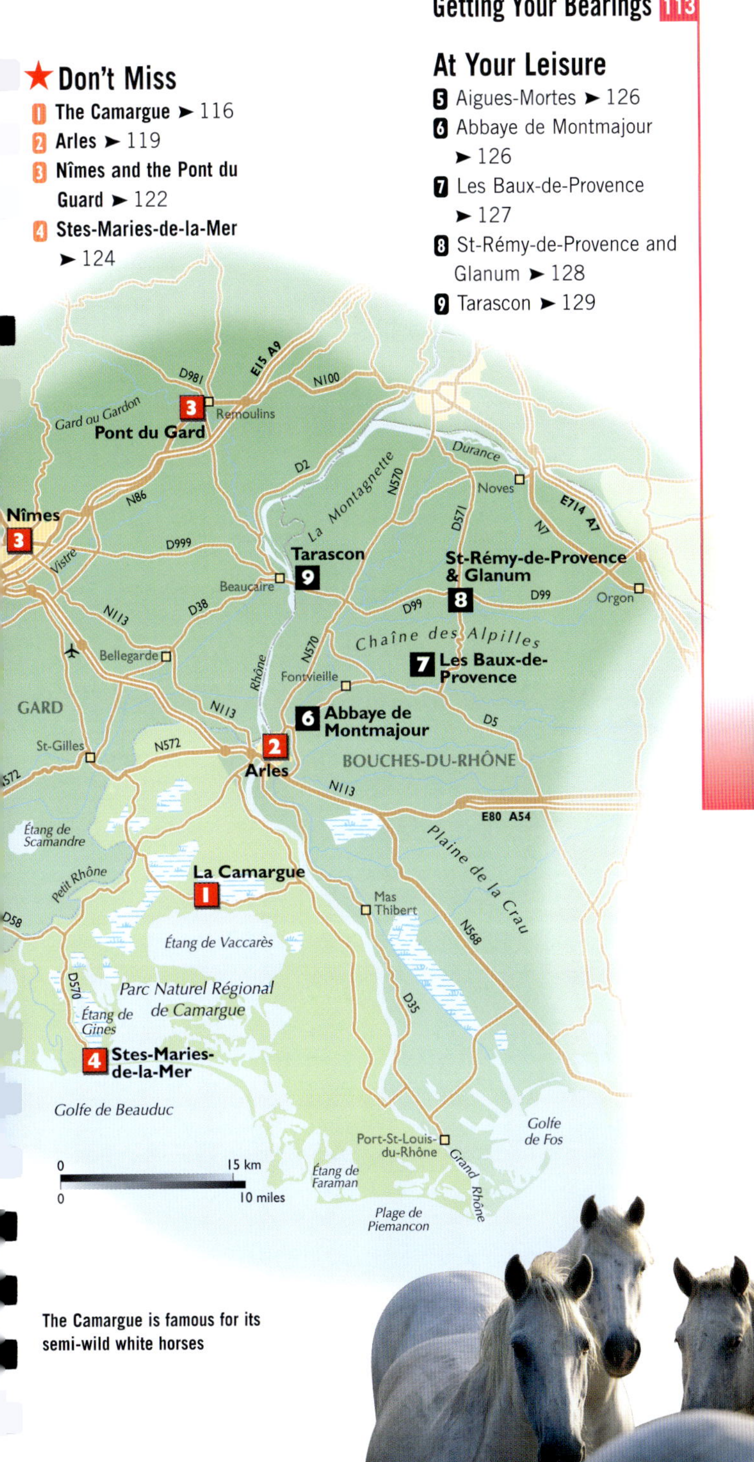

The Camargue is famous for its semi-wild white horses

Although there is a considerable amount of driving here, it will help you to appreciate the diversity of this region, both in its dramatically varied landscapes and in its customs, from the Languedoc city of Nîmes to the quintessential Provençal city of Arles, and the unique way of life in the Camargue.

The Camargue Area in Three Days

Day One

Morning

Spend the morning exploring the ancient monuments of 2 **Arles** (➤ 119–121). Make the Musée de l'Arles et de la Provence Antiques (➤ 121) your first port of call for a grasp of the town's history. The ruins of the Théâtre Antique (left) suggest it was even more lavish than the theatre in Orange in its heyday, while the beautifully preserved Les Arènes today stages frequent *Cours Camarguais* (Provençal bullfights).

Lunch

Enjoy a lunch of regional specialities at the popular locals' restaurant, L'Escaladou (➤ 131), or a snack at the lively Café la Nuit (11 place du Forum, tel: 04 90 49 83 30), subject of a famous Van Gogh painting.

Afternoon

Head out into Van Gogh country, past the 6 **Abbaye de Montmajour** (➤ 126–127), one of the most elaborate Romanesque churches in Provence, through the picturesque villages of Fontvieille and Maussane-les-Alpilles to the ancient ruined citadel of 7 **Les Baux-de-Provence** (➤ 127–128) – once called the Pompeii of Provence – set in a landscape of crumpled white limestone crags known as the Chaîne des Alpilles. From here it is a stone's throw to the chic market town of 8 **St-Rémy-de-Provence** and the ruins of **Glanum** (➤ 128–129), the nation's oldest classical buildings.

Evening

Enjoy simple Provençal flavours and local wines al fresco at Café des Arènes (right, ➤ 132) in St-Rémy-de-Provence.

Day Two

Morning

Visit the magnificent medieval château and the Souleïado museum of Provençal fabrics at 9 **Tarascon** (➤ 129).

Lunch

Tuck into regional cuisine in Tarascon's atmospheric restaurant, Abbaye St-Michel de Frigolet (➤ 132).

Afternoon

Marvel at the nearby 3 **Port du Gard** (above, ➤ 122–123), a remarkable feat of Roman engineering in the Languedoc region. Then drive to 3 **Nîmes** (➤ 122–123) to see the extraordinary oval-shaped Arènes, the best preserved Roman amphitheatre in the world.

Evening

Le Bouchon et l'Assiette (➤ 132) offers excellent-value set menus of regional specialities.

Day Three

Spend the day in the 1 **Camargue** (➤ 116–118), a land of salty marshes, rice fields, brackish lagoons and coastal dunes, renowned for its passionate people, its silver-cream horses, black bulls and salmon-pink flamingos. Join a pony trek (below) at one of the ranches, or while away the hours spotting exotic water birds. The quaint fishing village of **Stes-Maries-de-la-Mer** (➤ 124–125) is steeped in the tradition and folklore of the region, and Brûleur de Loups (➤ 132), with its fish dishes, is a good lunch venue.

The Camargue

The natural wilderness of the Camargue, the marshy flatland of the Rhône delta, is famous for its exotic wildlife, its semi-wild white horses, its little black bulls bred for fighting and its annual gypsy festival. Thousands of pink flamingos come to feed in the shallow waters here, and evaporating sea water leaves vast crystalline saltpans. Roads are few, so extend your exploration on foot or, better, by guided boat trip.

No area in France matches the Camargue for its landscape: brackish lagoons, flat rice fields and salty marshes, sand spits and coastal dunes, tufted with coarse, spiky grass and interlaced with shallow streams and canals. Even its boundaries – the Grand Rhône and Petit Rhône deltas and the sea – are forever shifting. This extraordinary landscape harbours an outstanding variety of wildlife and the unique lifestyle of the *Camarguais* cowboys.

Preserving traditions

The people of the Camargue are hardy folk. They live in low, thatched, white-washed cottages with bulls' horns over the door to ward off evil spirits. They proudly guard the *Camarguais* heritage, by wearing traditional costume and raising horses and cattle on ranches, or *manades*. Contrary to popular belief the famous white horses are not wild. They are actually owned by a *manadier* or breeder, but are left to roam semi-free. Some are also used for trekking expeditions. The small, black local bulls with their distinctive lyre-shaped horns, are bred for the ring (► 119). Watching a mounted *gardian* drive his herd through the marshes is a truly unforgettable sight!

Main picture: Reed beds fringe the waters of the Camargue
Below: A glossy ibis

Wildlife

The Camargue also offers sanctuary to some of Europe's most exotic water birds, including purple herons and stone curlews. The nature reserve centres on the shallow **Étang de Vaccarès**. The reserve of the Étang de Vaccarès itself is open only to visitors with a special permit, but there are vantage places off the surrounding roads (especially the D37) from where you can watch bird life. The reserve's headquarters is on the eastern side of the *étang*, where the superb **Centre d'Information La Capelière** has one of the best displays on the Camargue, with marked nature trails and information about the birds and plants of the area. There are three observatories within a few minutes of here, and a walking trail, 1.5km (1 mile) long.

On the west side of the *étang* is the Maison du Parc Naturel Régional de Camargue, 4km (2.5 miles) north of Stes-Maries-de-la-Mer, with displays and large viewing windows. To get closer to the bird life, go to the adjacent **Parc Ornithologique du Pont de Gau**, where there are half-hour trails around the Étang de Pont de Gau, or the Étang de Ginès sanctuary, where bulls graze in the summer. Large aviaries near the entrance to the park house birds of prey.

South of here, the salt marshes give way to sand dunes and ponds. It's great for bird-watching: look for flamingos, avocets and egrets feeding in the shallows; bitterns and herons in the reedbeds; and ducks, geese and waders on the shore.

Below right: Discovering the Camargue on horseback

Top: White storks perched on their nest
Above: Elegant pink flamingos

The Étang de Vaccarès

TAKING A BREAK

The **Domaine Paul Ricard** on the D37 at Méjanes rents out bicycles and ponies, and a large restaurant serves meals based on fresh local produce (tel: 04 90 97 10 51).

194 C2

Réserve Nationale de Camargue
Centre d'Information La Capelière, Arles
04 90 97 00 97; www.reserve-camargue.org
Daily 9–1, 2–6, Apr–Sep; Wed–Mon 9–1, 2–5, Oct–Mar Inexpensive

Maison du Parc Naturel Régional de Camargue
Pont de Gau
04 90 97 86 32
Daily 10–6, Apr–Sep; Sat–Thu 9.30–5, Oct–Mar

Parc Ornithologique du Pont-de-Gau
D570 from Arles or Stes-Maries-de-la-Mer 04 90 97 82 62; www.parcornithologique.com
Daily 9 to sunset, Apr–Sep; daily 10–5, Oct–Mar Moderate

Manade Jacques Bon, Camargue
Le Mas de Peint, Le Sambuc
04 90 97 20 62
Professional ranch with rodeos and tours on horseback

Musée Camarguais
Mas du Pont de Rousty
04 90 97 10 82
Daily 9:30–6, Apr–Sep; 10–5 Wed–Mon, Oct–Mar. Closed 1 Jan, 1 May, 25 Dec
Inexpensive

Sailing the blue waters of the Mediterranean

THE CAMARGUE: INSIDE INFO

Top tips Take precautions against **mosquitoes**, which breed prolifically in the marshes.

- Always take plenty of **drinking water** with you when you set out to explore the area.
- The best months for **bird-watching** are from April to June and September to February.
- For a **drive** in the Camargue ➤ 168–169.
- For **guided tours** in the Camargue ➤ 134.

2 Arles

Arles, at one time the Roman capital of Provence, then a medieval ecclesiastical centre, is today a lively, popular city, largely due to a variety of cultural events and influences. These include an internationally renowned photographic fair, and the influence of local fashion designer, Christian Lacroix, whose imaginative creations reflect the colourful traditional Arlésian costumes (► 8).

The Roman arena at Arles is used today for bullfights and performances

Arles has many historical places, most of which are in the largely traffic-free old quarter and can be reached on foot. Especially notable are the Roman arena and, next to it, the Roman theatre, but there are medieval sights too. The boulevard des Lices, the busy main street, runs alongside the old quarter and it is here that you'll find many shops, bars, hotels and restaurants, as well as the tourist office.

Arles' Highlights

Built during the first century AD, **Les Arènes** was the largest amphitheatre in Gaul (136m/149 yards long and 107m/117 yards wide), and scene of bloodthirsty contests between gladiators and wild animals. Originally, it had three storeys, but during the Middle Ages the stones from the third level were used to build churches and houses inside the arena to shelter the poor. These were demolished in 1825, leaving the amphitheatre once again free for bullfights. Near the arena is the **Théâtre Antique**. Much of the stonework of this Roman theatre was also dismantled to build houses and churches. The remaining rows of seats and two columns of the stage wall are, today, the setting for concerts, drama and the July folklore festival.

According to custom, the Roman necropolis of **Les Alyscamps** (from the Latin *elisii campi*, elysian fields) was built outside the city walls along the Via Aurelia. Christians took over the cemetery and several miracles are said to have taken place here, including the appearance of Christ. Formerly the necropolis had 19 chapels and several thousand tombs – all that remains today is a tranquil, poplar-lined alleyway dotted with moss-covered tombs.

The city's **Cathédral St-Trophime**, on place de la République, is a masterpiece of Provençal Romanesque architecture. The original church was built in the

Right: Visitors exploring a corner of the Roman necropolis Les Alycamps

Vincent Van Gogh

In 1888, the artist Vincent Van Gogh (1853–90) left Paris and came to Arles, where he fell under the spell of the Provençal light and landscapes. He lived in a modest cottage – the little yellow house which featured in his paintings – which was destroyed by bombing in 1944. It was at this productive time that he painted masterpieces, including the famous *Sunflowers* series. The following year, after a row with his friend Paul Gauguin over the founding of an artists' colony at Arles, and cutting off part of his own left ear, Van Gogh was committed to hospital, which has now become the Espace Van Gogh (above). It stands opposite the Muséon Arlaten, and still has the garden seen in his painting *Jardin de l'Hôpital à Arles*. In 1889, Van Gogh was moved to the mental hospital out of town at St-Paul-de-Mausole (➤ 129). A year later he returned north, and in 1890 he committed suicide at Auvers-sur-Oise, near Paris.

5th century, then rebuilt at the end of the 11th century, and the ornate tympanum, depicting the Last Judgement, was added in the next century. The cloister of St-Trophime, with rich carvings and sensitively illuminated chapels hung with Aubusson tapestries, is among the treasures of Provence. The **Muséon Arlaten**, on rue de la République, was founded by poet Frédéric Mistral in 1896. Displays cover aspects of everyday life in the region during the 17th to the 19th centuries and include a fascinating exhibition of Arlésian costume.

Musée de l'Arles et de la Provence Antique, beside the Rhône about 2km (1.2 miles) from the centre of Arles, is an absolute must see. It is built over the Cirque Romaine, an enormous second century chariot racecourse, which has been excavated. It is a modern museum covering the history of the area from Roman rule to the Christian era. On display are numerous Classical items found in the city, including Roman mosaics, sculptures of Augustus and Venus of Arles, and a fine collection of carved marble sarcophagi.

TAKING A BREAK

The rustic **La Mamma** restaurant near the arenas (20 rue de l'Amphithéâtre, tel: 04 90 96 11 60) serves tasty Italian and regional cuisine, including pizzas and beef with olives.

---

194 C3

Tourist Information Office
Esplanade Charles de Gaulle, boulevard des Lices
04 90 18 41 20; www.tourisme.ville-arles.fr
Daily 9–6:45, Apr–Sep; Mon–Sat 9–4:45, Sun 10–1, Oct–Mar

Les Arènes
Rond-Point des Arènes 04 90 49 38 20
Daily 9–6, May–Sep; 9–5:30, Oct and Mar–Apr;10–4:30, Nov–Feb. Closed 1 Jan, 1 Nov, 25 Dec and for occasional bullfights Moderate

Musée de l'Arles et de la Provence Antiques
Presqu'île du Cirque-Romain
04 90 18 88 88; www.arles-antique.org
Daily 9–7, Apr–Oct; 10–5, Nov–Mar. Closed some public hols Moderate

The Thermes de Constantin in Arles is one of the largest bath-houses in Provence

ARLES: INSIDE INFO

Top tips The **Pass Monuments**, available from the tourist office, covers nine sights in Arles.

- Browse around the town's huge **Saturday morning market** on boulevard des Lices. The second-hand market, on the same street, is on the first Wednesday of every month.

One to miss You won't see paintings by Van Gogh in Arles's **Fondation Van Gogh**, near the amphitheatre. However, the gallery has some interesting art by other modern painters, including Francis Bacon, which takes its inspiration from Van Gogh's works.

3 Nîmes and the Pont du Guard

Just 20km (12.5 miles) apart, the town of Nîmes, a vital part of Roman Provence, and the spectacular aqueduct that was built to channel water to its citizens, combine to form one of the great sights of France.

Around Nîmes

There are interesting buildings in the city's old quarter, but what makes this a must see site is the 2,000-year-old amphitheatre, **Les Arènes**. It's the best preserved Roman amphitheatre in the world, and it's still in regular use for bullfights and other events. As a concession to modern requirements, an inflatable roof can be added in wintertime. Inside, the three tiers of stone seats are designed for around 20,000 spectators – but be warned, there's no safety rail on the top tier.

Nîmes's Roman temple, the **Maison Carrée**, is less spectacular in scale, but still amazingly well preserved. There are some exquisite small mosaics in the interior, and the whole structure dates from the first century BC. The temple is next door to the contemporary art gallery, known as the **Carrée d'Art**. This light and spacious modern building, designed by English architect Sir Norman Foster in 1984, displays a collection of modern art and temporary exhibitions.

The Pont du Gard

This huge, honey-coloured marvel of engineering strides across the River Gardon in three imposing tiers. Close examination from the bridge immediately beside it shows that there's no mortar holding it up, just the skill of the Romans who constructed it around 19 BC, using stone blocks that weigh

La Garrigue

The low-growing vegetation found around the Pont du Gard is called *la garrigue*. In these tough, dry conditions, the plants that thrive are often tough and dry themselves, like box and holm oak, or with spiny leaves, such as thistles and gorse. Growing among these are the aromatic herbs that create the scents and flavours of Provence – thyme, marjoram, rosemary, sage and lavender.

6 tonnes. Projecting stones were built into the design, to hold scaffolding in place for repairs. The water channel is the top tier, part of an ambitious but successful scheme to transport water from the spring near Uzès 50km (31 miles) to the Roman settlement at Nîmes, where it could be used for bathing and fountains, as well as drinking. You can learn more about the context of its building and 19th-century restoration in the excellent exhibition centre on the left bank.

TAKING A BREAK

Drop in for a light meal and a glass of wine at the art-filled **Vintage Café** in Nîmes, located at the back of a tiny square with a fountain, between the arena and the Maison Carée (7 rue de Bernis, tel: 04 66 21 04 45).

---

194 B4

Tourist Information Office
6 rue Auguste 04 66 58 38 00; www.ot-nimes.fr Mon–Wed and Fri 8:30–8, Thu 8:30–9, Sat 9–7, Sun 10–6, Jul–Aug; Mon–Fri 8:30–7, Sat 9–7, Sun 10–6, Easter–Sep; Mon–Fri 8:30–7, Sat 9–7, Sun 10–5, Oct–Easter

Les Arènes
Place des Arènes 04 66 21 82 56
Daily 9–6 or 7, Apr–Sep; 9:30–4:30, Oct–Mar Inexpensive

Maison Carrée
Place de la Comédie 04 66 21 82 56
Daily 10–7, summer; 9:30–12:30, 1:30–4:30, winter Free

Musée d'Art Contemporain (Carrée d'Art)
Place de la Maison Carré
04 66 76 35 70
Tue–Sun 10–6
Inexpensive

Pont du Gard
194 C4
Exhibition Centre, Pont du Gard
08 20 90 33 30; www.pontdugard.fr
Site open all year 6 am–1 am; exhibition hall open daily 9:30–7, Easter–Sep; 10–5:30, Oct–Easter. Closed Mon am all year and 2 weeks in Jan
Exhibition hall: moderate

NÎMES AND THE PONT DU GARD: INSIDE INFO

Top tips In midsummer the **heat can be intense**, so it pays to plan your visit around a shady lunch stop in Nîmes, visiting the Pont du Gard either early in the morning or later in the afternoon, when the sun is not so fierce.

- For a great **overview of Nîmes**, head straight for the **Magne tower**, in the Jardin de la Fontaine.
- At the **Pont du Gard**, the car park fee (inexpensive) also pays for access to the aqueduct. Entry to the exhibition centre costs more, and there's also the option of an informative 25-minute video. **Ludo** is a discovery zone for kids.

4 Stes-Maries-de-la-Mer

The picture-postcard resort of Stes-Maries-de-la-Mer, steeped in the tradition and the folklore of the Camargue, makes a perfect base for visits into the heart of the region.

With sandy beaches to the east, the town is a good base for activities including bicycle rental, horse-back riding and watersports, while the nearby marshy flatlands and lagoons are famous for their bird life and white horses.

According to legend, the Virgin Mary's half-sisters Maria Jacobé and Maria Salome landed here in AD 40 with their black serving maid Sarah, patroness of gypsies. When they died, a chapel was built over their graves (later replaced by **Notre-Dame-de-la-Mer**) and the village has been a place of pilgrimage ever since. The main pilgrimage takes place on 24–25 May. Gypsies, dressed in brilliant skirts and shawls, ribbons and flowers, carry statues of the Marias and the bejewelled black Sarah in a small blue boat into the sea to be blessed, led by handsome mounted *gardians* in full Camargue cowboy dress. This is

A Gypsy Capital

Although they come from all over Europe, most of the gypsies who attend the annual pilgrimage are Spanish. Colourful gypsy caravans are a permanent feature of the area around the town, as is the Spanish entertainment such as flamenco, which is put on for visitors.

Looking out over the gently sloping rooftops of Stes-Maries-de-la-Mer

A forest of masts in the busy marina of Stes-Maries-de-la-Mer

followed by a festival of bullfighting, rodeos, flamenco and fireworks.

A tower, in rue Victor Hugo next to the church, houses the **Musée Baroncelli** (currently closed for renovations), which displays local historical finds. Both the museum tower and the church tower give views of the town and the Camargue.

TAKING A BREAK

Enjoy fresh seafood at **Les Embruns**, 11 avenue de la Plage (➤ 132).

194 B1

Tourist Information Office

5 avenue Van-Gogh

04 90 97 82 55; www.saintesmaries.com

Musée Baroncelli

Rue Victor Hugo 04 90 97 87 60

Closed for renovations, telephone for details

STES-MARIES-DE-LA-MER: INSIDE INFO

Top tips Get close to the pastures and the *manade* (herds of bulls and horses) of the Camargue on a 90-minute **boat trip** on the Petit Rhône river. Contact A.C.T. Tiki III, Le Grau d'Orgon–D38, 13460 Stes-Maries-de-la-Mer (tel: 04 90 97 81 68/04 90 97 81 22; www.tiki3.fr).

- The best place to find **somewhere to park** is the area beside the beach.

At Your Leisure

5 Aigues-Mortes

The impressive medieval town of Aigues-Mortes stands in the flat Camargue landscape, enclosed within its perfectly preserved powerful **ramparts**, built in the 13th century at the command of Philip III. The ramparts, which include 15 towers and 10 gateways, stretch for more than 1.5km (1 mile) around the town.

Park outside the walls beside the Porte de la Gardette, enter the town through the gate and you'll find a simple grid system of streets leading to the busy main square, the place St-Louis, dominated by a statue of Louis IX. This is the heart of the town where the Tourist Information Office and many of the cafés and restaurants are located. The **Tour de Constance**, built as part of the town's defences, is the most impressive of the towers. It became a prison, and in the 17th century hundreds of Protestant women were locked up here in appalling conditions. The tower can be reached only via the Logis du Gouverneur, starting point for the official tour of the ramparts.

The impressive Tour de Constance, part of Aigues-Mortes' remarkable fortifications

In July and August, trips by boat, horse-and-carriage or *petit train* leave from outside the town's main gate and take you into the Camargue's salt marshes. Wednesday and Sunday are market days.

194 A2

Tourist Information Office

Place St-Louis

04 66 53 73 00; www.ot-aiguesmortes.fr

Daily 9–8, Jul–Aug; Mon–Fri 9–12, 1–6, Sat–Sun 10–12, 2–6, rest of year

6 Abbaye de Montmajour

Set on a small hill 3km (2 miles) north of Arles, Montmajour was among the most powerful monasteries in medieval Provence and, even in ruins, it's still an impressive sight.

St Trophimus, an early Christian saint, fled here from Arles to hide in a cave, which became a holy place. Later, a group of hermits took up residence to safeguard the site where he had lived. The community grew, which led to the founding of the monastery in the 10th century. Under Benedictine rule, the abbey prospered, establishing priories and reclaiming the surrounding marshlands, and became an important site of pilgrimage. The abbey became very wealthy – and corrupt. In 1639, the Benedictines sent a group to rectify matters, but the monks in residence, reluctant to leave, sacked the abbey. The community was disbanded in 1786. Restoration began in 1907.

Today you can explore the extensive ruins and marvel at the sheer scale of the buildings. The impressive, incomplete 12th-century Upper Church is austere. The crypt, to the right of the nave, is partly built into the hillside, and has finely detailed carvings of wild beasts and demons on the colonnades. Look out for masons' marks in the church vaulting and the graffiti dating back to medieval times in the cloister.

The **keep**, 26m (85 feet) high, is an impressive fortified structure built in 1369. The reward for climbing the 124 steps is the panoramic views across to the Alpilles, Arles, Tarascon and the Plaine de la Crau. From here, go down the hill to see the 11th-century **Ermitage St-Pierre**, in the hillside caves where St Trophimus sought refuge.

190 A4
Route de Fontvieille, Arles
04 90 54 64 17
Daily 10–6:30, Apr–Sep; Tue–Sun 10–5, Oct–Mar
Moderate, under 18 free

The Abbaye de Montmajor

7 Les Baux-de-Provence

The ancient ruined **citadel** of les Baux-de-Provence is sited on a stony plateau on one of the highest ridges of the Chaîne des Alpilles. Les Baux is divided into two: the bustling inhabited lower village, where elegant Renaissance houses line the shiny cobbled streets, and the deserted **Ville Morte** (Dead City) perched above, its ruined buildings hardly distinguishable from the surrounding limestone crags.

During the Middle Ages, this was the seat of the **seigneurs de Baux**, one of

Place Louis Jou in Les Baux-de-Provence

southern France's most powerful families. Their Cour d'Amour – a society of lords, ladies and wandering troubadours – was renowned throughout the Midi and, ever since, Les Baux has been a pilgrimage centre for poets and painters.

A map directs you around the site of the Ville Morte, to the 13th-century keep and other medieval towers, an olive musuem and reconstructions of medieval siege

Pathways meander through the ruins of the citadel in Les Baux-de-Provence

machines. But it is the views from this high cliff-edge location that are the main attraction, taking in a landscape of wild, rocky terrain broken up with vineyards and woods.

Alongside the ruins of the Dead City is the handsome, busy **"modern" Les Baux**, which dates mainly from the 16th to 17th centuries. This area outside the original fortress contains shops, houses, art galleries, a folksy *santons* (traditional clay figurines) museum and a 16th-century town hall.

The **Val d'Enfer** (the Valley of Hell), a spectacular gorge to the north of the village, is also worth a visit. Here, an underground cavern, **Cathédrale des Images**, offers an amazing sound and light experience.

190 A5

Tourist Information Office

Passage Porte Mage 04 90 54 34 39; www.lesbauxdeprovence.com

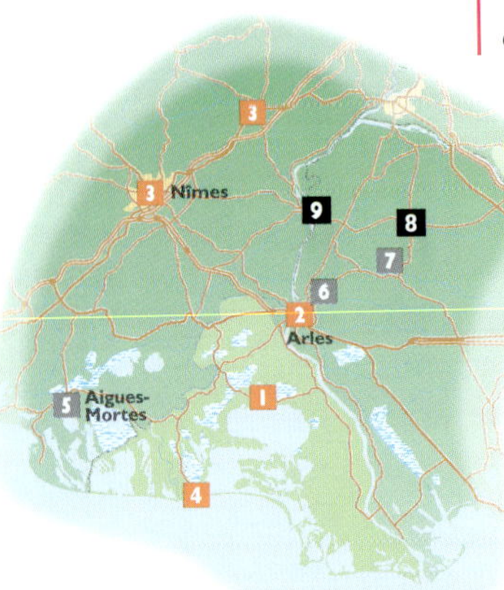

Les-Baux-de-Provence Citadelle

Ville Morte

04 90 54 55 56

Daily, 9–6:30, spring; 9–7:30, summer; 9:30–6, autumn; 9–5, winter

Expensive

8 St-Rémy-de-Provence and Glanum

In St-Rémy you will find the true flavour of Provence – the warm peaches-and-cream coloured buildings, the maze of lanes, the fountains, quiet shaded squares and the tree-lined boulevards. There are few sights of importance within the town itself, but many fine 16th- to 18th-century mansions can be seen in the

old quarter, and there are some small art galleries and museums.

Nostradamus was born here in 1503, but today St-Rémy owes its popularity to Van Gogh, who convalesced in an asylum just south of town after his quarrel with Gauguin and the ear-cutting incident in Arles. He produced 150 canvases and more than 100 drawings during his one year's stay here, including *Starry Night*, *The Sower* and his famous *Irises*. From April to October the tourist office runs a 90-minute **guided tour** visiting sights that he painted (Tue, Thu, Sat at 10 am). The tour also gives reduced entry fees for **St-Paul-de-Mausole** (the sanitorium where Van Gogh committed himself for treatment and rest in 1898) and the **Centre d'Art Présence Van Gogh**. Alternatively, get a map from the tourist office for a self-guided tour.

Near the sanitorium lie the extensive remains of the wealthy Greco-Roman town of **Glanum**, the oldest classical buildings in France. The area was first settled in 6 BC and the city was abandoned in the third century when it was overrun by

Tarascon's red-tiled rooftops

barbarians. Buildings near by, called Les Antiques, were also part of the Roman town. They include the oldest and smallest triumphal arch in France, dating from 20 BC and the best-preserved mausoleum of the Roman world, erected as a memorial to Caesar and Augustus.

190 A5

Tourist Information Office

Place Jean-Jaurès 04 90 92 05 22; www.saintremy-de-provence.com

Glanum

Avenue Vincent van Gogh, Route des Baux 04 90 92 23 79 Daily 10–6:30, Apr–Aug; Tue–Sun 10:30–5, Sep–Mar. Closed 1 Jan, 1 May, 1 Nov, 11 Nov, 25 Dec Expensive

For Kids

- **Tarascon** The châteaux was used as a prison up until the 1920s – look for graffiti by 18th-century English prisoners.

9 Tarascon

Most people visit Tarascon, former frontier town of the kingdom of Provence, to see the fortress of Good King René. Built between 1400 and 1449 on the banks of the Rhône, with a moat and turreted towers and an elegantly styled interior, it is now one of the finest **medieval châteaux** in France. The town is also famous for its dreaded **Tarasque**, a man-eating monster who, according to legend, was vanquished by the town's patron, Ste Marthe. On the last Sunday in June the green, dragon-like, papier-mâché Tarasque parades around town, starting four days of fun with festivities, fireworks, bonfires and bullfights. Tarascon also has several markets and fairs during the year, including an Orchid Festival in February, a medieval fête in September and a market in November dedicated to *santons* (traditional clay figurines).

The **Musée Souleïado**, at 39 rue Proudhon, in the old quarter (daily 10–6, May–Sep; Tue–Sat 10–5, Oct–Apr) is worth a look to find out about the town's traditional cloth-making industry, using vivid colours in the Provençal style.

194 C3

Tourist Information Office

59 rue des Halles

04 90 91 03 52; www.tarascon.org

Château de Tarascon

Boulevard de Roi-René

04 90 91 01 93

Daily 9–7, Apr–Aug; Tue–Sun 10:30–5, Sep–Mar. Closed 1 Jan, 1 May, 1 Nov, 11 Nov, 25 Dec Moderate

Where to... Stay

Prices
Expect to pay per night for a double room
€ under €100 **€€** €100–€200 **€€€** over €200

ARLES

Arlatan €€–€€€
This charming 16th-century residence of the comtes d'Arlatan is one of the region's most beautiful historic hotels, and has 30 rooms individually decorated with Provençal antiques. You can take breakfast in the peaceful walled garden. There is private parking.
194 C3 ✉ 26 rue Sauvage ☎ 04 90 93 56 66; www.hotel-arlatan.fr ⏲ Closed early Jan–early Feb

Hôtel Calendal €€
A two-star hotel located close to the arenas in Arles, the Calendal makes a comfortable and inexpensive base for exploring the town and the wider area. There are 38 air-conditioned bedrooms, with views to the arenas or over a garden courtyard. Inside, you'll find the tiled floors and wrought iron typical of Provence. Breakfast can be eaten in the garden.
194 C3 ✉ 5 rue Porte-de-Laure ☎ 04 90 96 11 89; www.lecalendal.com ⏲ Closed Jan

Nord-Pinus €€€
This hotel, in the centre of the Old Town, is a classified national monument. It has strong literary connections as it was once a favourite haunt of the Félibres poets and other literati, including Stendhal, Mistral, Cocteau and Henry James. Today it is popular with Christian Lacroix, top matadors and other wealthy aficionados, and is decorated accordingly with bullfighting posters and trophies alongside antique furniture and various *objets d'arts*. For people who want to feel truly Arlésian!
194 C3 ✉ Place du Forum ☎ 04 90 93 44 44; www.nord-pinus.com ⏲ Closed Jan–Feb

Le Mas de Peint €€€
This was the house of 17th-century Lyon draper, Antoine Peint. It became a farm in the 19th century – rice is still grown on the estate and cattle are bred here. There are eight bedrooms and three suites, some with beamed ceilings and others with a Victorian bathroom. Enjoy farm-grown food in the evenings.
194 C3 ✉ Le Sambuc ☎ 04 90 97 20 62; www.masdepeint.com ⏲ Closed Jan to mid-Mar, mid-Nov to mid-Dec

LES BAUX-DE-PROVENCE

Le Mas d'Aigret €–€€
If you want to see the dawn rise over Les Baux, then you'll need to stay in the village, and this unusual hotel carved into the rocky hillside is a great place to be, with wonderful views. There are 16 air-conditioned bedrooms, simply but tastefully furnished, with cool, white-painted furniture and pretty bedcovers. Facilities at this three-star hotel include a lounge, a bar and an outdoor swimming pool.
190 A5 ✉ 13520 Les Baux-de-Provence ☎ 04 90 54 20 00; www.masdaigret.com ⏲ Closed Jan

NÎMES

Hôtel Imperator Concorde €€€
There's more than a touch of extravagance in this beautiful hotel, which overlooks Jardin de la Fontaine and place Picasso in the heart of Nîmes. Its roadside setting is made up for by the superb

gardens. There are 62 spacious rooms, well designed and comfortable, with air-conditioning. Sip a cocktail before dinner with the ghosts of Ava Gardner and Ernest Hemingway, who both stayed here in the past. Breakfast is not included in the room price.

194 C3 Quai de la Fontaine 04 66 21 90 30; www.hotel-imperator.com All year

ST-RÉMY-DE-PROVENCE

Château de Roussan €

This former residence of the Marquis de Gange was built on land owned by his famous ancestor, Nostradamus. A hotel since 1951, it has beautifully decorated rooms. The surrounding parkland has ancient trees, streams, ornamental ponds with swans and ducks, and is ideal for a leisurely stroll. The restaurant serves Provençal cuisine.

190 A5 Route de Tarascon 04 90 92 11 63; www.chateau-de-roussan.com All year

Hotel Les Ateliers de L'Image €€€

This four-star hotel is an oasis of sophisticated minimalism at the heart of the town. It has 32 bedrooms and 4 suites, all with every modern amenity. There is a garden, an outdoor pool and an exotic Franco-Japanese restaurant.

190 A5 36 boulevard Victor Hugo 04 90 92 51 50 Closed Dec

STES-MARIES-DE-LA-MER

Hotel de Cacharel €€

A former *gardian* ranch in the heart of the marshes, with 15 comfortable bedrooms, each with bath or shower. Facilities include a swimming pool, and there is accompanied horse-back riding to explore the wetlands of the Camargue and to see the local black bulls.

194 B1 Route de Cacharel 04 90 97 95 44; www.hotel-cacharel.com All year

Where to... Eat and Drink

Prices
Expect to pay for a three-course meal for one, excluding drinks and service
€ under €25 €€ €25–€50 €€€ over €50

ARLES

L'Escaladou €

This authentic, down-to-earth, Arlésian restaurant in the centre of Arles is usually packed with locals, who enjoy hearty helpings of tasty Arles sausages and *boeuf gardian* (a spicy beef stew with olives, served with Camarguais rice).

194 C3 23 rue Porte-de-Laure 04 90 96 70 43 12–2:30, 6:30–11 Closed Wed

Corazon €€–€€€

This delightful restaurant is situated in a 16th-century town house complete with a courtyard and fountain. A calm and intimate atmosphere is created in a number of small dining rooms, which are decorated in subdued tones to match the exposed stonework. The menu features fine regional cuisine and offers a good choice of Camargue specialities such as beef served with a pepper and anchovy sauce. A bottle of house wine with your meal will cost around €20

194 C3 1 bis rue Réattu 04 90 96 32 53 Tue–Sat 12–2:30, 7:30–10. Closed Nov and 1–15 Jan

La Mamma €–€€
This restaurant, near the amphitheatre, has a tiled floor, wicker chairs and a pizza oven. The menu lists Italian and regional dishes such as sautéed beef with olives, crudités with anchovy sauce and pizzas.

194 C3 · 20 rue de l'Amphithéâtre · 04 90 96 11 60; www.lamammaarles.com · Tue–Sat 12–2:30, 7–10:30, Sun 12–2:30

LES BAUX-DE-PROVENCE

La Reine Jeanne €€
The large windows of this small restaurant give fine views of the valley. The regional cuisine includes peppers marinated in olive oil, leg of lamb with garlic pickles, and a Provençal platter with olive tapenade. A cod and poached vegetable *aïoli* is served every Friday.

190 A5 · Grande Rue · 04 90 54 32 06; www.la-reinejeanne.com · Daily 12–3, 7–9:30

NÎMES

Le Bouchon et l'Assiette €–€€
Situated in an attractive old building beside the Fontaine gardens, this restaurant offers great value *prixe-fixe* menus. The furnishings in the dining room may be simple, but the cooking is richly flavoured and beautifully presented – try the *foie gras*, served grilled with peppers and grape caramel.

194 B4 · 5 rue de Sauve · 04 66 62 02 93 · Thu–Mon noon–1:30, 7:30–10. Closed 1–15 Jan and 3 weeks in Aug

Le Vintage Café €–€€
Situated between the arena and La Maison Carrée, in a tiny square with a fountain, this delightful bistro has a dining room which is also used as a gallery for local artists.

194 B4 · 7 rue de Bernis · 04 66 21 04 45 · Tue–Fri 11–2:30, 7–11, Sat 7–11. Closed 2 weeks in Aug

STES-MARIES-DE-LA-MER

Brûleur de Loups €€
The tempting menu at this seafront restaurant includes *bourride* (a creamy, garlicky fish soup), fresh grilled "catch of the day" and even *carpaccio* of bull (thinly sliced and raw).

194 B1 · 1 avenue Gilbert-Leroy · 04 90 97 83 31 · 12–1:45, 7–9:30. Closed Tue eve, Wed

Les Embruns €€
Enjoy the best local ingredients at this restaurant, with its rustic yet refined interior. Fresh seafood is served in a variety of guises, including in paella, one of the specialities. *Prixe-fixe* menus are available, including a *menu gourmand*. Around €15 for a bottle of house wine.

194 B1 · 11 avenue de la Plage · 04 90 97 92 40; www.chez.com/embruns · Daily 12–2, 7:30–10 in season; lunch only low season; closed mid-Nov to mid-Feb

ST-RÉMY-DE-PROVENCE

Café des Arènes €
This small bar-cum-restaurant serves tasty local cuisine. Try a bull steak followed by crème brûlée with thyme. The pavement terrace enjoys the late-afternoon sun.

190 A5 · 9 boulevard Gambetta · 04 32 60 13 43 · Closed Sun eve, Mon Nov–Mar

TARASCON

Abbaye St-Michel de Frigolet
This restaurant is situated at the heart of a 12th-century abbey. The dining rooms are Provençal in style, and in fine weather you can dine out on the terrace. The cuisine has a regional flavour: try the red mullet with basil mayonnaise, and Frigolet liqueur crème brûlée.

194 C3 · Communauté des Prémontrés, Abbaye St-Michel de Frigolet · 04 90 90 52 70; www.frigolet.com · Daily 12–1:30, 7–8:45. Hotel guests only Mon–Tue

Where to... Shop

SOUVENIRS AND GIFTS

Quality reproductions of original Provençal jewellery can be found at the family-run **Bijoux Dumont** in Arles (3 rue du Palais, tel: 04 90 96 05 66, open Tue–Sat 9–12, 2:30–7), where they use mostly 18-carat gold, silver or semiprecious stones and incorporate the emblems of the region into their designs. You can choose from Provençal crosses, Stes-Maries-de-la-Mer cross pendants and cicada brooches. Alternatively, you might try **Bijouterie Pinus**, which also sells a range of necklaces, bracelets and crosses in traditional Provençal designs (6 rue Jean-Jaurès, tel: 04 90 96 04 63).

In St-Rémy-de-Provence, **Les Olivades** (28 rue Lafayette, tel: 04 90 92 00 80) is the place to go for colourful printed fabrics, traditional Provençal clothing and gift ideas.

FASHION

Christian Lacroix, the celebrated haute-couture designer, was born in Arles and his vibrant collections capture the spirit of Provence. The the fashions, jewellery, hats and handbags of his boutique at the heart of Arles' pedestrian zone are a major draw for the rich and fashionable (52 rue de la République, tel: 04 90 96 11 16, open Mon 2:30–7, Tue–Sat 9–12, 2–7).
L'Arlésienne (12 rue du Président-Wilson, tel: 04 90 93 28 05) is the place to go to kit yourself out in traditional *Camarguais* costume.

Maria Maria, in Stes-Maries-de-la-Mer, is a boutique with an ochre-walled and Spanish blue-tiled interior, and a *feria* (festival) atmosphere. It specialises in Andalucian costumes, embroidered shirts and *gardian* clothes. You'll find some big names (Christian Lacroix, Tomar Artesania) alongside the work of local designers (7 place des Remparts, tel: 04 90 97 71 60, open daily 10–12:30, 2–6, and 9 am–9 pm in summer and during special events).

At **Boutique du Gardian**, also in Stes-Maries-de-la-Mer, you'll find the clothes to get outfitted like a *gardian*: felt hat, broad belt and tall boots made of soft leather. You'll also find a range of well-known outdoor brands (9 rue Victor Hugo, tel: 04 90 97 85 34, summer daily 9–8, winter 9:30–12, 2–6).

FOOD AND DRINK

Chocolate-maker **Joël Durand** in St-Rémy-de-Provence combines chocolate with the region's local produce; one option is chocolate with black olives (3 boulevard Victor Hugo, tel: 04 90 92 38 25, open Mon 9:30–12:30, 2:30–6:30, Tue–Sat 9:30–12:30, 2:30–7:30, Sun 10–1, 3–6). Glacé fruit has been the speciality at **Lilamand**, also in St-Remy, since 1866. Try the glacé chestnuts or glacé fruit jam (5 avenue Albert Schweitzer, tel: 04 90 92 11 08, open Tue–Sat 10–12:30, 2:30–7). For traditional pottery, including hand-painted plates, carafes and other dishes, drop into **Terre è Provence** (1 rue Lafayette, tel: 04 90 92 28 52, open 9:30–1, 2–7, closed Sun–Mon and 15–31 Jan).

ART, ANTIQUITIES AND BOOKS

In Arles, **Antiquités Maurin** is a treasure trove of regional furniture, paintings and ceramics dating from the 17th to the 20th centuries (4 rue de Grille, tel: 04 90 96 51 57, closed Sun, and Mon morning).

You can browse through framed pictures and cards of Provence at **Galerie du Pharos** in St-Rémy-de-Provence (35 rue Carnot, tel: 04 90 92 08 24).

Where to... Be Entertained

Most of the nightlife in the region centres around Arles. **Théâtre d'Arles** presents a mixture of contemporary drama and ballet from companies around France and beyond. There are also regular children's shows (boulevard Clemenceau, tel: 04 90 52 51 55; ticket line: 04 90 52 51 51. Ticket office open Mon–Fri 11–1, 3–6:30, Sat–Sun 3–6, Aug–Dec; Mon–Fri 3–6, Jan–Jul). At **El Patio**, on the banks of the Rhône, you'll be entertained by Chico, leader of the celebrated band the Gypsy Kings. Here you can enjoy gypsy evenings with flamenco and rumba. Reservations are essential (Le Patio de Camargue, tel: 04 90 49 51 76, open Sat 8pm).

La Café la Nuit is a popular meeting place at the heart of Arles, and the subject of a famous Van Gogh painting (11 place du Forum, tel: 04 90 49 83 30, open 9 am–midnight).

Le Krystal, with its modern steel and pink décor and blue neon lights, hosts various theme nights. The choice includes zouk, go-go dancers and Latin. Or you can dance to an orchestra every Sunday and Monday (Hameau de Moulès, tel: 04 90 98 32 40, open Fri–Sat 10:30 pm–6 am, dancing Sun 2.30–8, Tue 7 pm–2 am).

Discothèque La Haute Galine, in St-Rémy-de-Provence, is one of the few late-night options for partying in this part of Provence. It offers a variety of music styles (chemin Cante Perdrix et Galine, tel: 04 90 92 00 03, open Fri–Sat from 9 pm).

SPORTS AND ACTIVITIES

At Arles you can get off the beaten track and discover the region's wildlife on an exciting four-wheel-drive tour, with **Camargue Safaris Gallon**. You'll go to the inland waterways and see the white horses, small black bulls and pink flamingos for which the area is famous. Some deals include biking and horse-back riding (36 avenue Edouard Herriot, tel: 04 90 93 60 31, open all year by appointment).

Horses and bulls are bred at **La Cabano dis Ego**, and the owners organise various activities, including traditional horse-back riding, French cowboy games and even hot-air balloon flights (Le Sambuc, tel: 04 90 97 20 62, open all year).

The village of Stes-Maries-de-la-Mer is a good base for activities. With **A.C.T. Tiki III** you can go on a 90-minute boat excursion on the Petit Rhône river to discover a landscape typical of the Camargue and get close to the herds of bulls and horses. Reservations are advised (Le Grau d'Orgon–D38, tel: 04 90 97 81 68/04 90 97 81 22; www.tiki3.fr, open Mar–Nov).

If you prefer to be on horse-back then you can discover the scenery of the Camargue's inland waters, beaches and wildlife, including flamingos, on 2-hour or full day excursions with **Promenade des Rièges**. The stables have the white horses for which the Camargue is so well known (route de Cacharel, tel: 04 90 97 91 38; www.promenadedesrieges.com, by appointment).

For a complete change, try the wide range of treatments on offer at **Thalacap Camargue**. At this thalassotherapy spa you can benefit from the therapeutic values of sea water, including seaweed and mud wrap, and hydromassage. Facilities include a gym, Turkish bath and sauna (avenue Jacques-Yves Cousteau, tel: 04 90 99 22 22; www.thalacap.fr; open daily 9–12, 2–8, closed early to mid-Dec).

The Vaucluse

Getting Your Bearings 136 – 137
In Four Days 138 – 139
Don't Miss 140 – 154
At Your Leisure 155 – 158
Where to... 159 – 164

Getting Your Bearings

The Vaucluse is one of France's smallest *departéments*, but also among its most popular, due to its wealth of ancient history and variety of scenery, from the delicate lacy silver crags of the Dentelles de Montmirail and the bleak, awesome massif of Mont Ventoux to the rolling, verdant hills of the Lubéron. The timeless quality of the Rhône valley's sun-bleached landscape is reinforced by some of the finest Roman remains, at Orange and Vaison-la-Romaine, and the entire region is saturated in medieval buildings, from the remotest hilltop village to the papal grandeur of historic Avignon – the other Rome – enriched by art and architecture over the centuries, and papal property up until the French Revolution.

For many, the Lubéron region epitomises the real magic of Provence, with its sleepy, medieval villages, hidden in a lush, green landscape. Peter Mayle's celebrated books present life here as idyllic and, despite the region's popularity, it is still possible to escape the tourist hordes and discover your own delights – a dusty game of pétanque in a fountain-splashed square; a stroll through olive groves and vineyards; coffee and croissants in a café; romantic, crumbling castle ruins; and pastis in the local bar are all a part of life here.

Vaucluse's colourful markets offer the opportunity to taste the specialities of this region (Cavaillon melons, Carpentras truffles, crystallised fruits in Apt) and no visit is complete without trying some of France's finest wines, in the villages of Châteauneuf-du-Pape, Gigondas and Beaumes-de-Venise.

Top: A Roman soldier

Above: A basket of lavender for sale

★ Don't Miss

1 **Avignon** ➤ 140
2 **Châteauneuf-du-Pape** ➤ 144
3 **Orange** ➤ 146
4 **Vaison-la-Romaine** ➤ 148
5 **Gordes and the Abbaye de Sénanque** ➤ 150
6 **The Lubéron** ➤ 152

At Your Leisure

7 Cavaillon ➤ 155
8 Roussillon ➤ 155
9 Fontaine-de-Vaucluse ➤ 156
10 Mont Ventoux ➤ 157
11 Dentelles de Montmirail ➤ 158

Page 135: The village of Brantes, in the foothills of Mont Ventoux

This itinerary embraces the must-see sights of Vaucluse, including historic Avignon and Orange and the heart-achingly beautiful landscapes of the Lubéron.

The Vaucluse in Four Days

Day One

Morning

Spend a day in the medieval, walled city of 1 **Avignon** (➤ 140–143). Start at the UNESCO-listed Palais des Papes (➤ 141), the jewel in Avignon's crown. From here, it is a short stroll down to the river and the celebrated Pont St-Bénézet (left, ➤ 141).

Lunch

Enjoy a classy Mediterranean lunch at No 75 (75 rue Guillaume Puy, tel: 04 90 27 16 00) in the picturesque ancient quarter of the city.

Afternoon

Soak up the atmosphere of Avignon's lively, main square – place de l'Horloge – abuzz with cafés, artists and buskers, or spend time window-shopping in rue Joseph Vernet, named after Avignon's most famous painter (whose seascapes can be seen in the Musée Calvet here, ➤ 141).

Evening

Dine in style at Hiély-Lucullus (5 rue de la République, tel: 04 90 86 17 07), one of Avignon's top gourmet temples.

Day Two

Morning

Spend the morning admiring two of the finest Roman monuments in Europe – the Arc de Triomphe, a grand three-arched monument, (➤ 147) and the massive Théâtre Antique, built into the slope of Colline St-Eutrope, (➤ 146) – in the historic town of 3 **Orange**.

Lunch

Restaurant des Princes (➤ 162) is a reliable lunch stop.

Afternoon

Tour the pretty wine villages of Haut Vaucluse – Beaumes-de-Venise, Vacqueyras, Gigondas – on the slopes of the Dentelles de Montmirail, en route to 4 **Vaison-la-Romaine** (left, ➤ 148–149), to visit the former city of Vaisio Vocontiorum, one of the best-preserved Roman sites of Provence.

Evening

Enjoy an evening of Provençal cuisine and top-notch wines at La Fontaine (➤ 162) in Vaison-la-Romaine.

Day Three

Morning

Visit the photogenic hilltop village of 5 **Gordes** (➤ 150–151). Hunt out the extraordinary stone *bories* (prehistoric settlements) on the outskirts of the village, and visit the 5 **Abbaye de Sénanque** (right, ➤ 150–151), set in a field of lavender.

Lunch

Hostellerie Le Phebus (➤ 162) is a delightful place for an al fresco lunch.

Afternoon

Head to 8 **Roussillon** (➤ 155–156), with its celebrated ochre quarries and follow the 1km (half-mile) Sentier des Ocres (Ochre Trail).

Evening

Enjoy a rustic meal overlooking the brilliant red ochre cliffs at David (place de la Poste, tel: 04 90 05 60 13).

Day Four

Morning

Explore the picturesque hilltop villages of the 6 **Lubéron** (➤ 152–153). Start at Oppède-le-Vieux, with its ruined château, and progress through Ménerbes and Lacoste to Bonnieux.

Lunch

Try Le Galoubet (➤ 162) in Ménerbes, or Le Pont Julien (➤ 161) in Bonnieux, for robust regional cuisine.

Afternoon

Leave your car and ramble through the lavender fields, pine woods and vineyards of the beautiful Parc Naturel Régional du Lubéron.

Evening

There are plenty of choices for dinner in Lourmarin. Le Moulin de Lourmarin (➤ 162) is especially well rated.

1 Avignon

The historic quarter of Avignon, enclosed within its impressive medieval walls and dominated by a huge papal palace, is a cheerful and lively tourist area. The town's famous bridge, immortalised in a popular children's song, is an essential stop.

Tromp-l'oeil in the place de l'Horloge

Avignon has been the scene of countless conflicts since Roman times, and for over a century it was the seat of the popes and centre of a religious and political power struggle. It was a French pope, Clement V, who first moved his residence from the Vatican to Avignon in 1309. From then on, a succession of French popes and cardinals built up a powerful base here, and the enduring legacy of this exciting period, when culture and scholarship flourished, is the magnificent fortified palace, the **Palais des Papes**. When the popes eventually returned to Rome in 1403, they took many of their treasures with them, and today there is a bleak emptiness about it. The entire complex is so vast that it has been described as "a city within a city", and takes at least a day to visit. Don't miss the fanciful Audience Hall, the frescoes of the Stag Room, the princely papal bedroom, St Martial's Chapel and the Hall of the Consistory.

A walk along the **ramparts** reveals the two sides of Avignon today – the village-like atmosphere of the historic walled Old Town, its skyline adorned with steeples and monuments; and the sprawling factories and bustling modern suburbs beyond, accommodating the city's 100,000 inhabitants. It is a busy place, especially in July when the narrow lanes and pedestrian zones resound with buskers, street theatre and café cabarets during the renowned arts festival.

Around the town, you'll find the best shopping along rue de la République, while the cafés of the **place de l'Horloge**, a lively square abuzz with artists and buskers, offer the chance to relax with a coffee and watch the world go by. There are several museums to explore, including the beautifully restored 14th-century **Petit Palais**, an art museum with a remarkable collection of medieval works, as well as Romanesque and Gothic sculpture and frescoes. The **Musée Calvet** is Avignon's main museum, with collections of French, Italian, Flemish and Duch paintings, sculpture and porcelain from the last five centuries. Be sure to make time for the **Pont St-Bénézet** – the Pont d'Avignon immortalised in song. It was originally a wooden structure, built in 1177 by

Left: Taking a break beneath the magnificent Palais des Papes

Below: The view across the Rhône from the gardens of Rocher des Doms

Sur le Pont d'Avignon

The cheerful **children's song** about dancing on the bridge dates back to the 15th century, but its composer is unknown. It came to wider attention in 1853, when Adolphe Adam (better remembered for his ballet, *Giselle*) included it in an operetta, *Le Sourd ou l'Auberge Pleine*. The song proved so popular that it became the focus of its own operetta in 1876. Crooner Jean Sablon recorded a famous swing version of the song in 1939, and it is said that BBC radio played it 14 times in one day as a coded message before the D-Day landings. Recorded hundreds of times in different ways, it has even inspired classical piano variations. Today it is used widely around the world to teach children the French language.

the young shepherd St Bénézet, and was rebuilt in stone after a siege in 1226. It was constantly buffeted by the strong flow of the Rhône, and in the mid-17th century, most was washed away. Now just four picturesque arches remain.

One of the best vantage points to appreciate Avignon's medieval grandeur is the 13th-century **Fort St-André at Villeneuve-lès-Avignon**, on the other side of the river. The view is especially spectacular at sunset, as the golden southern light bathes the town, and it is a very popular place for an evening out.

TAKING A BREAK

Enjoy tea and cakes, or perhaps a light lunch at **Le Simple Simon**, a decorative English-style tea room and restaurant in the heart of the Old Town (26 rue Petite-Fusterie, tel: 04 90 86 62 70, open Tue–Sat 9–7).

---

195 B1

Tourist Information Office
41 cours Jean-Jaurès
04 32 74 32 74; www.ot-avignon.fr
Mon–Sat 9–6 (7 Jul), Sun 10–5, Apr–Oct; Mon–Fri 9–6, Sat 9–5, Sun 10–12, Nov–Mar

Palais des Papes
Place du Palais
04 90 27 50 00; www.palais-des-papes.com
Daily 9–7, 8 or 9, mid-Mar to Oct; 9:30–5:45, rest of year
Expensive mid-Mar to Oct; moderate Nov to mid-Mar

Musée Calvet
65 rue Joseph Vernet
04 90 86 33 84
Wed–Mon 10–1, 2–6
Moderate

The surviving arches of Pont St-Bénézet

Petit Palais
☎ 04 90 86 44 58 Wed–Mon 10–1, 2–6, Jun–Sep; Wed–Mon 9:30–1, 2–5:30, Oct–May
Moderate

AVIGNON: INSIDE INFO

Top tips The **Avignon Passport**, available from the tourist office or at participating sights, gives reduced price entry to the main sights.

- The **Palais des Papes** offers guided tours in English (tel: 04 90 27 50 73).
- For a relaxing way to see the town take one of the little **sightseeing land trains** which set off frequently throughout the day from place du Palais (Apr–Oct).
- The **Festival d'Avignon** (Avignon International Festival of Theatre) offers top-name entertainment, plus many fringe shows for three weeks in July (www.festival-avignon.com).

Hidden gem The **Fondation Angladon Dubrujeaud**, in an elegant city mansion on rue Laboureur, includes paintings by Sisley, Manet, Cézanne and Picasso, and Provence's only original Van Gogh (tel: 04 90 82 29 03, www.angladon.com; open Wed–Sun 1–6; also Tue, May–Nov).

2 Châteauneuf-du-Pape

Set amid the stony, sun-baked, red soil of the southern Rhône, the picturesque, old fortified village of Châteauneuf-du-Pape, surrounded by its famous vineyards, is dedicated to the production of the world-famous red wines which bear its name.

Châteauneuf-du-Pape is a popular visitor destination, with people coming to see the village and more importantly, to taste the wines. At the bottom of the village in Cave Brotte, the **Musée Père Anselme** is dedicated to the history of local viticulture, and visitors can indulge in wine tastings and are offered the chance to buy. Among the best-known vineyards in the town are Château Le Nerthe, Château Rayas, Château de la Gardine, Château de Beaucastel and the Château des Fines Roches. The **Fête de la Véraison** (Grape-ripening Festival)

CHÂTEAUNEUF-DU-PAPE: INSIDE INFO

Top tip The tourist office can **arrange visits** to vineyards and wineries.

Wine routes

Numerous wine routes in the region lead you through charming yellow-stone villages with shady squares, old fountains and red-tiled roofs, hidden in a sea of vineyards and largely given over to restaurants and cellars offering free wine tasting.

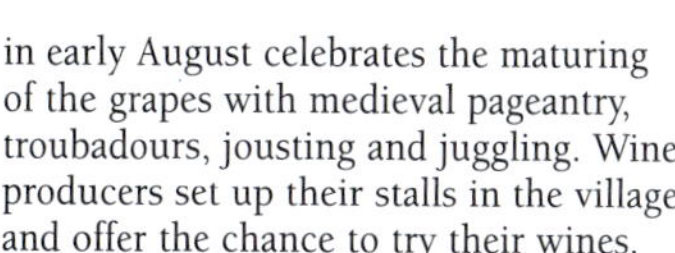

in early August celebrates the maturing of the grapes with medieval pageantry, troubadours, jousting and juggling. Wine producers set up their stalls in the village and offer the chance to try their wines.

Left: Vineyards surround Châteauneuf-du-Pape

The wines of Châteauneuf-du-Pape are world renowned, largely thanks to 13th-century Pope Jean XXII of Avignon. It was he who built the now-ruined château, with its splendid views of the Rhône valley, as a summer residence, and then went on to plant the first vineyards.

184 B3

Tourist Information Office
Place du Portail ☎ 04 90 83 71 08
Mon–Sat 9:30–7, Sun 10–1, 2–6, Jun–Sep; Mon–Sat 9:30–12:30, 2–6, Sun 10–1, 2–6, Oct–May

Musée Père Anselme
Cave Brotte ☎ 04 90 83 70 07
Daily 9–1, 2–7, mid-Jun to mid-Sep; daily 9–12, 2–6, mid-Sep to mid-Jun Free

Left: Séguret, one of the pretty villages on the wine routes

Winemaking

Many Côtes du Rhône wines are made from just one grape variety, but vintners here blend up to 13 different grapes to produce their distinctive wines of unique complexity. The vines are widely spaced, and the soil is covered with pebbles to magnify the heat of the sun during the day and release it at night. This results in a wine with a high alcohol content (12.5 per cent or higher). Most of the 13 million bottles of wine made here are a full-bodied red, although it's worth trying one of the 700,000 bottles of white. Look out for the crossed keys of the château embossed on the bottle, as this signifies that it is an authentic bottle of Châteauneuf-du-Pape.

3 Orange

Historic Orange, the "Gateway to Provence", lies in the fertile plain of the Rhône river. Its main claims to fame are two of the finest Roman monuments in Europe – the great triumphal arch and the massive theatre. Today, Orange is an important centre for Côtes du Rhône wines and produce such as olives, honey and truffles. The heart of the town dates from medieval times and is lively and bustling, with picturesque lanes and squares. It is small and easily explored on foot, and the tourist office organises guided tours.

The Théâtre Antique

One of the best surviving theatres from the ancient world, the Théâtre Antique was built over 2,000 years ago, with seating for up to 10,000 spectators. Although all that remains of the theatre is a mere shadow of its former splendour, it is nevertheless easy to imagine the theatre in its heyday. The monumental stage wall (*frons scanae*), made from red sandstone and measuring 103m (113 yards) long, 37m (40 yards) high and nearly 2m (6.5 feet) thick, is the only one in the world to survive completely from ancient times. Originally the theatre was used for meetings and lectures, and staged anything from circus acts to Greek tragedies. Its excellent acoustics are demonstrated every July and August in the **Chorégies**, a world-famous festival of opera, drama and ballet, held here since 1869. Classical, jazz and pop concerts are also held here throughout the summer.

Above: The Roman Arc de Triomphe stands in the middle of modern Orange

Left: The view from Colline St-Eutrope

The Arc de Triomphe

The massive 22m (71-foot) Arc de Triomphe was constructed as a symbol of Roman power following Caesar's conquest of the Gauls and victory over the Greek fleet. Its three archways are covered with intricate carvings and nautical symbols portraying maritime supremacy. The arc is on a roundabout surrounded by traffic from the busy N7.

The first-rate **Municipal Museum** gives a detailed insight into life in Roman Gaul. The most remarkable exhibit is a huge marble slab depicting the Romans' remarkable land survey of the region, which detailed boundaries, land owners and tax rates. There is also a full history of the city, and some interesting portraits of the royal House of Orange. The museum is a splendid introduction to the Théâtre Antique.

TAKING A BREAK

Le Yaka, at 24 place Sylvian, near the Théâtre Antique, is a Provençal bistro with wooden beams, floral table-cloths, generous portions and a jolly atmosphere (tel: 04 90 34 70 03; closed Wed, Tue dinner and Nov).

---

184 A4

Tourist Information Office
5 cours Aristide-Briand
04 90 34 70 88; www.ville-orange.fr
Mon–Sat 9:30–7, Sun and public hols 10–4, Apr–Sep; Mon–Sat 10–1, 2–5, Oct–Mar

Théâtre Antique
Place des Frères-Mounet
04 90 51 17 60
Daily 9–8, Jun–Aug; 9–7, Apr–May, Sep; 9–6, Mar, Oct; 10–4:30, Jan–Feb, Nov–Dec
Moderate, also valid for Musée Municipal

Arc de Triomphe
Avenue de l'Arc-de-Triomphe/N7

Municipal Museum
Rue Madeleine-Roch
04 90 51 17 60
Daily 9–8, Jun–Aug; 9–7, Apr–May, Sep; 9–6, Mar, Oct; 10–4:30, Jan–Feb, Nov–Dec Expensive

Today the Théâtre Antique is the venue for festivals and concerts

ORANGE: INSIDE INFO

Top tips There is **parking** alongside cours Aristide Briand and in cours Pourtoules near the Théâtre Antique.

- Telephone **Théâtre Antique** for details of guided tours (Jul–Aug only), and concert and theatre information.
- To the west of the theatre, **Colline St-Eutrope** is well worth the climb to reach its cool, shady park with magnificent views over Orange, the theatre and the Rhône plain beyond.

4 Vaison-la-Romaine

Undisputedly one of Provence's best-preserved Roman sites, Vaison is an extraordinary blend of modern town, medieval village and former Roman city – Vaisio Vocontiorum – now the town's greatest attraction.

Soaking up the atmosphere at the restored Roman theatre

Archaeological sites

The two Roman sites, Villasse and Puymin, are separated by a modern road. The **Puymin quarter**, the higher and larger of the two sites, has a visible street layout, some surviving walls and remains of frescoes and mosaic floors. The highlight is the 1st-century AD **Roman theatre**, which was restored in the 20th century and is now the venue for a range of events. Its tiered rows of seating, joined by stairs and topped with a portico, could accommodate 6,000 spectators. Other points of interest on this site include the extensive House of Apollon Lauré; the even larger Tonnelle House; the public space known as the Sanctuary; and an area of smaller houses and workshops.

The smaller, lower site, called **quartier de la Villasse**, has an important street of small shops, workshops and villas with mosaic floors. One notable structure is the ruins of the House of the Silver Bust, the largest house excavated in Vaison. The archaeology museum fee is included in the entry ticket for Villasse.

The medieval quarter

Once you've explored the Roman sites, walk down the main street, Grande Rue, and cross the Roman bridge over the Ouvèze River to the **medieval quarter**. Clinging to a lofty jagged rock, the houses of Vaison's medieval village have been lovingly restored by artists and crafts-people. It is a steep climb to the ruined 13th-century château through a maze of twisting cobbled streets, rewarded by sweeping views across Ouvèze Valley and the Côtes du Rhône vineyards as far as the snow-topped Alps.

TAKING A BREAK

Sit on the terrace at **Vieux Vaison** (8 place du Poids, in the medieval quarter, tel 04 90 36 19 45) and tuck into pizzas from the wood-fired oven, pasta dishes and grills.

---

184 C5

Tourist Information Office
Place du Chanoine-Sautel
04 90 36 02 11; www.vaison-la-romaine.com

Roman sites
Avenue Général-de-Gaulle 04 90 36 02 11
Daily 9:30–6:30, Jun–Sep; 9:30–6, Apr–May; 10–12, 2–5 or 6, Oct–Mar Moderate, covers both sites

Above: Pont Romain spans the Ouvèze River
Right: Old houses overlook the Roman ruins

VAISON-LA-ROMAINE: INSIDE INFO

Top tips The Roman sites, archaeological museum and other sights may be visited on a single ticket, **Billet Tous Monuments**, available from the ticket office adjacent to the Roman sites.
- There are **large parking areas** next to the Roman sites.
- A large, lively **street market** takes place every Tuesday morning.
- A **summer festival** of drama, music and dance is held at the Roman theatre from early July to mid-August. Every three years, there is also a **Festival of Choral Music**.

Hidden gem The Romanesque cathedral, **Notre-Dame de Nazareth**, on avenue Général-de-Gaulle, has lovely 12th-century cloisters. It is about 10 minutes' walk from the quartier de la Villasse site.

5 Gordes and the Abbaye de Sénanque

Famous for its artists' colony, magnificent Cistercian abbey and ancient *borie* village, Gordes makes an ideal centre for touring the Lubéron.

Gordes is justifiably rated one of the most beautiful villages in France. Its grandiose church and Renaissance château rise from a golden plinth on a spur of Mont Ventoux, surrounded by narrow cobbled streets and tiers of sandstone houses that spill down the steep, stony slopes. During World War II, the village fell into decline, but in the 1960s artists brought new life to the village, restoring the delightful Renaissance houses and setting up attractive galleries, studios and boutiques. Now considered a chic place to have a second home, it is well served with shops and restaurants. The château currently contains the tourist office, on the first floor, along with the **Museum of Pol Mara**, a Flemish contemporary artist and honorary citizen of Gordes.

Abbaye de Sénanque

In a secluded valley north of Gordes, bathed in a sea of lavender, is one of the great symbols of Provence, the Cistercian abbey of Sénanque. The honeyed stone abbey was built in the 12th century by the Cistercian Order, as the third – and last – of their monasteries in Provence. The three monasteries were known as the "Three Cistercian Sisters of Provence" (the other two are Silvacane ➤ 103–104 and du Thoronet ➤ 80). The monks here still follow a

Bories

Southwest of Gordes, the most famous collection of *bories* in France lies in dusty scrubland. These extraordinary beehive-shaped, dry-stone huts sheltered the earliest farmers and semi-nomadic shepherds as early as the 3rd century BC.

secret medieval recipe to concoct a pungent, herb-flavoured yellow liqueur called Sénancole. Notices advise that Sénanque abbey is not a tourist site but a place of monastic life, with a pious atmosphere and a rule of silence which visitors are requested to respect. At present, all visitors must join a guided tour (available in French only).

TAKING A BREAK

La Pause, a tiny, café-cum-teashop in Gordes' village centre, serves light meals and snacks (Route Neuve, tel: 04 90 72 11 53; closed Sun evening).

Above: Intriguing stone huts at Village des Bories
Left: Abbaye de Sénanque nestles peacefully in an attractive wooded valley

184 C3
Abbaye de Sénanque
Gordes
04 90 72 05 72; www.senanque.fr
Guided tours start 10 am. Up to 11 tours per day Jul–Aug, 2 in winter. Closed Sun am and Jan
Moderate. Advance reservations recommended

184 C3
Tourist Information Office
Le Château, Gordes
04 90 72 02 75; www.gordes-village.com Mon–Sat 9–12, 2–6, Sun 10–12, 2–6

Château de Gordes
04 90 72 02 75 Daily 10–12, 2–6. Closed 1 May, 25 Dec
Inexpensive

Village des Bories
D2 from Gordes 04 90 72 03 48 Daily 9–sunset Moderate

Below: Exploring the narrow, cobbled streets in Gordes

GORDES AND THE ABBAYE DE SÉNANQUE: INSIDE INFO

Top tips Gordes has a lively two-week **music festival** in August.
- All visitors to the abbey must join a **guided tour** (in French). Dress modestly. Closure at 12 and 5 or 6 is very prompt.
- After your visit, take the opportunity to **buy lavender oils and soaps**, handmade by the monks.

6 The Lubéron

The Parc Naturel Régional du Lubéron is a protected region of cedar and pine countryside interspersed with lavender fields, almond and olive groves, fragrant herbs, *garrigue* scrub and vineyards, draped across a compact range of small mountains that stretch from Cavaillon to Manosque.

The dramatic wooded gorge of the Combe de Lourmarin (road D943) splits the region in two. The high, wild Grand Lubéron mountains lie to the east. Walkers tackling the strenuous climb from Auribeau to the uppermost peak of Mourre Nègre (1,100m/3,609 feet) will be well rewarded with dizzy views from the Basse-Alpes to the Mediterranean. To the west, many of the pretty hilltop villages of the Petit Lubéron have been restored and are now fashionable second homes.

The busy old market town of **Apt**, north of the Lubéron mountains, makes an ideal centre for touring the area. The best place to start is at the **Maison du Parc Naturel Régional du Lubéron**, which details walks and other outdoor activities, together with a small local natural history museum. The town itself is renowned for its jams and crystallised fruit – try some at the bustling Saturday market. Apt is also well known for its lavender essence and hand-made pottery, and is an important centre for the truffle trade in winter.

The Lubéron Villages

The neighbouring villages of Bonnieux, Lacoste, Ménerbes and Oppède-le-Vieux vie for the title of prettiest Lubéron village.

Right: The village of Lourmarin, in the south of the Lubéron

Bonnieux, overlooking the vineyards, cherry trees and lavender fields of the Coulon valley, has many fine monuments, including the Town Hall, a bakery museum and some notable Renaissance paintings in its two churches.

Lacoste is rich, exclusive and crowned by an 11th-century fortress, which in its heyday was one of the region's grandest.

The Luberón's highest-profile village, **Ménerbes**, has long attracted celebrities, including Picasso's mistress Dora Maar and, more recently, François Mitterand and British writer Peter Mayle. The village, the setting for Peter Mayle's bestseller, *A Year in Provence* (1989), is a lively place with a vibrant weekly market, 13th-century fortress and 14th-century church.

At first glimpse **Oppède-le-Vieux** appears a typical hilltop village, but on closer inspection you will see that many of the houses are in ruins, overrun with weeds. Some of the old cottages and the Romanesque church have been restored by resident artists, and Oppède is returning to its former glory.

To the South

The imposing Renaissance château, medieval houses, tiny fountain-filled squares and inviting restaurants of **Lourmarin** create a picturesque ensemble on the southern slopes of the Lubéron. French novelist and philosopher Albert Camus bought a house here after winning the Nobel Prize for literature in 1957. His simple grave can be visited in the village cemetery.

The pretty village of **Ansouis**, on a rocky crest, is dominated by the keep of its great château, home of the Sabran family for the last 800 years. The 12th-century fortress was modernised during the Renaissance, and is today more of a large country house than a castle. On the ground floor there are displays of weapons and armour, while upstairs you'll find Flemish tapestries and elegant pieces of Italian-Renaissance furniture.

Pine forests cling to slopes of the the Lubéron

TAKING A BREAK

When visiting the village of **Lacoste** stop at the cheap and cheerful Café de France, where you can enjoy a light lunch such as *salade Niçoise* or omelette and fries (Le Village, lunch only).

Left: Bonnieux, one of the pretty Lubéron villages

Maison du Parc Naturel Régional du Lubéron
185 D2
60 place Jean Jaurès, Apt
04 90 04 42 00;
www.parcduluberon.com
Mon–Fri 8:30–12, 1:30–7, Sat 8:30–12, 1:30–7, summer; Mon–Fri 8:30–12, 1:30–6, winter Inexpensive

Tourist Information Office
185 D2
20 avenue Philippe-de-Girard, Apt
04 90 74 03 18;
www.ot-apt.fr
Mon–Sat 9–7, Sun 9:30–12.30, Jul–Aug; Mon–Sat 9–12, 2–6, Sun 9.30–12:30, Oct–Apr; Mon–Fri 9–12, 2–6, May–Jun, Sep

Tourist Information Office
185 D2
7 place Carnot, Bonnieux
04 90 75 91 90;
www.bonnieux.com
Mon Sat 9:30–12:30, 2–6

Top: Vineyards in the Lubéron hills
Above: An archway frames a narrow street in Apt

Tourist Information Office
185 E2
Place du Château, Ansouis
04 90 09 86 98; www.ansouis.fr
Daily 10–12, 2–6, Feb–Dec. Closed every second Mon

THE LUBÉRON: INSIDE INFO

Top tips Drop into the **Maison du Parc Naturel Régional du Lubéron** for information on walks and other activities in the park.
- Pause at the terrace near the 12th-century church in **Bonnieux** and enjoy the stunning views of the valley and nearby hilltop villages.
- In **Oppède-le-Vieux** you can walk the overgrown pathways in the upper part of the village to the summit, but take care as there are many unprotected drops.

One to miss Don't expect to find **Peter Mayle** in Ménerbes – he lived near by until he was driven away by visiting fans.

At Your Leisure

7 Cavaillon

Cavaillon is France's greatest market garden – its very name synonymous with those delicious, sweet, pink-fleshed melons – and boasts one of Europe's largest wholesale fruit and vegetable markets. The vast, mouth-watering **market** for the general public every Monday morning is considered the most important market in the Vaucluse.

The town's agricultural wealth stems from its location in the fertile Durance valley. From the Colline St-Jacques, a one-time neolithic site at the top of the town, there are spectacular views across the valley to the distant highlands of the Lubéron and the Alpilles.

In the town centre, numerous Roman finds have been assembled in the **Musée Archéologique**. The former cathedral is also worth visiting, as is the beautifully preserved 18th-century synagogue, with its small museum illustrating the region's traditional protection of Jewish communities.

184 C2
Tourist Information Office
Place François-Tourel
04 90 71 32 01;
www.cavaillon-luberon.com
Mon–Sat 9–12:30, 2–6:30, Sun 10–12, Jul–Aug; Mon–Sat 9–12:30, 2–6:30, mid-Mar to Jun, Sep–Oct; Mon–Fri 9–12, 2–6, Sat 9–12, Nov to mid-Mar

The town of Cavaillon, viewed here from the neolithic site of Colline St-Jaques, is known as the melon capital of France

8 Roussillon

Once known worldwide for its ochre dyes, Roussillon is now considered one of

Roussillon is a jumble of ochre buildings of various hues

France's most beautiful villages. Perched on a platform of rich rust-coloured rock called Mont Rouge, the village is hidden amid dark pine forests and scrub, and surrounded by jagged cliffs and hollows of every shade of ochre imaginable, from blood red, gold, orange and pale yellow to white, pink and violet. For here lie the richest deposits of ochre in all France.

The ochre industry began here at the end of the 18th century, bringing prosperity to the villagers until 1958, and although today very few quarries are worked, Roussillon still holds its merry Ochre Festival at Ascensiontide. Visitors can explore the old opencast quarries along the 1km (0.5-mile) **Sentier des Ocres** (Ochre Trail, open daily 9–6, Mar to mid-Nov; daily 10–5:30, mid-Nov to Feb), which has information sign-boards along the way. To make the most of the trail, you'll need to be able to walk well in difficult terrain.

The picturesque houses, built by the ochre miners over the centuries, present a full palette of ochre shades, which create a special glow in the streets. The hub of the village is the small, lively square beside the Mairie (town hall), where the Roussillonais gather in the outdoor cafés. Narrow lanes and winding stairways lead up to a Romanesque church, offering a sweeping panorama of the ochreous Vaucluse scenery, with its hill villages and distant mountains.

185 D3

Tourist Information Office

Place de la Poste

04 90 05 60 25; www.roussillon-provence.com

Mon–Sat 10–12, 2–5:30

9 Fontaine-de-Vaucluse

Tucked away at the end of the narrow *vallis clausa* (enclosed valley), Fontaine-de-Vaucluse is famous for its emerald-green spring, a 15-minute walk along the traffic-free Chemin de la Fontaine, beside the Sorgue river. The spring gushes from a huge cave-like abyss at the foot of a sheer cliff into a strange, still and very deep pool, surrounded by rocks and vegetation and often by a dense, dripping spray. Research has proved that this is one of the world's largest and most powerful natural springs. It consists of a vast underground labyrinth of rivers and is able to produce up to

The swift waters of Fontaine-de-Vaucluse

630 million cubic metres (22,260 million cubic feet) of water each year, flowing down the narrow valley to become the Sorgue. For maximum effect, come in March or April.

Fontaine's other main tourist attractions include a **paper mill**, and a small **museum** dedicated to the famous 14th-century Italian poet Petrarch. He wrote most of his poetry here, inspired by the solitude and wilderness he found in the valley.

184 C3
Tourist Information Office
Chemin du Gouffre
04 90 20 32 22
Tue–Sat 9:30–12:30, 1:30–5:30

Moulin à Papier Vallis Clausa
Chemin de Gouffre
04 90 20 34 14
Daily 9–6. Closed 1 Jan, 25 Dec

Musée Pétrarque
Left bank of the Sorgue
04 90 20 37 20
Wed–Mon 10–12, 2–6, Apr–Oct
Inexpensive

10 Mont Ventoux

The awesome, isolated massif of Mont Ventoux – the "Giant of Provence" – rises 1,909m (6,261 feet) above the Plateau de Vaucluse, making it the highest peak between the Alps and the Pyrénées. Italian poet Francesco Petrarch was the first recorded man to reach its summit, in 1336. It is a good 5-hour hike (for organised walks and excursions contact Bedoin Tourist Office, tel: 04 90 65 63 95, or Malaucène Tourist Office, tel: 04 90 65 22 59), but most people drive to the summit of the mountain, where high-tech

Above: The village of Bedoin, near Mont Ventoux

For Kids

• **Roussillon** Older children might enjoy scrambling over the rough terrain of the quarries, but this may be more difficult for young children. Make sure they wear something that you don't mind being stained with ochre.

• **Fontaine-de-Vaucluse** On the way to see the spring, **Le Monde Souterrain de Norbert Casteret** (tel: 04 90 20 34 13, open daily 10–12, 2–6, Apr–Aug; Wed–Sun 10–12, 2–5, Feb–Mar, Sep to mid-Nov) displays collections of rocks and minerals, but also deals vividly with efforts to discover the source of the water flowing from the Fontaine.

observation and communications equipment is installed. From here the vista takes in the Alps, the Rhône Valley, the Vaucluse Plateau, the Cévennes and the Mediterranean. Wrap up warm, even in summer. Its bleak limestone peak, totally devoid of vegetation, has been blasted white by icy *mistral* winds of up to 160km/h (100mph). For much of the year the summit is snow-clad and popular with skiers.

185 D4

Mont Ventoux Information

Chalet d'Accueil du Mont Ventoux

04 90 63 42 02

11 Dentelles de Montmirail

The higher part of the slopes of this small range of hills in northern Vaucluse is wild wooded country, but most of the lower slopes are covered with vines producing Côtes du Rhône red wines. Among the prettiest and most evocative wine villages are Séguret and Gigondas. The ochre cottages of **Séguret** house craftspeople renowned for their dried flowers and *santons* (traditional clay figurines). The wines of the small, unspoiled village of **Gigondas**, set against the jagged backdrop of the Dentelles, are reputed to be the best in the area, notably the intense red Grenache wines. Others wine villages worth a visit include Vacqueyras and Beaumes-de-Venise. Majestically framed by the lacy silver crags of the Dentelles, **Beaumes** is known for its sweet, golden Muscat wines. Taste them at the Cave des Vignerons or during the region's annual wine festivals, accompanied by goat's cheese, *foie gras* and melons in Muscat. Wine tasting is available in all the villages.

The pinnacles of Dentelles de Montmirail

184 C4

Tourist Information Office

Place du Portail, Gigondas

04 90 65 85 46

Tourist Information Office

Maison des Dentelles, place du Marché, Beaumes-de-Venise

04 90 62 94 39

Mon–Sat 9–12, 2–6 or 7

Where to... Stay

Prices
Expect to pay per night for a double room
€ under €100 **€€** €100–€200 **€€€** over €200

APT

Auberge du Lubéron €€

Apt's top hotel, decorated in warm terracotta and cream shades, is full of Provençal charm and character. The bedrooms are in two houses located on a small square with a fountain. All rooms are furnished with pretty floral fabrics and have a private bath or shower and TV. Some also have a mini-bar and air-conditioning. The spacious dining room opens out onto the terrace, where meals may be served in good weather.

185 D2 8 place du Faubourg du Ballet 04 90 74 12 50 Closed Nov and 25 Dec

AVIGNON

Auberge de Cassagne €€€

This delightful four-star hotel, just five minutes outside Avignon, is tastefully decorated and offers a high standard of comfort. The spacious bedrooms are furnished with Provençal antiques and fabrics, and have luxurious bathrooms. All rooms have satellite TV and a mini-bar. The hotel is set in beautiful gardens, with an outdoor pool and a tennis court. There is a restaurant of international renown, and you can chose to dine on the terrace.

184 B3 450 allée de Cassagne, le Pontet 04 90 31 04 18 Closed Jan

Camping de Bagatelle €

Situated on the Île de la Barthelasse, an island on the Rhône connected to Avignon by a bridge, this large camping ground can accommodate tents or caravans (trailers), and is surrounded by greenery. Facilities include a grocery store, bars, a restaurant, pool, bicycle rental and kids' playgrounds. There's also a youth hostel. It's €11 to pitch a two-man tent, €35 for a caravan.

184 B3 Île de la Barthelasse 04 90 86 30 39; www.campingbagatelle.com All year

La Ferme €

This old farmhouse is on the Île de la Barthelasse – once a hunting reserve and then a fashionable place to promenade and picnic. Gypsy caravans in the garden are popular with actors during the summer festival.

184 B3 Chemin des Bois, Île de la Barthelasse 04 90 82 57 53 Closed Nov to mid-Mar

Hôtel d'Europe €€–€€€

Follow in the steps of Napoleon Bonaparte, Pablo Picasso and Salvador Dalí, and stay at the Marquis of Graveson's former house, which was built in 1580 and turned into a hotel in 1799. The hotel is furnished with antiques, candelabra, paintings and Persian carpets. There are 44 bedrooms, and the 3 suites have a terrace with wonderful views over Avignon. There's a restaurant and parking.

184 B3 12 place Crillon 04 90 14 76 76; www.heurope.com All year

La Mirande €€€

This is an elegant four-star hotel in a medieval cardinal's palace, on a quiet cobbled square at the foot of the Palais des Papes, within the walled city of Avignon. The hotel has been carefully restored and is furnished with antiques and paintings. The bedrooms are luxurious, with beautiful marble bathrooms, and most overlook the square or

the garden with the Palais des Papes in the background. There is a candlelit bar, an excellent restaurant (you have the option of dining on the terrace in summer), a tea room and a garden.
184 B3 ✉ 4 place de la Mirande ☎ 04 90 85 93 93; www.la-mirande.fr All year

BONNIEUX

De l'Aiguebrun €€

A beautiful old, stone farmhouse just a few kilometres east of the village of Bonnieux, in the peaceful heart of the Lubéron National Park. Ten bedrooms decorated in authentic Proveçal style, and a restaurant.
185 D2 ✉ Relais de la Canube ☎ 04 90 04 47 00 Closed Jan–Feb

GORDES

Le Mas de la Beaume €€

This beautiful stone *mas* (farmhouse) overlooks the village. Inside you'll find baskets of flowers hanging from the old beams, embroidered lampshades and lots of polished wood. There are five bedrooms, all traditionally furnished with consummate taste. The picturesque garden has a swimming pool and a terrace where a fantastic farmhouse-style breakfast is served with home-made jams.
184 C3 ✉ 84220 Gordes Village ☎ 04 90 72 02 96 All year

LOURMARIN

Hostellerie le Paradou €€

A small stream runs through the wooded gardens of this small, sleepy hotel beneath the gorges of Lourmarin on the road to Apt. Le Paradou is a friendly place with nine comfortable bedrooms. There are a number of dining options: you can eat in the restaurant, in the conservatory or on the terrace.
185 D2 ✉ Combe de Lourmarin (D943) ☎ 04 90 68 04 05 Closed Jan

ORANGE

Arène €€

This small, three-star hotel, in a quiet traffic-free square in the historic centre of Orange, offers 30 good-value bedrooms, each with a safe, air-conditioning and a mini-bar. There is a small breakfast room and a separate restaurant. There is a private garage (parking fee).
184 A4 ✉ 8 place de Langes ☎ 04 90 11 40 40; www.hotel-arene.fr

ROUSSILLON

Mamaison €€

The delightful rooms at this small, old farmhouse were indivdually decorated by local artists. There is a restaurant here, too, which specialises in tasty, home-grown, organic vegetarian dishes.
185 D3 ✉ Quartier Les Devens ☎ 04 90 05 74 17; www.mamaison-provence.com Closed Nov–Feb

VAISON-LA-ROMAINE

Hostellerie Le Beffroi €€

Set in a 16th-century mansion and an adjoining building that dates from the 17th century, this three-star hotel is full of local character. There are beamed ceilings, tiled floors and fine furniture. The 22 comfortable bedrooms have private bath or shower, satellite TV and a mini-bar. Some of the rooms have panoramic views of the medieval town of Vaison-la-Romaine, while others overlook the terraced gardens (where breakfast is served in good weather). The restaurant creates original dishes prepared from seasonal local produce, which can be accompanied by a choice of wines, including Côtes du Ventoux and Côtes du Rhône. There is a swimming pool in the gardens and a private garage (parking fee).
184 C5 ✉ Rue de l'Evêché, Cité Médiévale ☎ 04 90 36 04 71; www.le-beffroi.com Closed Feb–Mar

Where to...
Eat and Drink

Prices
Expect to pay for a three-course meal for one, excluding drinks and service
€ under €25 **€€** €25–€50 **€€€** over €50

APT

Auberge du Lubéron €€€
The dining room in this old inn is decorated in pastel colours and complements the furniture and beautiful fabrics. There are wonderful views of the Apt valley from the terrace. Lubéron regional cuisine features on the menu in dishes such as pan-fried duck *foie gras* with regional glacé fruits – one of the chef's specialities.

185 D2 8 place du Faubourg du Ballet 04 90 74 12 50; www.auberge-luberon-peuzin.com Tue–Sun 12–2, Tue–Sat 7:30–9:30; closed 10 Nov–10 Dec, first 2 weeks in Jan

AVIGNON

Christian Étienne €€
The food does not come cheap at this Avignon restaurant, but the quality is excellent and the setting superb. It's housed in a 14th-century palace, complete with painted ceilings and frescoes, and with a view out from the terrace over the fabulous Palais des Papes. Truffles are a significant feature of the menu, and the black truffle omelette is not to be missed.

184 B3 10 rue de Mons 04 90 86 16 50 Tue–Sat noon–1:15, 7:30–9:15

La Fourchette €€–€€€
You'll find wood panels, comfortable wicker chairs and a multitude of forks (*fourchettes*) decorating the walls at this restaurant. Smoked haddock ravioli, or sardines marinated in coriander and thyme custard could be some of the delicious dishes prepared here, but the choice varies depending on what's available at the local market each day. Reservations are essential.

184 B3 17 rue Racine 04 90 85 20 93 Mon–Fri 12:15–1:45, 7:15–9:45; closed first 3 weeks in Aug

BONNIEUX

Le Pont Julien €€
In a traditional Provençal house, with lamps and paintings decorating the unpretentious interior, at the heart of the Lubéron's regional park. There are two dining rooms and a terrace for the warmer weather. The menu offers a choice of Mediterranean specialities, from bouillabaisse (the fish stew that originated in Marseille) to Lubéron goat's cheese to roast leg of lamb, typical of Haute-Provence.

185 D2 N100 04 90 74 48 44; www.lepontjulien.com Wed–Mon Jul–Aug; Thu–Tue lunch Apr–Jun, Sep; daily lunch, Fri–Sat eve, Oct–Mar. Closed mid-Dec to mid-Jan.

CAVAILLON

Prévot €€€
Chef Jean-Jaques Prévot's lavish dining room is matched by the equally rich cuisine. Try his *artichaut soufflé* and his succulent Cavaillon melon desserts, or his menu entitled Flavours of Lubéron.

184 C2 353 avenue Verdun 04 90 71 32 43; www.restaurant-prevot.com Closed Sun–Mon

CHÂTEAUNEUF-DU-PAPE

La Mère Germaine €€

This is one of the the village's most popular restaurants, with views of the vineyard from the traditional dining room. The wine list includes the best *crus* of the *appellation*.

184 B3 Avenue du Commandant-Lemaître 04 90 83 54 37; www.lameregermaine.com Lunch and dinner daily

GORDES

Hostellerie Le Phebus €€€

Le Phebus is both a restaurant and a four-star hotel. Chef Xavier Mathieu's sophisticated regional cuisine includes dishes such as fillet of sole pan-fried in salt butter with tangy jasmine and vanilla, and farmhouse duck *foie gras*. You can choose to eat in the elegant dining room, which has beamed ceilings, or, weather permitting, you may prefer the terrace with its fabulous views. You can expect to pay around €28 for a bottle of the house wine.

184 C3 Route de Murs, 84220 Joucas-Gordes 04 90 05 78 83; www.lephebus.com Mon, Fri–Sat 12–1:30, 7–9:30, Tue–Thu, Sun 7–9:30, early Apr to mid-Oct

La Pause €

This friendly café-cum-teashop in the village centre is an ideal place to stop for a tasty snack or light meal.

184 C3 Route Neuve 04 90 72 11 53 Closed Sun pm

LOURMARIN

Le Moulin de Lourmarin €€€

This restaurant is set in a beautiful converted 18th-century oil mill. Under an impressive vaulted stone roof, the candle-lit tables are dressed with blue and yellow fabric. Chef Edouard Loubet uses vegetables from the restaurant's garden, along with herbs and spices typical of the Lubéron, in dishes such as wheat and clam risotto with spices from the Apt region, and pigeon from the Alpilles with a reduction of rocket (arugula). The four extravagant menus are a feast for the senses.

185 D2 Rue du Temple, 84160 Lourmarin 04 90 68 06 69; www.moulindelourmarin.com Lunch and dinner daily, May–Aug; phone at other times. Closed mid-Oct to Feb

MÉNERBES

Le Galoubet €€

Exquisite regional cuisine served in a small, cheerful dining room or al fresco under the olive trees.

185 D2 104 avenue Marcellin Poncet 04 90 72 36 08 Closed Wed

ORANGE

Restaurant des Princes €€

There has been a hotel/restaurant on this site in the heart of the Old Town since the 17th century. Today the Restaurant des Princes has a light, modern dining room which offers a menu of French dishes alongside a few regional specialities. An extensive buffet is also available.

184 A4 Hôtel des Princes, 86 avenue de l'Arc de Triomphe 04 90 51 87 87; www.amarys-orange.com Daily 12–2:30, 7–10:30

VAISON-LA-ROMAINE

La Fontaine Restaurant €€€

This hotel/restaurant, situated in a 16th- and 17th-century building in the old part of town, has an ornate dining room. The menu concentrates on traditional Provençal dishes, and the wine cellar stocks predominantly local Côtes du Rhône and Ventoux labels.

184 C5 Le Beffroi, rue de l'Evêché, Cité Médiévale 04 90 36 04 71; www.le-beffroi.com Wed–Mon 12–2, 7:30–9:30, Apr–Oct

Where to... Shop

MARKETS

The markets of Avignon are ideal for buying those essential picnic supplies. At the **Marché des Halles** (place Pie, open Tue–Sun 6 am–1:30 pm) you can purchase a wide range of local produce, or try the **Marché des Remparts St-Michel** (Porte St-Michel, open Sat–Sun 6 am–1 pm). This is Avignon's biggest market for exotic North African spices, vegetables and fruit.

Antiques dealers mix with locals who sell the contents of their cellars at the **Marché aux Puces**, also in Avignon. Arrive early for the pick of the best bargains at this large bazaar (place des Carmes, open Sun 7–1).

SOUVENIRS AND GIFTS

Look for individual shops selling beautiful printed fabrics of the region, including tableware and clothing. In Vaison-la-Romaine try **Souléiado** (2 cours Henri Fabre, tel: 04 90 36 38 33, open Tue–Sat 10–12, 3–7).

Drop into **Cannelle** in Roussillon, a small shop full of fun gift ideas, regional produce (olive oils, liqueurs, saffron), books and perfumes (place de la Poste, tel: 04 90 05 71 27).

In Avignon, visit **Scènes Intérieures** (41 rue d'Amphoux, tel: 04 90 86 46 31), a beautiful interior design and gift shop.

FOOD AND DRINK

If you're shopping for edible treats try crystallised fruits in Apt. **Apt Union** (quartier Salignan, BP 137, tel: 04 90 76 31 31, open Mon–Sat 9–12, 2–6) is a world leader when it comes to the glacé cherry. **Aptunion Apt** is another top shop in town (N100, direction Avignon, tel: 04 90 76 31 43).

One of the best Provençal snacks is *fougasse* bread, and in Avignon at **Boulangerie Trouillas** you'll find a variety of *fougasses* with olives, *grattelons* (bacon) and nuts (14 place des Châtaignes, tel: 04 90 86 10 84, open Mon–Sat 6 am–8 pm). **La Tropézienne** (22 rue St-Agricole; tel: 0 490 86 24 72, www.la-tropezienne.fr.st; open Tue–Sun, daily in Jul) is famous for its *papalines* (black chocolates) filled with liquor scented with 60 regional spices. They also sell glacé fruits, jams and the house speciality – *tropézienne* – a delicious cake filled with cream.

Au Goût du Jour in Roussillon is an upmarket deli specialising in regional honeys, oils, wines, cheeses, tea and champagne (5 rue Richard Casteau, tel: 04 32 52 17 68).

Lou Canestéou is considered Vaison-la-Romaine's best cheese shop. It offers a wide choice of locally made goat's cheese, including *banon* (wrapped in oak leaves), *picadon* and *cachat* (10 rue Raspail, tel: 04 90 36 31 30).

ART, ANTIQUES AND BOOKS

Stop off at **Shakespeare Librairie**, in Avignon, for a book and a cup of tea. This discount English bookshop and tea shop also hosts occasional readings and recitals (155 rue Carreterie, tel: 04 90 27 38 50, open Tue–Sat 9:30–12:30, 2–6:30). **Hervé Baum**, also in Avignon, sells all sorts of objects for the home and garden, modern and antique, chic and rustic (19 rue Petite Fusterie, tel: 04 90 86 37 66).

In L'Isle-sur-la-Sorgue, **L'Isle aux Brocantes** has more than 35 dealers trading in an "antiques village" (passage du Pont, 7 avenue des 4-Otages, tel: 04 90 20 69 93).

Gifts and paints in every imaginable shade of ochre can be found at **Galerie des Ocres** in Roussillon (Le Castrum, tel: 04 90 05 62 99).

Where to... Be Entertained

BARS, CLUBS AND CASINOS

In Avignon, **Opéra Café**, a contemporary chic bar-restaurant, on the city's busiest square, is a hit with the hip crowd. There is a DJ every evening (24 place de l'Horloge, tel: 04 90 86 17 43, open 9 am–1 am, 3 am Jul). You can choose from two bars and two dance floors at **Le Blues**, which hosts karaoke nights, disco, live rock, jazz and blues (25 rue Carnot, tel: 04 90 85 79 71, open 11 pm–5 am). **Cadillac Café** is decorated with 1950s Americana. There are frescoes of Marilyn and Elvis, pool tables, video games, as well as theme nights and barbecues in summer (11 bis route de Lyon, tel: 04 90 86 99 57, open daily 2 pm–1 am). Che Guevara posters adorn the walls at **Cubanito's Café**, where you can try a free salsa class any evening at 9 pm (51 rue Carnot, tel: 04 90 27 90 59, open Tue–Sun 5 pm–1 am).

THEATRE AND MUSIC

Orange's Roman **Théâtre Antique** is the spectacular setting for concerts, opera and theatre (rue Madeleine Roch, tel: 04 90 51 17 60).

Opéra Théâtre d'Avignon is the venue for concerts by the Orchestra Lyrique de Région Avignon-Provence and ballet productions (1 rue Racine; enquiries 11–6, tel: 04 90 82 42 42; tickets tel: 04 90 82 81 40 for performances on Tue–Sat 8.30 pm, Sun 2.30 pm).

If you are in Avignon during the festival in July you can enjoy cabaret and live music most evenings aboard **Peniche Dolphin Blues**, a café-theatre on a barge moored on the Rhône near the bridge in Avignon (chemin de l'Île-Piot, tel: 04 90 82 46 96). **Le Rouge Gorge** hosts cabaret-style dinner theatre, with dancers and fine food on Fridays and Saturdays. On other days there's jazz, rock, samba and flamenco (place de la Mirande, tel: 04 90 14 02 54, open Sep–Jul, show nights 8 pm–3 am).

In Cavaillon, **Le Grenier à Sons**, a 350-seat concert hall, stages jazz, rock, blues, reggae and more by established musicians and budding talents (157 avenue du Général-de-Gaulle, tel: 04 90 06 44 20; www.grenier-a-sons.org).

SPORTS AND ACTVITIES

Take to the skies with **Aéroclub d'Avignon** and discover Avignon and its surroundings. Flights can take you as far as Mont Ventoux (Aéroport d'Avignon-Caumont, tel: 04 90 84 17 17).

There are 16 computerised bowling alleys at **Bowling**; snacks are available (avenue Paul-Claudel, tel: 04 90 88 50 11, open 3 pm–2 am (to 4 am Fri–Sat). You can rent skates at **Patinoire d'Avignon** ice rink, where the local ice-hockey team, the *Castors* (Beavers), are based (2483 chemin de l'Amandier, tel: 04 90 88 54 32; www.patinoire-avignon.com; open Mon–Fri 9:30–12, 3–5:30, also Fri 9 pm–11:30 pm, Sat 3–5:30, 9–11:30, Sun 3–6, early Sep to mid-May).

Balloon flights with **Hot Air Balloon Provence**, in Gordes, will take you over the villages of the Lubéron. The flight lasts between 60 and 90 minutes (Le Mas Fourniguière Joucas, tel: 04 90 05 79 21; www.avignon-et-provence.com/ballooning/fr/infos.htm).

Vélo Loisir en Lubéron cycling club organises tours in the Parc Naturel Régional du Lubéron (BP14, 04280 Céreste, tel: 04 92 79 05 82; www.veloloisirluberon.com).

Walks and Tours

1 The Heart of Provence 166 – 167
2 The Camargue 168 – 169
3 Vaison-la-Romaine 170 – 171
4 Gorges du Verdon 172 – 174

1 The Heart of Provence

Drive

DISTANCE 135km (84 miles) **TIME** Allow a full day
START/END POINT Aix-en-Provence 191 E3

From Aix-en-Provence this tour heads into Montagne Ste-Victoire before turning south towards the Massif de la Ste-Baume. The roads are narrow in places and hilly in others, which makes the drive interesting rather than arduous.

1–2

Leave **Aix-en-Provence** on the **D10**, towards St-Marc-Jaumegarde and Vauvenargues, to reach the **Barrage de Bimont** after about 7km (4 miles). The lake behind the Barrage de Bimont dam provides water for local towns.

2–3

Continue on the **D10** to the pretty village of **Vauvenargues**, famous for its Renaissance **château**, inherited by Pablo Picasso in 1958. The artist died here in 1973 and is buried in the grounds. The park and château are not open to the public. Rejoin the **D10** by driving through the village (there is only one road).

The **D10**, now signed **Jouques and Rians**, runs along the northern flank of the Montagne Ste-Victoire, which inspired artist Paul Cézanne.

3–4

Bear right shortly, following the **D223** signed Rians. The road narrows, climbs and offers good views all the way. At the next intersection, turn left (no sign). This is the **D23** towards Rians, which ends at a T-junction with the D3. Turn right, signed **Ollières and St-Maximin-la-Ste-Baume**. Approaching **St-Maximin**, turn left at the traffic lights, then right and left again as you cross St-Maximin. The **basilica** here is the best example of Gothic architecture in Provence.

4–5

Go over a roundabout to take the **N560** signed **Nans-les-Pins**. Bear right as the main road bears left. This smaller road goes under a railway bridge and is signed **Aubagne, Marseille and St-Zacharie**. Continue for 100m (110 yards), turn left at traffic lights. Go over at the next traffic lights onto the **D64** signed **Mazaugues**. Follow the **D64** to the **D1** and turn right towards **Rougiers**. Turn left off the D1 into the village at the sign for **Rougiers centre**, and left again at the café/*tabac* up rue Ste-Anne. Go uphill towards a **ruin and a church** on top of the hill ahead. Bear sharp left and go through an open barrier, before continuing up the valley. Go over a crest and down to an intersection. Turn right onto the **D95** (only the back of the sign is visible, to check that you are on the right road make sure the wrong side indicates Plan-d'Aups). Go past signs warning of deer, and continue to the **Hôtellerie at La Ste-Baume**, a 19th-century restoration of a Dominican friars' pilgrim hostel, dating from medieval times, now a base for spiritual studies. Continue on the **D80** through **Plan-d'Aups**, after which the road widens. At the next intersection, bear right onto a road signed Auriol, which joins the D45a to make a long, twisting descent around hairpin bends. When you reach the N560 at a roundabout, take the first exit signed **St-Zacharie**.

5–6

At the village, continue until a road on the left, the **D85**, is signed **Trets and Col du Petit Galibier**. Stay on this road, later the **D12**, which climbs providing fine views, to reach **Trets**. Here are the remains of medieval walls, as well as square 14th-century towers and a 15th-century castle and church.

6–7

Approaching **Trets**, turn left at a roundabout, go straight over a mini-roundabout, and bear left at the next intersection to approach a roundabout with a fountain. Bear left here onto the **D908** signed **Peynier**, a village with a pleasant Romanesque church.

7–8

Pass **Peynier** to the south and climb through wooded hills. After 4km (2.5 miles) take the **D46C** to the right, signed for **Belcodène**, and go through the village following signs for **Fuveau**. At a fork in the road, keep right, go over the *autoroute* and enter **Fuveau**. Turn left and right into the main square, then, almost immediately, take the first street on the left, the road to **Aix-en-Provence and Gardanne**. At a roundabout with a central fountain, take the exit signed for **Aix** and continue to the **N96**. Turn right and follow this road and the **N7** to Aix.

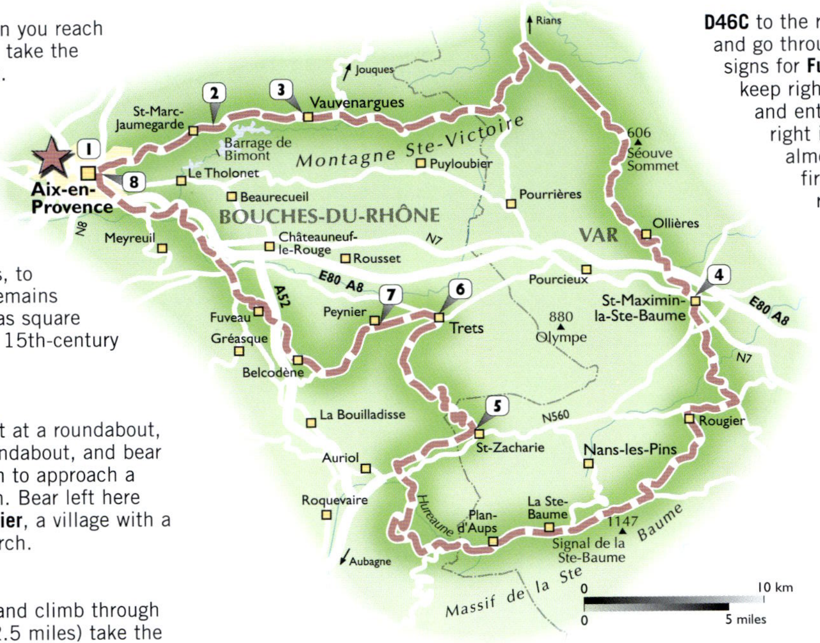

Taking a break

There are many restaurants and brasseries to choose from in St-Maximin-la-Ste-Baume.

2 The Camargue

Drive

DISTANCE 95km (59 miles) **TIME** Allow a full day
START/END POINT Arles ✚ 194 C3

The Camargue, Provence's best-known wildlife location and one of Europe's most important wetlands, is famous for its hardy white horses, black bulls, pink flamingos and some of Europe's most exotic birds.

1–2

Head west from Arles and cross the Grand Rhône. Take the **D570** (signed for Stes-Maries-de-la-Mer) to Albaron, once a powerful stronghold but now fighting off the sea with pumping stations rather then repelling human invaders. From here take the **D37** to Méjanes.

Taking a Break

Restaurant de Méjanes
✉ Domaine de Méjanes, on the D37, 4km (2.5 miles) south of Albaron ☎ 04 90 97 10 51 ⏲ Lunch daily, dinner by reservation

2–3

Méjanes is a small lakeside resort with a narrow-gauge railway, a bullring and ponies and horses for hire. From here, follow the **D37** as it runs past the Étang de Vaccarès, the largest of the Camargue's lagoons.

3–4

The Étang de Vaccarès (➤ 117) is part of a nature reserve called the Réserve Nationale de Camargue, which has its

Golfe de Beauduc

0 10 km
0 5 miles

Salin-de-Giraud 4

Étang de Faraman

the west of the sluggish Grand Rhône. Eventually it joins the **D570**, and continue which leads northeast back to Arles.

Wildlife of the Camargue

The Camargue is home to countless birds, including ducks, waders and geese. The shallow lagoons provide excellent feeding grounds for swans, avocets and egrets, while the freshwater marshes, with their extensive reed beds, are used as nesting sites by herons, moorhens, coots and mallards. Among the most spectacular sights are the colonies of resident pink flamingos.

visitor office and headquarters at La Capelière. On this stretch, stop the car at any of the laybys (turnouts) and the distinctive smell of marsh immediately becomes apparent – a combination of salt, rotting vegetation and growing plants. At Villeneuve, turn south towards **La Capelière**. It's easy to miss the excellent **visitor centre** – keep a lookout for the sign and be ready to turn off the road on the left. There are marked nature trails, and the 1.5km (1-mile) path around the building has signs giving details about the area's plants and animals. Continue south past Salin-de-Badon, noted for its birds, to Salin-de-Giraud.

Plane trees line the route near Arles

4–5

Salin-de-Giraud is the best known of the region's salt-producing towns. The tree-lined avenues are dominated by the Solvay refinery, where glittering piles of salt can be glimpsed through the railings. Now take the **D36** north as it slices through the marshy land to

3 Vaison-la-Romaine

Walk

The town of Vaison-la-Romaine (➤ 148–149), which straddles the River Ouvèze, is a mixture of Roman city, medieval village and modern town. This walk, which has some steep climbs, takes you past the town's Roman bridge, the medieval gateway and the 12th-century cathedral.

DISTANCE 3.5km (2 miles) **TIME** 1.5 hours
START/END POINT Main parking area, avenue Général-de-Gaulle ✚ 184 C5

1–2

Start from the main parking area, next to the **Roman sites** on **avenue Général-de-Gaulle**. Walk through the heart of town down to the ancient **Pont Romain**, a Roman bridge 17m (56ft) long. Note the level of the Ouvèze River below the bridge; in the floods of September 1992 the river flowed over the top of the Pont Romain.

2–3

Take the road opposite the bridge, which leads up to the **Haute Ville**. Go through the **arched gateway**, a remnant of the medieval ramparts. Upper Vaison is an almost complete medieval town, with attractive alleys of houses dating from the 13th and 14th centuries. Turn sharply left, backtracking a little, up the narrow **rue de l'Horloge**. Continue climbing, looking towards the **clock tower** that gives the road its name. Follow the road around to the right, and turn left at a T-junction onto **rue de l'Église**, following

The medieval town of upper Vaison rises on a hill above the River Ouvèze

Taking a break
You will find plenty of cafés and restaurants on and around the Grande Rue and place Chanoine-Sautel, near the Roman sites.

signs for the château. There is a viewpoint to the left, near the **church**. Pass the church and continue uphill to Plan Pascal and on again, up some steps, to the **rue de la Charité**. This road narrows into a rough track. At the end of the stone wall on the left, turn left and climb to the ruins of the **château**.

3–4

The château (closed to the public) gives you wonderful views of the Roman ruins and the lower town. Return to the stone wall. Turn right and then left under an arch, go down the rough-hewn steps to a beautiful square with a fountain and the **Hôtel de Prévôt**. Leave the square to the left and go down

A statue of Empress Sabina excavated from Vaison's Roman ruins

rue des Fours, one of the prettiest streets in old Vaison. When a road leads off to the right, keep straight ahead. Turn right at the next junction to reach a T-junction. Turn left, then take the next turn on the right, which opens up to a view of the lower town. Descend the steps on the left and then more steps to the right, to reach **rue du Château**. Turn left and follow the road to a main road junction. Bear right and cross the River Ouvèze by the **Pont**

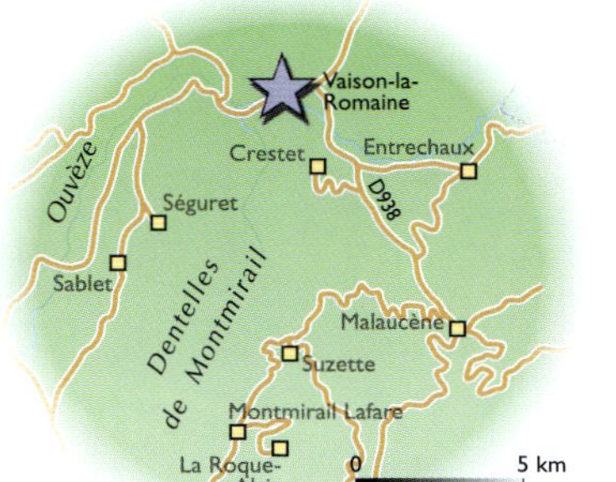

Neuf. Take the first right into avenue Jules Ferry and then go left to reach the **cathedral**.

4–5

Inside the 12th-century Romanesque **Cathédrale Notre-Dame de Nazareth**, the old bishop's throne sits behind the altar and on the north side of the cathedral there are lovely cloisters. Return to **avenue Jules Ferry** and walk 500m (545 yards) to **avenue Général-de-Gaulle** and the entrance to the **quartier du Puymin**.

5–6

The quartier du Puymin has some fascinating **Roman ruins**, including several villas and a theatre that held around 6,000 people. After visiting this extensive Roman site, cross the road to enter the other major area, the **quartier de la Villasse**, where you'll find the Roman baths. The parking area is near by.

Top tip
You can do this walk at any time of year. On clear days there are good views of Mont Ventoux (➤ 157–158) from the château ruins.

4 Gorges du Verdon

Drive with walks

DISTANCE 137km (85 miles) **TIME** One day (excluding walks)
START/END POINT Castellane 192 B5

This drive offers spectacular views of the Gorges du Verdon (➤ 74–76) as you follow the river west from Castellane to the Lac de Ste-Croix. After stopping in Moustiers-Ste-Marie for refreshment, you follow the Verdon's south bank, a slightly easier drive, with equally dramatic views.

1–2

Leave **Castellane**, a popular base for walkers and climbers, from the roundabout by the **Grand Hôtel du Levant**, on the **D952** signed **Moustiers-Ste-Marie**. The road splits at the **Pont de Soleils**; this is the bridge you'll reach on the return route to Castellane. Bear right to stay on the **D952** signed **Moustiers**; soon you'll enter a short tunnel. Immediately at the tunnel exit a sign on the left indicates the **D23B** to the **Belvédère du Couloir Samson**. A short, dead-end road takes you to this **view-point** with parking spaces, at the bottom of the Verdon valley.

Be prepared

If you intend to do any **walking**, ask for the walking routes from the **tourist office** at Castellane or Moustiers-Ste-Marie before you set out. Always check the **weather conditions** and take a torch (flashlight), water and food.

2–3

From Belvédère du Couloir Samson you can follow part of a seven-hour **walk** to a summit called **La Maline** at 1,460m (4,788 feet). Noticeboards emphasise the need for careful preparation, professional equipment and proper attention to the rapidly changing water level of the river. Back in your car, return to the **D952** and turn left. Bear left in the village of **Rougon** and about 1km (less than a mile) before reaching the small village of **La Palud-sur-Verdon**, a sign left indicates the **Route des Crêtes**.

3–4

The Route des Crêtes offers dramatic views of the canyon as it climbs to the highest points of the north bank of the river, with numerous *belvédères* (viewpoints) where you can stop. A sign indicates whether the Route des Crêtes is *ouvert* (open) or *fermé* (closed) because of snow. If it is closed, skip to point 4–5. Otherwise, turn off onto the dramatic road. When you reach the **Pas de la Baou** (1,285m/4,215 feet), the river is 715m (2,345 feet) below. From these heights, the road descends and there are views to the west. Take care as there are few safety barriers or walls around these hair-pinned descents and you are likely to encounter walkers until the road returns to **La Palud-sur-Verdon**.

4–5

At La Palud-sur-Verdon you can **rent mountain bicycles** or find a **guided walk** or **climb**. The town hall, in a small **château**, has an exhibition explaining the geology, flora and fauna of the area. Turn left on the **D952**, signed for Moustiers. As the road reaches the end of the Grand Canyon, there are views to the **Lac de Ste-Croix**. At a roundabout, bear right to **Moustiers-Ste-Marie**, an ideal place to eat lunch.

5–6

Moustiers-Ste-Marie (➤ 80–81) is known for its ***faïence*** (fine glazed ceramics) and for a silver star suspended on a chain between two rock faces. Legend tells that it was first erected by a knight grateful for his return to the village after being held prisoner by the Saracens. Leave Moustiers by retracing your route back to the roundabout, going straight over on the **D957** and following the sign for Aiguines. The road crosses a bridge where the Verdon River flows into the lake; here you can rent kayaks and electric boats. Shortly, take a left turn onto the **D19** to **Aiguines**.

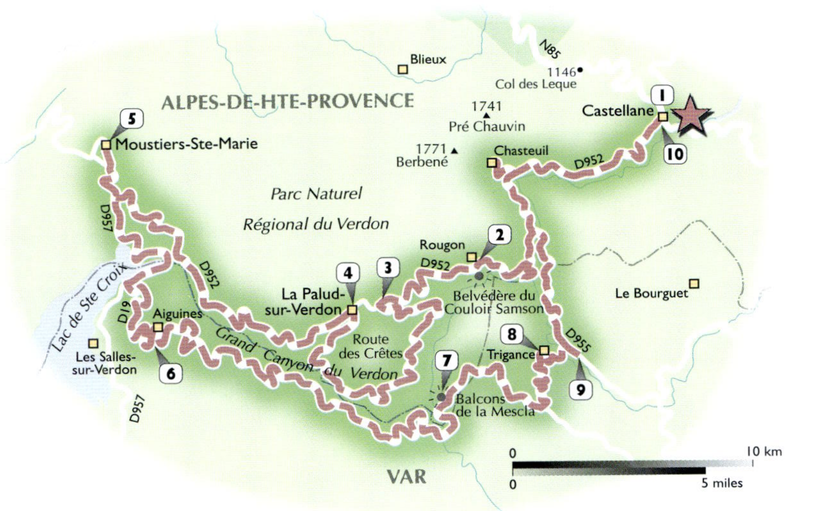

6–7

Park on the road in the heart of Aiguines and go down steps on the right to a small arcade of artisanal shops. One of these specialises in wood-turning, once the village's single but prosperous industry. Continue along the **D19** as it climbs out of Aiguines and stop at the **orientation table** about 1km (less than a mile) further on. The river and views are now mainly on your left, with numerous stopping places and viewing points. Care should be taken on these sometimes narrow corners, and especially at a short series of mini-tunnels cut into the rock face, the **Tunnel de Fayet**. The last of the viewing opportunities is at the **Balcons de la Mescla**.

7–8

The Balcons de la Mescla has a **bar-restaurant** where you can stop for refreshments and enjoy more superb views. After several kilometres, watch for signs to **Trigance** and a **Maison de l'Information**. Turn left to descend to the village.

8–9

Trigance has small shops, a well, an art gallery and the last working water-powered **flour mill** in Provence, all dominated by a sombre château (closed to the public). The **tourist office** is a further 5km (3 miles) out of the heart of the village. Follow the road as it skirts Trigance to the south. At a T-junction with the **D955**, turn right; the tourist office is on the right after 500m (545 yards).

9–10

The tourist office has excellent displays about local geology and you can also buy local produce there, including wonderful Provençal soap. Head back along the **D955** until you reach the Pont de Soleils; turn right on the **D952** to return to Castellane.

Left: The attractive hillside village of Trigance

Taking a break

Ma Petite Auberge
✉ Boulevard de la République, Castellane
☎ 04 92 83 62 06 ⌚ Fri–Tue 12–2:30, 7–10:30, Mar–early Nov.

La Treille Muscate
✉ Place de l'Église, Moustiers-Ste-Marie
☎ 04 92 74 64 31 ⌚ Mid-Feb to mid-Nov. Closed Wed Jul–Aug, also Wed pm and Thu rest of year.

Practicalities

GETTING ADVANCE INFORMATION

Tourist Information

- Alpes-Maritimes: www.guideriviera.com
- Marseille and Carmargue (Bouches du Rhône) area: www.visitprovence.com
- Var: www.tourismevar.com
- Haute Provence: www.alpes-haute-provence.com
- Vaucluse: www.provenceguide.com

In the UK

French Tourist Office
178 Piccadilly
London W1V 0AL
☎ 09068 244 123

BEFORE YOU GO

WHAT YOU NEED

● Required
○ Suggested
▲ Not required
△ Not applicable

Some countries require a passport to remain valid for at least six months beyond the date of entry – contact their consulate or embassy or your travel agent for details.

	UK	Germany	USA	Canada	Australia	Ireland	Netherlands	Spain
Passport (or National Identity Card where applicable)	●	●	●	●	●	●	●	▲
Visa (regulations can change – check before your journey)	▲	▲	▲	▲	▲	▲	▲	▲
Onward or Return Ticket	▲	▲	▲	▲	▲	▲	▲	▲
Health Inoculations (tetanus and polio)	▲	▲	▲	▲	▲	▲	▲	▲
Health Documentation	●	●	●	●	●	●	●	●
Travel Insurance	○	○	○	○	○	○	○	○
Driver's Licence (national)	●	●	●	●	●	●	●	●
Car Insurance Certificate	○	○	n/a	n/a	n/a	○	○	○
Car Registration Document	●	●	n/a	n/a	n/a	●	●	●

WHEN TO GO

Provence

High season: APR–SEP
Low season: JAN–MAR, OCT–DEC

JAN	FEB	MAR	APR	MAY	JUN	JUL	AUG	SEP	OCT	NOV	DEC
12°C	12°C	14°C	18°C	21°C	27°C	28°C	28°C	25°C	22°C	17°C	14°C
Cloud	Cloud	Cloud	Sun	Sun	Sun	Sun	Sun	Sun	Wet	Wet	Wet

Sun · Cloud · Wet · Sun/Showers

Temperatures are the **average daily maximum** for each month, although they can rise to 35°C (95°F) in July and August. Spring starts in March when the mimosa and almonds come into bloom on the coast, and it is usually warm enough to sit outside on the terrace in April. Mountain melt-water in spring brings the possibility of flash floods in the Rhône valley. Summers are hot and dry, and the coastal areas are very crowded. The autumn months (September and October) can be very pleasant, although there may be occasional thunderstorms. Colder weather arrives in November, with snow settling on high ground in December. The *mistral* wind blows down the Rhône valley during the winter months, but you can avoid it by heading east to the Côte d'Azur.

In the US
French Tourist Office
444 Madison Avenue
16th Floor, New York NY 10022
☎ 212/838-7800

In Australia
French Tourist Office
Level 20, 25 Bligh Street
Sydney, NSW 2000
☎ (02) 9231 5244

In Canada
French Tourist Office
1981 avenue McGill College, Suite 490
Montreal H3A 2W9
☎ 514/876-9881

GETTING THERE

By Air Nice-Côte d'Azur and Marseille-Provence are the main airports in the region, but there are also international flights from within Europe to the smaller airports: Toulon, Nîmes-Arles-Camargue and Montpellier.
From the UK carriers include France's international airline, Air France (tel: 0845 0845 111 in UK; 0802 802802 in France; www.airfrance.com), British Airways (tel: 0845 7733377; www.ba.com), easyJet (tel: 0871 750 0100; www.easyjet.com) and Ryanair (tel: 0870 156 9569; www.ryanair.com). The flight time from London to Provence is around 2 hours.
From the US and Canada Delta Air Lines operates a few direct flights between New York and Nice-Côte d'Azur, but passengers from most US and Canadian cities will usually have to change at Paris or London (Heathrow, Gatwick and Stansted). Delta Air Lines (tel: 1 800 241 4141 in US; www.delta.com), American Airlines (tel: 1 800 433 7300 in US; www.aa.com) and Air Canada (tel: 1 888 247 2262 in Canada; www.aircanada.com). The flying time direct from New York to Provence is around 8 hours.
By Rail Paris is the main railway hub, with six major railway stations. SNCF, the national carrier, operates high-speed train (TGV) services from the Gare de Lyon in Paris to Provence. The Eurostar passenger train service (tel: 08705 186186 in UK) from London Waterloo via the Eurotunnel to Paris Gare du Nord takes 3 hours.
By Sea Several ferry companies operate regular services from England and Ireland to north and northwest France. Crossing times from England vary from 35 minutes to 9 hours, and from Ireland around 14 to 18 hours.

TIME

France is on Central European Time, one hour ahead of Greenwich Mean Time (GMT +1). From late March, when clocks are put forward one hour, until late October, French summer time (GMT +2) operates.

CURRENCY AND FOREIGN EXCHANGE

Currency The euro (€) is the official currency of France and Monaco. Notes (bills) are issued in denominations of €5, €10, €20, €50, €100, €200 and €500 and coins are in denominations of 1, 2, 5, 10, 20 and 50 cents, and €1 and €2.

Exchange You can exchange travellers' cheques at some banks and at bureaux de change at airports, main railway stations or in some department stores, and exchange booths. All transactions are subject to a commission charge, so you may prefer to rely on cash and credit cards. Travellers' cheques issued by American Express and VISA may also be changed at many post offices.

Credit cards are widely accepted in shops, restaurants and hotels. VISA (Carte Bleue), MasterCard (Eurocard) and Diners Club cards with four-digit PINs can be used in most ATM cash dispensers. Some smaller shops and hotels may not accept credit cards – always check before you book in.

TIME DIFFERENCES

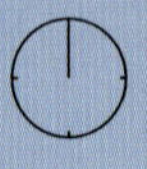

GMT
12 noon

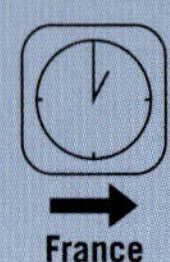

France
1 pm

Germany
1 pm

Spain
1 pm

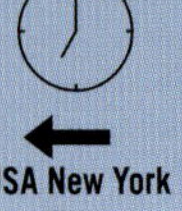

USA New York
7 am

Australia
Sydney 10pm

WHEN YOU ARE THERE

CLOTHING SIZES

UK	Rest of Europe	USA	
36	46	36	Suits
38	48	38	Suits
40	50	40	Suits
42	52	42	Suits
44	54	44	Suits
46	56	46	Suits
7	41	8	Shoes
7.5	42	8.5	Shoes
8.5	43	9.5	Shoes
9.5	44	10.5	Shoes
10.5	45	11.5	Shoes
11	46	12	Shoes
14.5	37	14.5	Shirts
15	38	15	Shirts
15.5	39/40	15.5	Shirts
16	41	16	Shirts
16.5	42	16.5	Shirts
17	43	17	Shirts
8	34	6	Dresses
10	36	8	Dresses
12	38	10	Dresses
14	40	12	Dresses
16	42	14	Dresses
18	44	16	Dresses
4.5	38	6	Shoes
5	38	6.5	Shoes
5.5	39	7	Shoes
6	39	7.5	Shoes
6.5	40	8	Shoes
7	41	8.5	Shoes

NATIONAL HOLIDAYS

1 Jan	New Year's Day
27 Jan	St Devote's Day (Monaco only)
Mar/Apr	Easter Sunday and Monday
1	May Labour Day
8	May VE Day (France only)
May/Jun	Whit Sunday and Monday
June	Corpus Christi (Monaco only)
14 July	Bastille Day (France only)
15 Aug	Assumption
1 Nov	All Saints' Day
11 Nov	Remembrance Day (France only)
19 Nov	Monaco National Holiday (Monaco only)
9 Dec	Immaculate Conception (Monaco only)
25 Dec	Christmas Day

OPENING HOURS

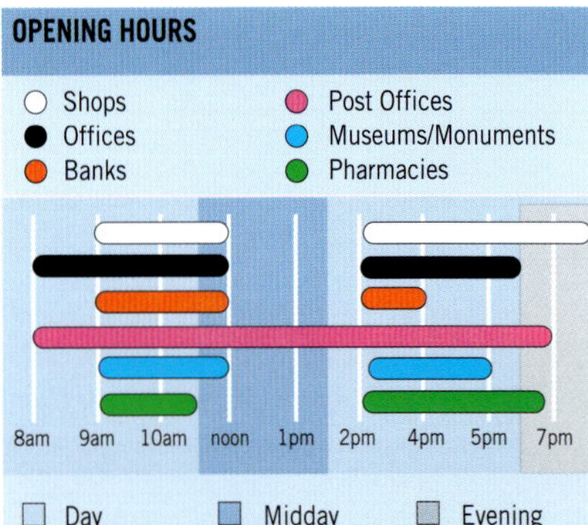

Shops In summer shops are open from 4 to 8 or 9 pm. Most shops close on Sunday and many on Monday. Small food shops open from 7 am and may open on Sunday morning. Large department stores do not close for lunch, and hypermarkets open 10 am to 9 or 10 pm, but may shut on Monday morning.
Banks Banks are closed on Sunday, as well as Saturday or Monday.
Museums Museums and monuments have extended summer hours. Many close one day a week; either Monday (municipal ones) or Tuesday (national ones).

EMERGENCY NUMBERS

POLICE 17

FIRE 18

AMBULANCE 15

PERSONAL SAFETY

The *Police Municipale* (blue uniforms) carry out police duties in cities and towns. The *Gendarmes* (blue trousers, black jackets, white belts), the national police force, cover the countryside and smaller places. The CRS deal with emergencies and also look after safety on beaches. Monaco has its own police.

To avoid danger or theft:

- Do not use unmanned roadside rest areas at night.
- Cars, especially foreign cars, should be secured.
- Beware of pickpockets.

Police assistance:
☎ 17 from any call box

TELEPHONES

All telephone numbers in France comprise ten digits (eight in Monaco). There are no area codes except for Monaco (377 precedes number when phoning from outside the principality). Most public phones use a phone card (*télécarte*), sold in units of 50 or 120 at France Telecom shops, post offices, tobacconists, newsagents and at railway stations. Cheap call rates generally apply Mon–Fri 7 pm–8 am, Sat–Sun all day.

International Dialling Codes
Dial 00 followed by

UK:	**44**
USA / Canada:	**1**
Irish Republic:	**353**
Australia:	**61**
New Zealand:	**64**

POST

Post Offices
The PTT (*Poste, Téléphone et Télécommunications*) deals with mail and telephone services. Outside main centres, post offices open shorter hours and may close 12–2. Letter boxes are yellow. Post offices usually have an ATM.

ELECTRICITY

The power supply in France is 220 volts. Sockets accept two-round-pin (or increasingly three-round-pin) plugs, so an adaptor is needed for most non-Continental appliances. A transformer is needed for appliances operating on 110–120 volts.

TIPS/GRATUITIES

Restaurant, café and hotel bills must by law include a service charge, so a tip is not expected, although many people do leave a few coins in restaurants.

Taxis	€0.50–€1.50
Tour guides	€0.50–€1.50
Porters	€0.50–€1.50
Usherettes	small change
Hairdressers	€0.50–€1.50
Lavatory attendants	small change

CONSULATES and EMBASSIES

 UK	 US	 Germany	 Ireland	 Canada
☎ 04 91 15 72 10	☎ 04 91 54 92 00	☎ 04 91 16 75 20	☎ 04 93 61 50 63	☎ 04 93 92 93 22
☎ 04 93 62 13 56	☎ 04 93 88 89 55	☎ 04 93 83 55 25		

HEALTH

Insurance Citizens of EU countries receive reduced-cost emergency health care with relevant documentation (European Health Insurance Card), but private medical insurance is still advised, and essential for all other visitors.

Dental Services As for general medical treatment (see above, Insurance), nationals of EU countries can obtain dental treatment at reduced cost. Around 70 per cent of standard dentists' fees are refunded, but private medical insurance is still advised for all.

Weather July and August are likely to be sunny and very hot. When sightseeing, cover up, apply a good sunscreen, wear sunglasses and a hat, and drink plenty of fluids.

Drugs Pharmacies – recognised by their green cross sign – possess highly qualified staff able to offer medical advice, provide first-aid and prescribe a wide range of drugs, although some are available by prescription (*ordonnance*) only.

Safe Water Tap water is safe to drink, and restaurants will often bring a carafe of water to the table, although you may prefer to buy bottled water. Never drink from a tap marked *eau non potable* (not drinking water).

CONCESSIONS

Students/Youths Holders of an International Student Identity Card (ISIC) are entitled to discounted admission to museums and sights, air and ferry tickets and meals in some student cafeterias. Holders of the International Youth Travel Card (or GO 25 Card) qualify for similar discounts as ISIC holders.

Senior Citizens If you are over 60 you can get discounts (up to 50 per cent) in museums, on public transport and in places of entertainment. You will need a *Carte Vermeil*, which can be purchased from the *Abonnement* office of any main railway station. You may get a discount if you show your passport.

TRAVELLING WITH A DISABILITY

France has made great headway in providing access and facilities for visitors with disabilities. However, some tourist offices, museums and restaurants that are in historic, protected buildings are still not fully accessible. A telephone call before going to a restaurant is a good idea to arrange for an easily accessible table. The Association des Paralysés de France (17 boulevard Auguste Blanqui, 75013, Paris, tel: 01 40 78 69 00; www.apf.asso.fr) provides information on wheelchair access.

CHILDREN

Children are welcomed in most hotels and restaurants. Baby-changing facilities are excellent in newer museums and attractions, but limited elsewhere.

TOILETS

Modern unisex, self-cleaning, coin-operated toilets are found on the streets of most major cities. In smaller towns and villages, free public toilets can normally be found by the market square or near tourist offices. Cleanliness varies, and some older or more remote establishments may have a squat toilet. Café toilets are for the use of customers only.

USEFUL WORDS AND PHRASES

Yes/no **Oui/non**
Hello **Bonjour/bonsoir**
Goodbye **Au revoir**
How are you? **Comment allez-vous?**
Please **S'il vous plaît**
Thank you **Merci**
Excuse me **Excusez-moi**
I'm sorry **Pardon**
You're welcome **De rien/avec plaisir**
Do you have...? **Avez-vous...?**
How much is this? **C'est combien?**
I'd like... **Je voudrais...**

DIRECTIONS

Is there a phone box around here? **Y a-t-il une cabine téléphonique dans le coin?**
Where is...? **Où se trouve...?**
...the nearest Métro **le Métro le plus proche**
...the telephone **le téléphone**
...the bank **la banque**
...the toilet **les toilettes**
Turn left/right **tournez à gauche/droite**
Go straight on **allez tout droit**
The first/second (on the right) **le premier/le deuxième (à droite)**
At the crossroads **au carrefour**

IF YOU NEED HELP

Could you help me, please? **Pouvez-vous m'aider?**
Do you speak English? **Parlez-vous anglais?**
I don't understand **Je ne comprends pas**
Could you call a doctor quickly, please? **Pouvez-vous appeler d'urgence un médecin, s'il vous plaît?**

RESTAURANT

I'd like to book a table **Puis-je réserver une table?**
A table for two please **Une table pour deux personnes, s'il vous plaît**
Do you have a fixed price menu? **Vous avez un menu prix fixe?**
Could we see the menu please? **Nous pouvons avoir la carte?**
Could I have the bill please? **L'addition, s'il vous plaît**
A bottle/glass of... **Une bouteille/un verre de...**

MENU READER

apéritifs appetisers
boissons alcoolisées alcoholic beverages
boissons chaudes hot beverages
boissons froides cold beverages
carte des vins wine list
coquillages shellfish
fromage cheese
gibier game
hors d'oeuvres starters
légumes vegetables
plats chauds hot dishes
plats froids cold dishes
plat du jour dish of the day
pâtisserie pastry
plat principal main course
potages soups
service compris service included
service non compris service not included
spécialités régionales regional specialities
viandes meat courses
volaille poultry

NUMBERS

0	**zéro**	12	**douze**	30	**trente**	110	**cent dix**
1	**un**	13	**treize**	31	**trente et un**	120	**cent vingt**
2	**deux**	14	**quatorze**	32	**trente-deux**	200	**deux cents**
3	**trois**	15	**quinze**			300	**trois cents**
4	**quatre**	16	**seize**	40	**quarante**	400	**quatre cents**
5	**cinq**	17	**dix-sept**	50	**cinquante**	500	**cinq cents**
6	**six**	18	**dix-huit**	60	**soixante**	600	**six cents**
7	**sept**	19	**dix-neuf**	70	**soixante-dix**	700	**sept cents**
8	**huit**	20	**vingt**	80	**quatre-vingts**	800	**huit cents**
9	**neuf**			90	**quatre-vingt-dix**	900	**neuf cents**
10	**dix**	21	**vingt et un**	100	**cent**		
11	**onze**	22	**vingt-deux**	101	**cent un**	1,000	**mille**

BRIEF A–Z

agneau lamb
ail garlic
ananas pineapple
anguille eel
banane banana
beurre butter
bifteck steak
bière (bière pression) beer (draught beer)
boeuf beef
boudin noir/blanc black/white pudding
brochet pike
cabillaud cod
calmar squid
canard duck
champignons mushrooms
chou cabbage
choucroute sauerkraut
chou-fleur cauliflower
choux de Bruxelles Brussels sprouts
citron lemon
civet de lièvre jugged hare
concombre cucumber
confiture jam
coquilles Saint-Jacques scallops
cornichon gherkin
côte/côtelette chop
côtelettes dans l'échine spare ribs
couvert cutlery
crevettes grises shrimps
crevettes roses prawns
croque monsieur toasted ham and cheese sandwich
cru raw
crustacés seafood
cuisses de grenouilles frogs' legs
cuit (à l'eau) boiled
eau mineral gazeuse/non gazeuse sparkling/still mineral water
ecrevisse crayfish
entrecôte sirloin steak
entrées first course
épices spices
épinards spinach
épis de maïs corn (on the cob)
escargots snails
farine flour
fenouil fennel
fèves broad beans
figues figs
filet de boeuf fillet
filet mignon fillet steak
filet de porc tenderloin
fines herbes herbs
foie gras goose liver
fraises strawberries
framboises raspberries
frit fried
friture deep-fried
fruit de la passion passion fruit
fruits de la saison seasonal fruits
gaufres waffles
gigot d'agneau leg of lamb
glace ice-cream
glaçons ice cubes
grillé grilled
groseilles redcurrants
hareng herring
haricots blancs haricot beans
haricots verts french beans
homard lobster
huîtres oysters
jambon blanc/cru/fumé ham (cooked/Parma style/smoked)
jus de citron lemon juice
jus de fruits fruit juice
jus d'orange orange juice
lait demi-écrémé/entier milk semi-skimmed/full-cream
langouste crayfish
langoustine scampi
langue tongue
lapin rabbit
lentilles lentils
lotte monkfish
loup de mer sea bass
macaron macaroon
maïs sweetcorn
marron chestnut
menu du jour/à la carte menu of the day/à la carte
morilles morels
moules mussels
mousse au chocolat chocolate mousse
moutarde mustard
myrtilles bilberries
noisette hazelnut
noix walnut
noix de veau fillet of veal
oeuf à la coque/dur/au plat egg soft/hard-boiled/fried
oignon onion
origan oregano
pain au chocolat croissant with chocolate centre
part portion
pêche peach
petite friture fried fish (whitebait or similar)
petits (biscuits) salés savoury biscuits
petit pain roll
petits pois green peas
pintade guinea fowl
poire pear
pois chiches chick peas
poisson fish
poivre pepper
poivron green/red pepper
pomme apple
pommes de terre potatoes
pommes frites chips
poulet (blanc) chicken (breast)
prune plum
pruneaux prunes
queue de boeuf oxtail
ragoût stew
ris de veau sweetbread
riz rice
rôti de boeuf (rosbif) roast beef
rouget red mullet
saignant rare
salade verte lettuce
salé/sucré salted/sweet
saumon salmon
saucisses sausages
sel salt
soupe à l'oignon onion soup
sucre sugar
thon tuna
thym thyme
tripes tripe
truffes truffles
truite trout
truite saumonée salmon trout
vapeur (à la) steamed
venaison venison
viande hachée minced meat/mince
vin blanc white wine
vin rosé rosé wine
vin rouge red wine
vinaigre vinegar
xérès sherry

Atlas

To identify the regions, see the map on the inside of the front cover

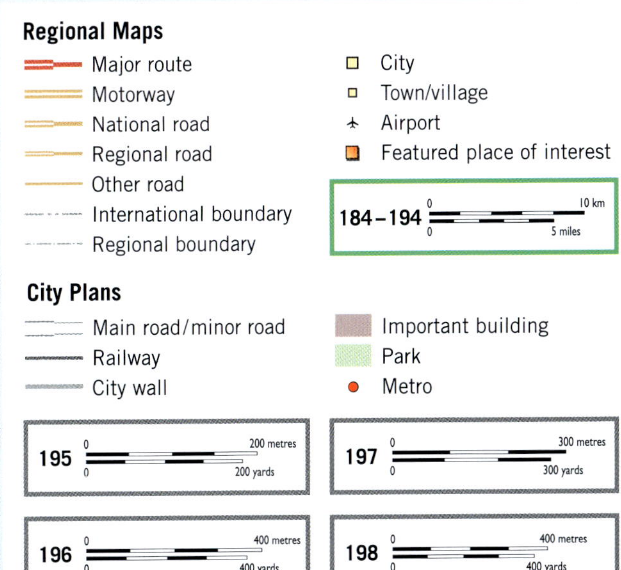

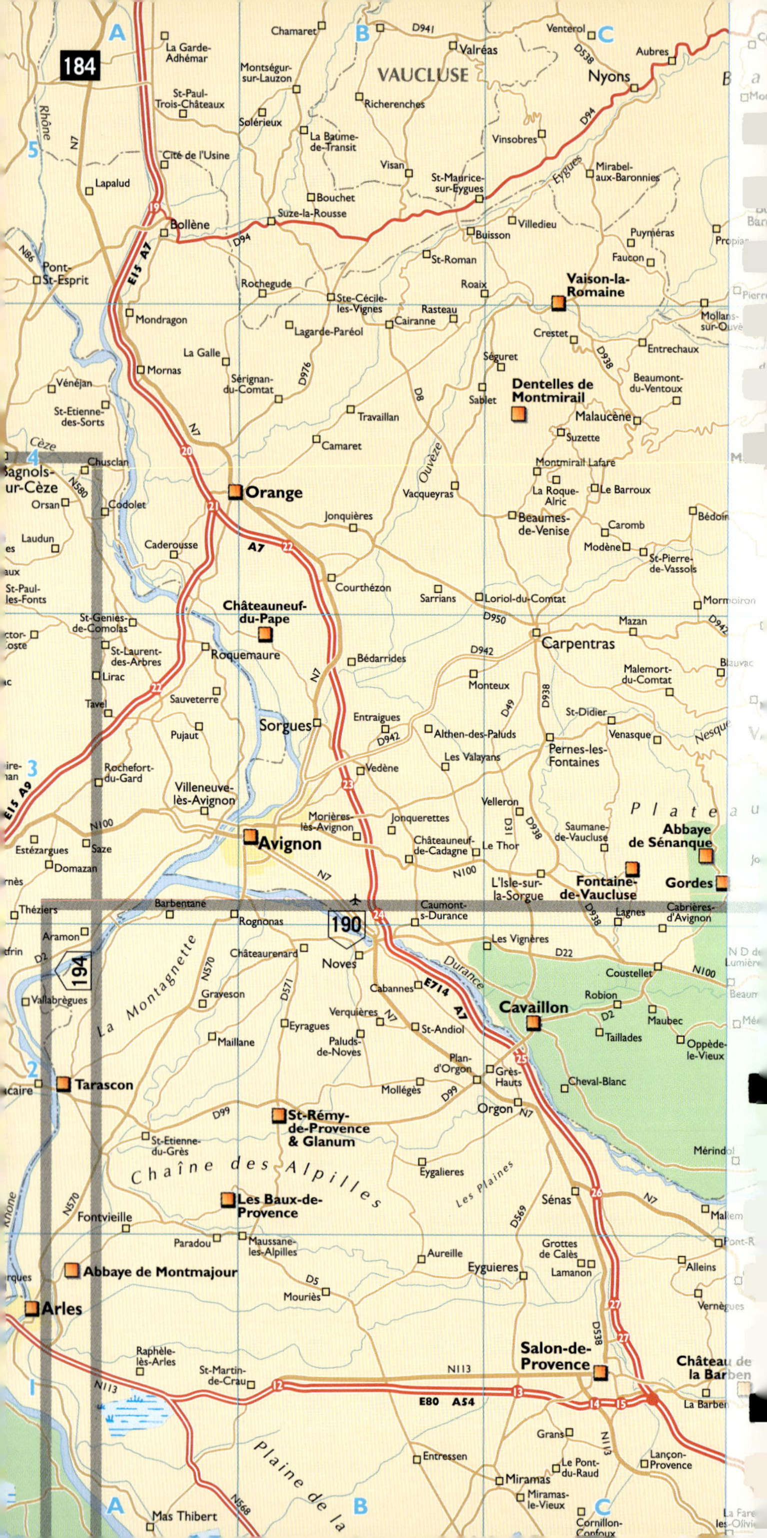

184
A
B
C
VAUCLUSE
La Garde-Adhémar
Chamaret
D941
Venterol
Valréas
Aubres
Nyons
Montségur-sur-Lauzon
St-Paul-Trois-Châteaux
Richerenches
Solérieux
La Baume-de-Transit
Vinsobres
D94
Rhône
N7
Cité de l'Usine
Visan
Mirabel-aux-Baronnies
Eygues
Lapalud
St-Maurice-sur-Eygues
Bouchet
Suze-la-Rousse
Bollène
Villedieu
Buisson
Puyméras
Propiac
N86
Pont-St-Esprit
E15 A7
Rochegude
St-Roman
Faucon
Roaix
Vaison-la-Romaine
Ste-Cécile-les-Vignes
Rasteau
Cairanne
Mondragon
Lagarde-Paréol
Crestet
Mollans-sur-Ouvèze
Entrechaux
La Galle
Séguret
D938
Mornas
Sérignan-du-Comtat
D976
Dentelles de Montmirail
Beaumont-du-Ventoux
Vénéjan
Sablet
D8
Malaucène
St-Etienne-des-Sorts
Travaillan
Suzette
Cèze
Camaret
Chusclan
Montmirail Lafare
Bagnols-sur-Cèze
N580
Orange
Ouvèze
Vacqueyras
La Roque-Alric
Le Barroux
Orsan
Codolet
Jonquières
Beaumes-de-Venise
Bédoin
Laudun
Caderousse
A7
Carombe
Modène
St-Pierre-de-Vassols
St-Paul-les-Fonts
Courthézon
Sarrians
Loriol-du-Comtat
Mormoiron
St-Genies-de-Comolas
Châteauneuf-du-Pape
D950
Mazan
St-Laurent-des-Arbres
Roquemaure
Carpentras
D942
Bédarrides
Monteux
Malemort-du-Comtat
Lirac
Sauveterre
N7
D49
D938
Tavel
Entraigues
St-Didier
Pujaut
Sorgues
Althen-des-Paluds
Venasque
Nesque
Les Valayans
Pernes-les-Fontaines
Rochefort-du-Gard
Vedène
E15 A9
Villeneuve-lès-Avignon
Velleron
Plateau
N100
Jonquerettes
D31
Estézargues
Saze
Morières-lès-Avignon
Saumane-de-Vaucluse
Abbaye de Sénanque
Avignon
Châteauneuf-de-Cadagne
Le Thor
Domazan
N100
L'Isle-sur-la-Sorgue
Fontaine-de-Vaucluse
Gordes
Théziers
Barbentane
Caumont-s-Durance
Lagnes
Cabrières-d'Avignon
Rognonas
190
Aramon
Les Vignères
D22
D2
194
Châteaurenard
Noves
Durance
Coustellet
N100
N570
Cabanes
E714
Vallabrègues
Graveson
D571
Robion
La Montagnette
Verquières
A7
Cavaillon
Maubec
Eyragues
St-Andiol
D2
Maillane
Taillades
Oppède-le-Vieux
Paluds-de-Noves
Plan-d'Orgon
Grès-Hauts
Tarascon
Mollégès
D99
Cheval-Blanc
Orgon
D99
St-Rémy-de-Provence & Glanum
St-Etienne-du-Grès
Eygalières
Mérindol
Chaîne des Alpilles
Les Plaines
Sénas
N7
Les Baux-de-Provence
D569
Mallemort
N570
Fontvieille
Paradou
Maussane-les-Alpilles
Grottes de Calès
Aureille
Lamanon
Eyguières
Abbaye de Montmajour
Alleins
D5
Mouriès
Arles
Vernègues
D538
Salon-de-Provence
Château de la Barben
Raphèle-lès-Arles
N113
St-Martin-de-Crau
N113
E80
A54
La Barben
Grans
Entressen
Le Pont-du-Raud
N113
Lançon-Provence
Plaine de la
Miramas
Miramas-le-Vieux
N568
Mas Thibert
Cornillon-Confoux

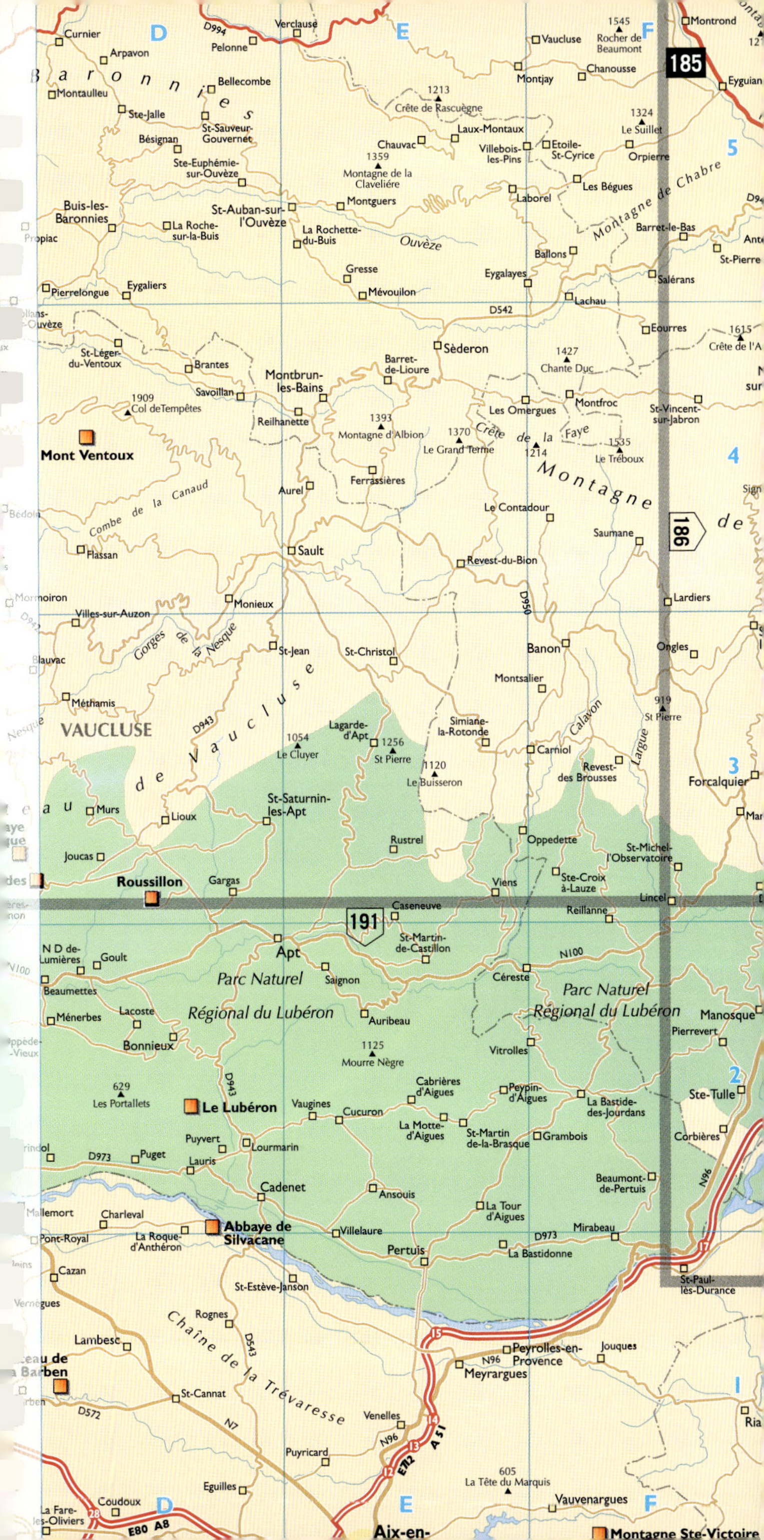
185
D
E
F
Curnier
Arpavon
D994
Verclause
Pelonne
1545
Rocher de Beaumont
Vaucluse
Montrond
Baronnies
Montaulleu
Bellecombe
Montjay
Chanousse
Eyguian
1213
Crête de Rascuègne
Ste-Jalle
St-Sauveur-Gouvernet
Bésignan
Laux-Montaux
1324
Le Suillet
Chauvac
1359
Montagne de la Claveliére
Villebois-les-Pins
Etoile-St-Cyrice
Orpierre
5
Ste-Euphémie-sur-Ouvèze
Les Bégues
Laborel
Montagne de Chabre
Montguers
Buis-les-Baronnies
St-Auban-sur-l'Ouvèze
La Roche-sur-le-Buis
La Rochette-du-Buis
Ouvèze
Barret-le-Bas
Propiac
St-Pierre
Ballons
Gresse
Eygalayes
Salérans
Pierrelongue
Eygaliers
Mévouilon
Lachau
D542
Eourres
1615
Crête de l'A
Sèderon
St-Léger-du-Ventoux
Barret-de-Lioure
1427
Chante Duc
Brantes
Montbrun-les-Bains
Savoillan
Montfroc
St-Vincent-sur-Jabron
1909
Col de Tempêtes
Reilhanette
Les Omergues
1393
Montagne d'Albion
1370
Le Grand Terme
Crête de la Faye
1214
1535
Le Tréboux
Mont Ventoux
4
Ferrassières
Montagne de
Aurel
Combe de la Canaud
Le Contadour
Bedoin
186
Saumane
Sault
Flassan
Revest-du-Bion
Mormoiron
Monieux
D950
Lardiers
Villes-sur-Auzon
Gorges de la Nesque
St-Jean
St-Christol
Banon
Ongles
Blauvac
Montsalier
Méthamis
Plateau de Vaucluse
919
St Pierre
VAUCLUSE
D943
Lagarde-d'Apt
1054
Le Cluyer
1256
St Pierre
Simiane-la-Rotonde
Carniol
Calavon
Largue
1120
Le Buisseron
Revest-des Brousses
3
Forcalquier
Murs
St-Saturnin-les-Apt
Lioux
Rustrel
Oppedette
Joucas
St-Michel-l'Observatoire
Roussillon
Gargas
Ste-Croix à-Lauze
Viens
Caseneuve
Lincel
Reillanne
191
Apt
St-Martin-de-Castillon
N D de-Lumières
Goult
N100
Saignon
Céreste
Beaumettes
Parc Naturel Régional du Lubéron
Parc Naturel Régional du Lubéron
Ménerbes
Lacoste
Auribeau
Manosque
Pierrevert
Bonnieux
1125
Mourre Nègre
Vitrolles
629
Les Portallets
D943
Cabrières d'Aigues
Peypin-d'Aigues
2
Le Lubéron
Vaugines
Cucuron
La Bastide-des-Jourdans
Ste-Tulle
La Motte-d'Aigues
St-Martin de-la-Brasque
Grambois
Corbières
Puyvert
Lourmarin
D973
Puget
Lauris
Cadenet
Ansouis
Beaumont-de-Pertuis
N96
Mallemort
Charleval
La Tour d'Aigues
Abbaye de Silvacane
Mirabeau
Pont-Royal
La Roque-d'Anthéron
Villelaure
D973
La Bastidonne
Pertuis
Cazan
St-Paul-lès-Durance
St-Estève-Janson
Vernègues
Rognes
D543
Chaîne de la Trévaresse
Lambesc
Peyrolles-en-Provence
Jouques
N96
Meyrargues
Château de la Barben
1
St-Cannat
D572
N7
Venelles
N96
A51
Puyricard
E712
605
La Tête du Marquis
Eguilles
Coudoux
Vauvenargues
La Fare-les-Oliviers
E80 A8
Aix-en-
Montagne Ste-Victoire

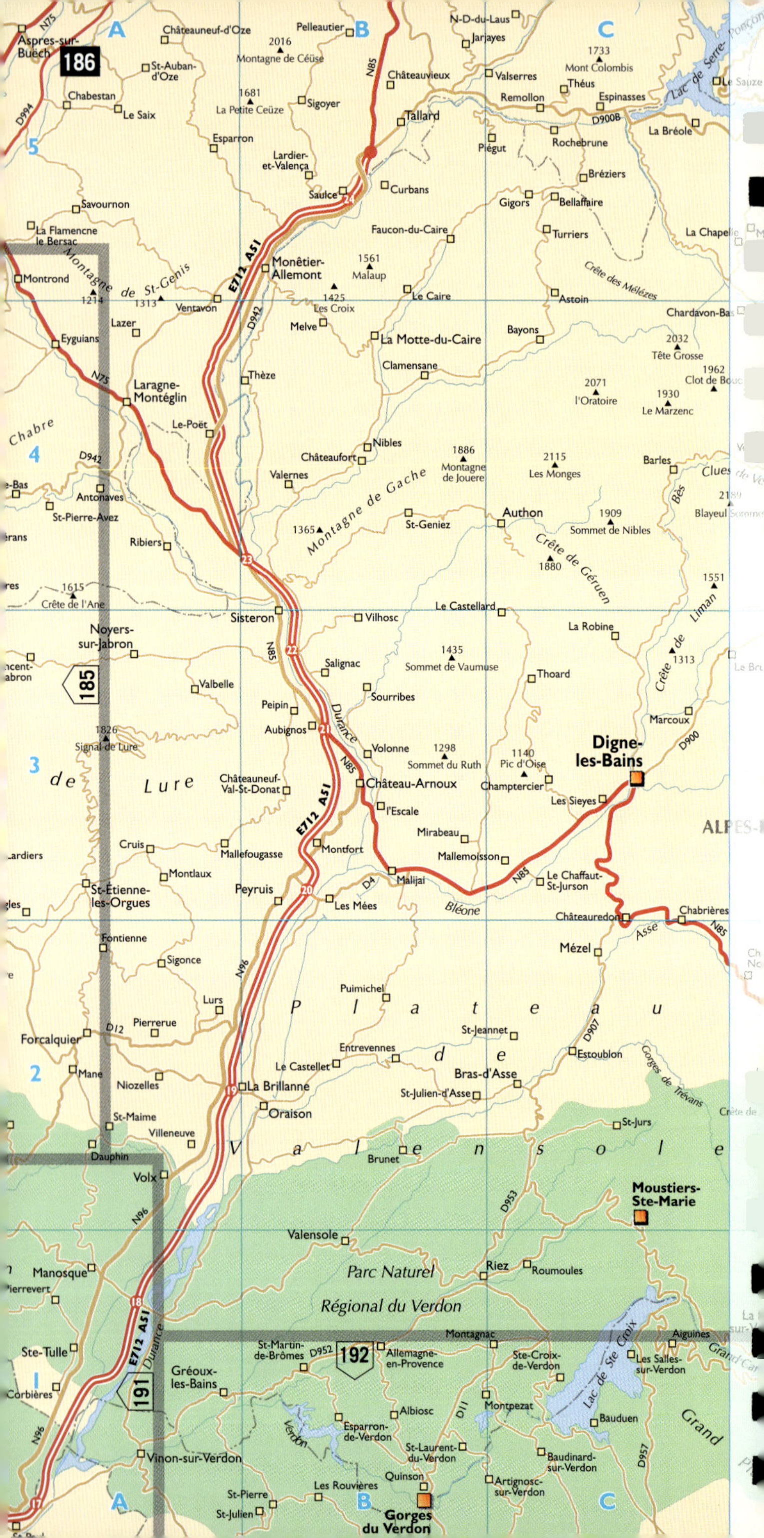
186
A
B
C
5
4
3
2
1
Aspres-sur-Buëch
N75
D994
Châteauneuf-d'Oze
St-Auban-d'Oze
Chabestan
Le Saix
Pelleautier
2016
Montagne de Céüse
1681
La Petite Ceüze
Sigoyer
Esparron
Lardier-et-Valença
Saulce
N85
Châteauvieux
Tallard
N-D-du-Laus
Jarjayes
Valserres
Remollon
Piégut
1733
Mont Colombis
Théus
Espinasses
D900B
Rochebrune
Lac de Serre-Ponçon
Le Sauze
La Bréole
Bréziers
Curbans
Gigors
Bellaffaire
Turriers
Faucon-du-Caire
La Chapelle
Savournon
La Flamencne
le Bersac
Montagne de St-Genis
Montrond
1214
1313
Ventavon
Monêtier-Allemont
E712 A51
1561
Malaup
1425
Les Croix
Le Caire
Astoin
Crête des Mélèzes
Chardavon-Bas
Lazer
Eyguians
D942
Melve
La Motte-du-Caire
Bayons
2032
Tête Grosse
Clamensane
1962
2071
l'Oratoire
1930
Le Marzenc
N75
Laragne-Montéglin
Thèze
Chabre
Le-Poët
Nibles
Châteaufort
1886
Montagne de Jouere
2115
Les Monges
Barles
Clues de Ve
Valernes
Montagne de Gache
Antonaves
St-Pierre-Avez
Ribiers
1365
St-Geniez
Authon
1909
Sommet de Nibles
Bès
2189
Blayeul
23
1615
Crête de l'Ane
Crête de Géruen
1880
1551
Sisteron
Vilhosc
Le Castellard
Crête de Liman
La Robine
Noyers-sur-Jabron
N85
22
Salignac
1435
Sommet de Vaumuse
1313
Thoard
185
Valbelle
Peipin
Sourribes
Marcoux
1826
Signal de Lure
Aubignos
21
Durance
Volonne
1298
Sommet du Ruth
1140
Pic d'Oise
Digne-les-Bains
D900
de
Lure
Châteauneuf-Val-St-Donat
N85
Château-Arnoux
Champtercier
Les Sieyes
l'Escale
E712 A51
Mirabeau
ALPES-
Cruis
Mallefougasse
Montfort
Mallemoisson
Montlaux
St-Étienne-les-Orgues
Peyruis
Malijai
D4
N85
Le Chaffaut-St-Jurson
20
Les Mées
Bléone
Châteauredon
Chabrières
Asse
N85
Fontienne
Mézel
Sigonce
N96
Puimichel
Lurs
Plateau
D907
St-Jeannet
Pierrerue
D12
Forcalquier
Entrevennes
de
Estoublon
Le Castellet
Gorges de Trévans
Mane
Niozelles
19
La Brillanne
Bras-d'Asse
St-Julien-d'Asse
Oraison
St-Maime
Villeneuve
St-Jurs
Dauphin
Valensole
Brunet
Volx
Moustiers-Ste-Marie
N96
D953
Valensole
Manosque
Parc Naturel
Riez
Roumoules
Pierrevert
Régional du Verdon
18
E712 A51
Durance
Montagnac
Aiguines
Ste-Tulle
St-Martin-de-Brômes
D952
192
Allemagne-en-Provence
Ste-Croix-de-Verdon
Lac de Ste Croix
Les Salles-sur-Verdon
Corbières
Gréoux-les-Bains
191
Albiosc
D11
Montpezat
Bauduen
Grand
N96
Esparron-de-Verdon
Verdon
St-Laurent-du-Verdon
Baudinard-sur-Verdon
D957
Vinon-sur-Verdon
Quinson
Artignosc-sur-Verdon
17
Les Rouvières
St-Pierre
A
B
C
St-Julien
Gorges du Verdon

D
E
F
Lac de Serre-Ponçon
2327
Pic de Morgon
Les Fabres
Melezet
2809
Pic de Boussolenc
2988
Grand Parpaillon
Tournoux
St-Ours
3193
Roche Blanche
Le Sauze
D954
2440
Le Petit Ferrand
2917
L'Aupillon
Montagne de Parpaillon
3048
Grand Bérard
La Condamine-Châtelard
Larche
3032
Tête de Siguret
5
St-Vincent-les-Forts
Le Lauzet-Ubaye
D900
Jausiers
2885
Tête de Fer
Serre Bouréou
Les Thuiles
St-Pons
Faucon
D900
Ubaye
Barcelonnette
2955
Tête de l'Enchastraye
Montclar
Montagne de la Blanche
Le Sauze
Pra-Loup
Super-Sauze
2820
Montagne de l'Alpe
2678
Col des Restefond
2727
Cime de Voga
2430
Pic de Bernardez
Seyne
D900
2909
Grande Séolane
2685
Le Chapeau de Gendarme
2802
Cime de la Bonette
1346
Col de Maure
2739
Roche Close
Le Villard-d'Abas
2240
Col d'Allos
Parc National du Mercantour
St-Dalmas-le-Selvage
2839
Le Grand Cheval de Bois
2961
Tête de l'Estrop
2327
Col de la Cayolle
2563
Mont Aunos
Le Vernet
Verdaches
3051
Mont Pelat
2916
Pointe Côte de l'Ane
4
Le Haut Vernet
2560
Tête Noire
Clues de Verbaches
1770
Set de la Croix
Bléone
Allos
1240
Col du Labouret
2654
Sommet du Caduc
D908
2818
Cime de Pal
Prads-Haute-Bléone
2560
Sangraure
2426
L'Autapie
Clignon
1667
Sommet de Chappe
Entraunes
2468
Cime de l'Aspre
2673
2403
Sommet de Denjuan
Colmars
Blégiers
Var
La Javie
Villars-Colmars
Le Brusquet
Beauvezer
Verdon
2434
Laupon
St-Martin-d'Entraunes
Montagne du Cheval Blanc
2305
Draix
2580
Le Petit Coyer
Villeneuve-d'Entraunes
2223
Thorame-Haute
2158
Le Couradour
Guillaumes
3
Thorame-Basse
Château-Garnier
La Bâtie
Tartonne
ALPES-DE-HTE-PROVENCE
188
1431
Col de la Colle St-Michel
2100
Le Ruch
2159
Tête de Travers
Gorges de Daluis
Lambruisse
Daluis
D902
Méailles
1789
Montagne de l'Allier
Clumanc
Sausses
D955
Le Fugeret
Castellet-lès-Sausses
Braux
La Croix-sur-Roudoule
Chaudon-Norante
St-Lions
La Mure
Annot
Moriez
St-André-les-Alpes
N202
Entrevaux
Barrême
N202
Rouainette
1620
La Barre
1725
Sommet du Castellard
Vergons
1124
Col de Toutes Aures
2
Senez
St-Julien-du-Verdon
1621
Crête de Montmuye
1941
Sommet de la Bernarde
Collongues
N85
Barrage de Castillon
Les Mujouls
1146
Col des Leque
Gars
Blieux
Briançonnet
Clues de Haute
1741
Pré Chauvin
Soleilhas
St-Auban
1474
1471
Castellane
1771
Berbené
Peyroules
Thorenc
Parc Naturel Régional du Verdon
Le Mousteiret
Valderoure
Rougon
Caille
La Palud-sur-Verdon
D952
Le Bourguet
Châteauvieux
Séranon
Andon
Brenon
193
La Marte
N85
1642
Montagne de l'Audibergue
Grand Canyon du Verdon
Trigance
1
Bargeme
La Bastide
La Roque-Esclapon
Comps-sur-Artuby
St-Vallier-de-Thiey
Mons
Plan de
Spéracèdes
D
E
F

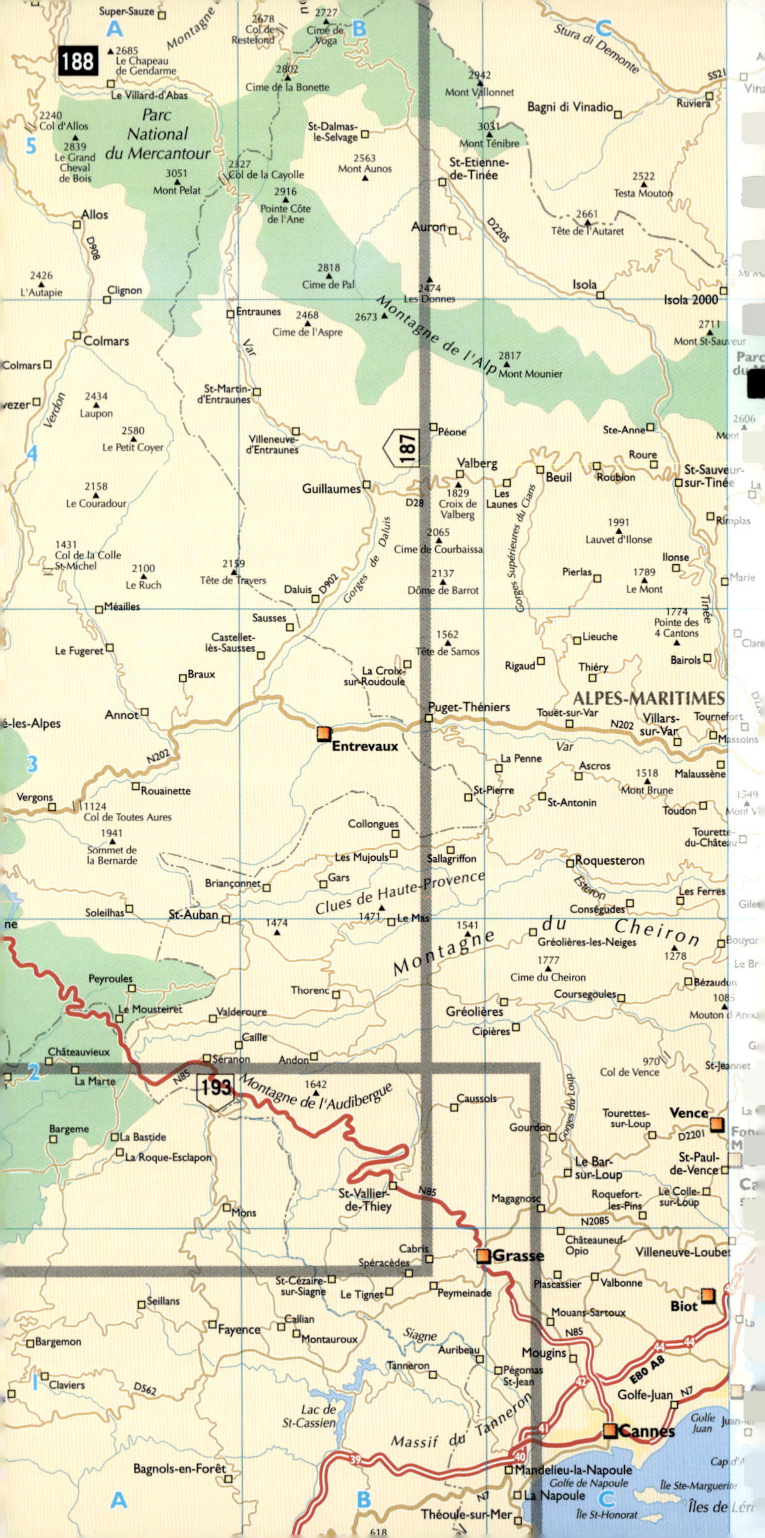

A
B
C
5
4
3
2
1
Super-Sauze
2685 Le Chapeau de Gendarme
Montagne
2678 Col de Restefond
2727 Cime de Voga
Stura di Demonte
SS21
Vina
2802 Cime de la Bonette
2942 Mont Vallonnet
Le Villard-d'Abas
Parc National du Mercantour
Bagni di Vinadio
Ruviera
2240 Col d'Allos
2839 Le Grand Cheval de Bois
St-Dalmas-le-Selvage
3031 Mont Ténibre
2327 Col de la Cayolle
2563 Mont Aunos
St-Etienne-de-Tinée
3051 Mont Pelat
2916 Pointe Côte de l'Ane
2522 Testa Mouton
Allos
D908
Auron
D2205
2661 Tête de l'Autaret
2818 Cime de Pal
2426 L'Autapie
Clignon
2474 Les Donnes
Isola
Isola 2000
Entraunes
2468 Cime de l'Aspre
2673
Montagne de l'Alp
Colmars
2711 Mont St-Sauveur
Var
2817 Mont Mounier
Colmars
Verdon
2434 Laupon
St-Martin-d'Entraunes
2580 Le Petit Coyer
Villeneuve-d'Entraunes
Péone
Ste-Anne
2606
187
Valberg
Roure
Beuil
Roubion
St-Sauveur-sur-Tinée
2158 Le Couradour
Guillaumes
D28
1829 Croix de Valberg
Les Launes
Gorges Supérieures du Cians
Rimplas
2065 Cime de Courbaissa
1991 Lauvet d'Ilonse
1431 Col de la Colle St-Michel
Gorges de Daluis
Ilonse
2100 Le Ruch
2159 Tête de Travers
Daluis
D902
2137 Dôme de Barrot
Pierlas
1789 Le Mont
Marie
Méailles
Tinée
1774 Pointe des 4 Cantons
Sausses
Castellet-lès-Sausses
1562 Tête de Samos
Lieuche
Le Fugeret
La Croix-sur-Roudoule
Rigaud
Thiéry
Bairols
Braux
ALPES-MARITIMES
Annot
Puget-Théniers
Touët-sur-Var
Villars-sur-Var
Tournefort
Massoins
Entrevaux
N202
Var
N202
La Penne
Ascros
1518 Mont Brune
Malaussène
Vergons
Rouainette
St-Pierre
St-Antonin
Toudon
1124 Col de Toutes Aures
1941 Sommet de la Bernarde
Collongues
Tourette-du-Château
Les Mujouls
Sallagriffon
Roquesteron
Briançonnet
Gars
Clues de Haute-Provence
Esteron
Les Ferres
Soleilhas
St-Auban
1474
1471 Le Mas
Conségudes
1541
Montagne du Cheiron
Gréolières-les-Neiges
1278
Bouyon
1777 Cime du Cheiron
Peyroules
Thorenc
Bézaudun
Coursegoules
Le Mousteiret
Valderoure
Gréolières
1085 Mouton d'Anou
Cipières
Caille
Châteauvieux
Séranon
Andon
970 Col de Vence
St-Jeannet
La Marte
N85
193
1642
Montagne de l'Audibergue
Caussols
Gorges du Loup
Gourdon
Tourettes-sur-Loup
Vence
D2201
Bargeme
La Bastide
La Roque-Esclapon
Le Bar-sur-Loup
St-Paul-de-Vence
St-Vallier-de-Thiey
N85
Magagnosc
Roquefort-les-Pins
Le Colle-sur-Loup
Mons
N2085
Châteauneuf-Opio
Cabris
Grasse
Villeneuve-Loubet
Spéracèdes
St-Cézaire-sur-Siagne
Le Tignet
Peymeinade
Plascassier
Valbonne
Seillans
Biot
Mouans-Sartoux
Fayence
Callian
Montauroux
Siagne
N85
Bargemon
Auribeau
Mougins
44
44
Tanneron
Pégomas
St-Jean
E80 A8
42
Claviers
D562
Golfe-Juan
N7
Lac de St-Cassien
Massif du Tanneron
41
Cannes
Golfe Juan
40
39
Bagnols-en-Forêt
Mandelieu-la-Napoule
Golfe de Napoule
Île Ste-Marguerite
La Napoule
N7
Îles de Lérins
Île St-Honorat
Théoule-sur-Mer
618

D
E
F
Gaiola
Bóves
Peveragno
Borgo S Dalmazzo
Moiola
SS21
Aisone
Demonte
Roccavione
SS20
Andonno
Robilante
Vinadio
I
Vigna
Prea
2231
Monte Besimáuda
S Bartolomeo
Valdieri
Roáschia
1768
Cima della Pigna
5
2404
Becco Costa Rossa
2450
Monte Bourel
2718
Tenuta di Caccia
Entrácque
Vernante
S Anna di Valdieri
1867
Monte Sapè
3088
Monte Matto
2687
Cima del Lausetto
2157
Pico Miráuda
2451
Monte Bussáia
Parco Regionale Alta Valle Pésio e Tánaro
2938
Mt Malinvern
Terme di Valdieri
Limone Piemonte
2306
Monte Garbella
2650
Pointe Marguareis
3297
Cima d'Argentera
Parco Regionale delle Alpi Marittime
1871
Col de Tende
Parc National du Mercantour
2241
Cime de l'Evêque
3143
Cime du Gélas
Le Boréon
2606
Mont Giraud
2250
Baus de la Frema
2786
Mont Neillier
E74 N204
Tende
4
1500
Col St-Martin
La Bolline
St-Martin-Vésubie
2873
Mont Bégo
2200
Monte Saccarello
La Brigue
2496
Cime de la Valette
St-Dalmas
Rimplas
D2565
Venanson
2685
Cime du Diable
2414
Pointe de la Corne de Bouc
2136
Cime de Marte
Roquebillière-Vieux
Roya
1677
Cima de Coss
Marie
2085
Mont Tournairet
Roquebillière
Belvédère
Fontan
1889
L'Authion
Ft de Cayrons
Saorge
2038
Mont Peyrevieille
La Bollène-Vésubie
Clans
1607
Col de Turini
1971
Mont Torrage
I
Lantosque
1610
L'Arpette
D2565
Moulinet
1587
Tête d'Alpe
D2205
La Tour
1606
Brec d'Utelle
Breil-sur-Roya
Pigna
1481
Pierre Plate
Peïra-Cava
879
Col de Brouis
Castel Vittório
Massoins
St-Jean-la-Rivière
Utelle
1504
Cime de Rocca Seira
D2566
Rocchetta Nervina
3
Piene
1026
Mont Colombin
1549
Mont Vial
Duranus
Apricale
Gorges de la Vésubie
Lucéram
1002
Col de Braus
Isolabona
Perinaldo
Sospel
Olivetta San Michele
1413
Mont Férion
Coaraze
Collabassa
SS20
Bonson
Dolceacqua
Levens
1281
Mt Razet
1378
Mont Grammont
D2566
Berre-des-Alpes
Seborga
Ferres
Gilette
Bendejun
Castillon
San Biagio d Cima
L'Escarène
St-Martin-du-Var
Camporosso
Bouyon
St-Antoine
La Garde
1264
Pic de Baudon
E80
A8
St-Blaise
Contes
Ste-Agnès
Le Broc
Peille
Châteauneuf-de-Contes
59
Ventimiglia
SS1
N202
Castagniers
Gorbio
Mortola
Bordighera
Carros
Tourrette-Levens
Peillon
Garavan
D2204
Menton
58
Roquebrune
Aspremont
Gattières
Laghet
Cap Martin
Riviera di Ponente
Colomars
Drap
La Turbie
A8
Falicon
E80
56-57
Monte-Carlo
2
54
55-55
MONACO
La Gaude
Les Corniches
Eze
Cap d'Ail
Fondation Maeght
57
Villefranche-sur-Mer
Beaulieu-sur-Mer
Villa Ephrussi de Rothschild
N202
N7
St-Jean-Cap Ferrat
Cagnes-sur-Mer
NICE
51
50
49
48
Plage de la Ville
Cap Ferrat
Nice (Cotê d'Azur)
47
46
La Brague
Antibes
1
Juan-les-Pins
Cap d'Antibes
D
E
F

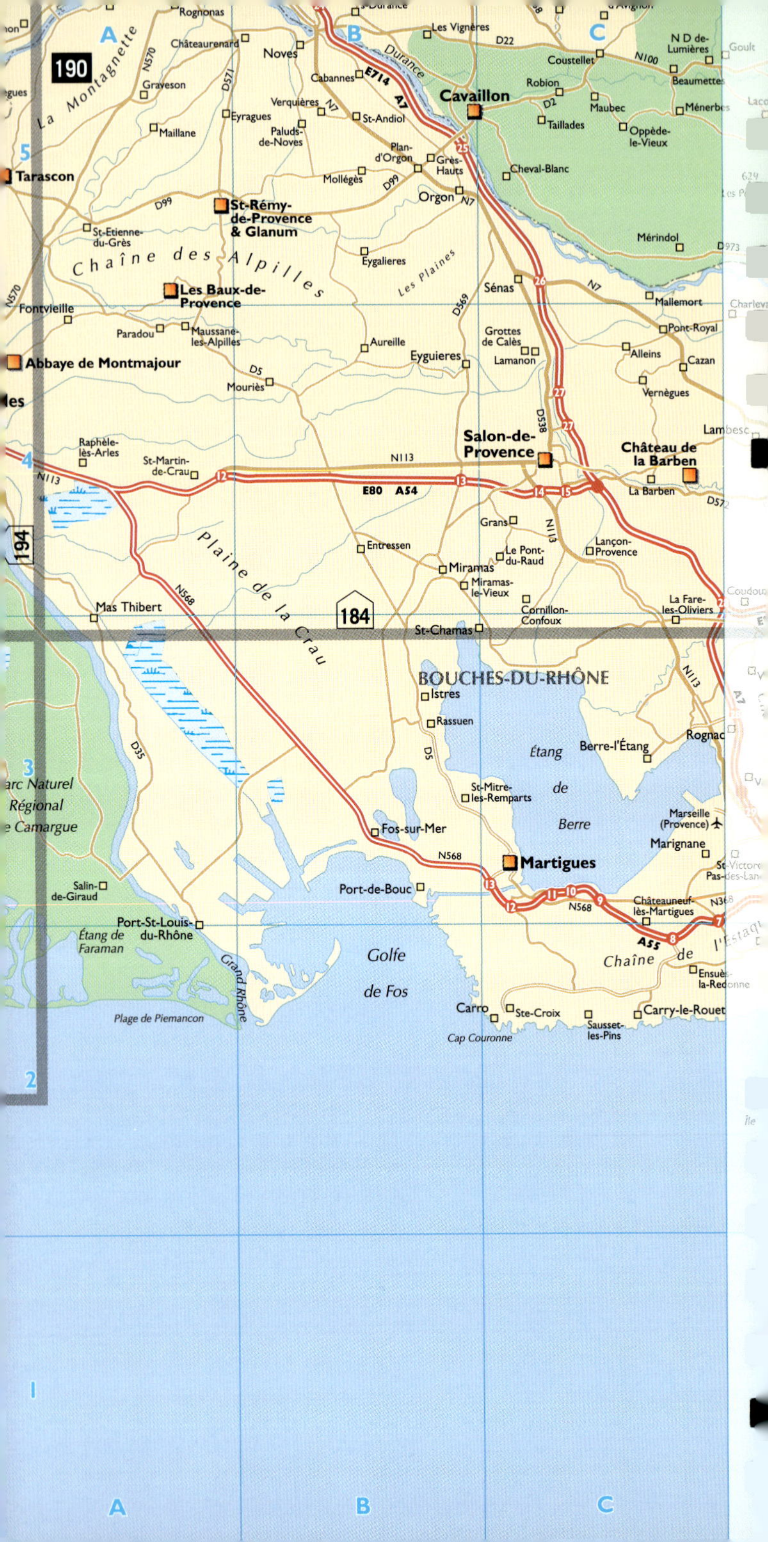
190
A
B
C
Rognonas
Châteaurenard
Noves
Les Vignères
D22
N D de-
Lumières
Goult
La Montagnette
N570
D571
Graveson
Cabannes
E714
A7
Durance
Coustellet
N100
Beaumettes
Robion
Cavaillon
Maubec
Ménerbes
Verquières
N7
Eyragues
St-Andiol
D2
Taillades
Oppède-
le-Vieux
Maillane
Paluds-
de-Noves
Plan-
d'Orgon
Grès-
Hauts
25
Cheval-Blanc
5
Tarascon
Mollégès
D99
Orgon
N7
D99
St-Rémy-
de-Provence
& Glanum
St-Etienne-
du-Grès
Mérindol
D973
Chaîne des Alpilles
Eygalieres
Les Plaines
Les Baux-de-
Provence
Sénas
26
N7
Mallemort
N570
Fontvieille
D569
Paradou
Maussane-
les-Alpilles
Grottes
de Calès
Pont-Royal
Aureille
Lamanon
Alleins
Cazan
Eyguieres
Abbaye de Montmajour
D5
Mouriès
Vernègues
27
D538
27
Lambesc
Salon-de-
Provence
Château de
la Barben
Raphèle-
lès-Arles
St-Martin-
de-Crau
N113
4
N113
12
E80
A54
13
14
15
La Barben
D572
194
Grans
Plaine de la Crau
Entressen
N113
Le Pont-
du-Raud
Lançon-
Provence
Miramas
Miramas-
le-Vieux
N568
Mas Thibert
184
Cornillon-
Confoux
La Fare-
les-Oliviers
St-Chamas
BOUCHES-DU-RHÔNE
N113
Istres
A7
Rassuen
D35
D5
Étang
Berre-l'Étang
Rognac
3
Parc Naturel
Régional
de Camargue
St-Mitre-
les-Remparts
de
Berre
Marseille
(Provence)
Fos-sur-Mer
Marignane
N568
Martigues
St-Victoret
Pas-des-Lanciers
Salin-
de-Giraud
Port-de-Bouc
13
11
10
9
12
N568
Châteauneuf-
lès-Martigues
N368
Port-St-Louis-
du-Rhône
Étang de
Faraman
A55
8
7
Golfe
de Fos
Chaîne de l'Estaque
Grand Rhône
Ensuès-
la-Redonne
Carro
Ste-Croix
Sausset-
les-Pins
Carry-le-Rouet
Plage de Piemancon
Cap Couronne
2
1
A
B
C

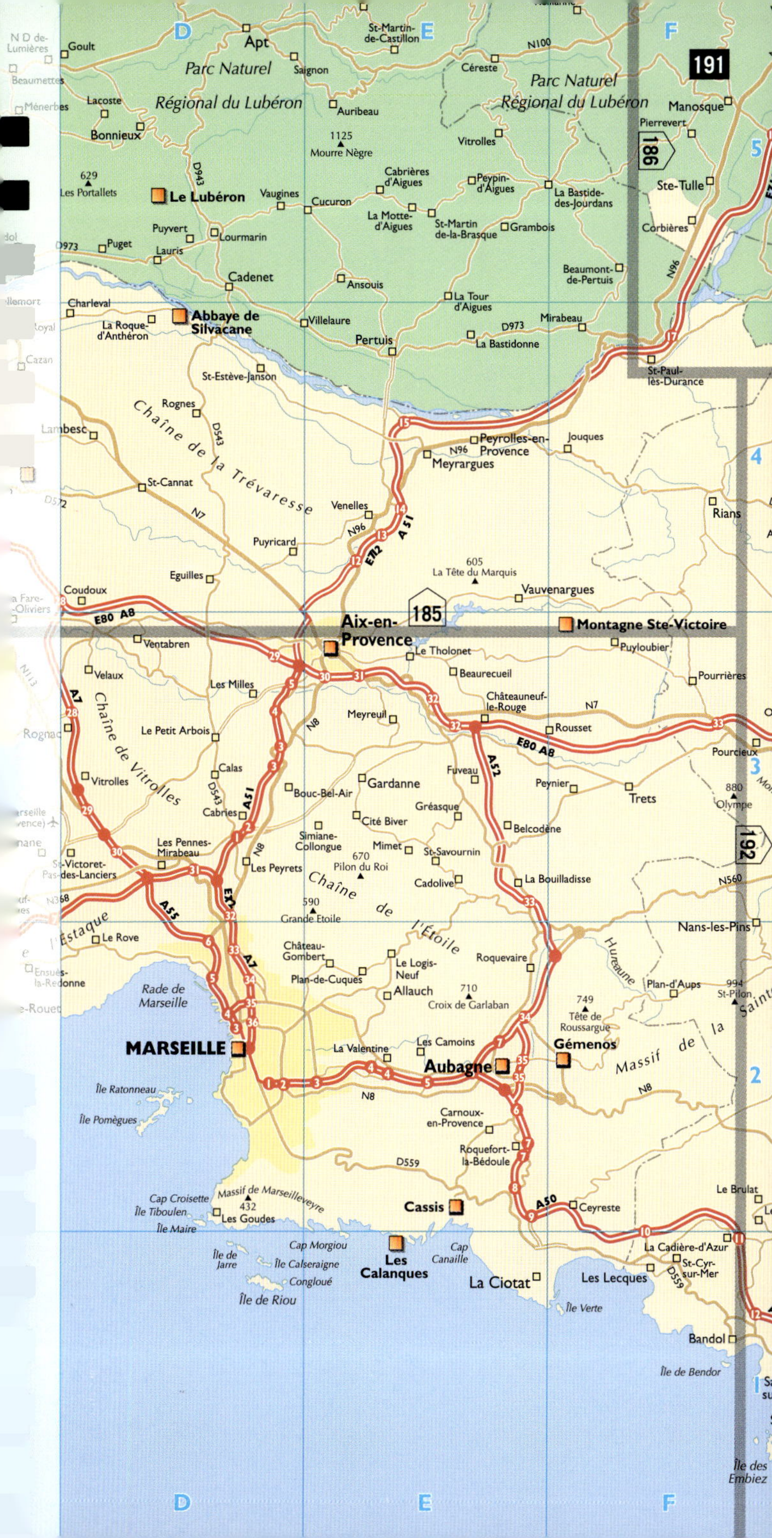
D
E
F
N D de-Lumières
Goult
Apt
St-Martin-de-Castillon
N100
Beaumettes
Parc Naturel Régional du Lubéron
Saignon
Céreste
Parc Naturel Régional du Lubéron
Ménerbes
Lacoste
Auribeau
Manosque
Pierrevert
Bonnieux
1125
Mourre Nègre
Vitrolles
186
5
629
Les Portallets
Le Lubéron
D943
Vaugines
Cabrières d'Aigues
Peypin-d'Aigues
Ste-Tulle
Cucuron
La Bastide-des-Jourdans
Puyvert
Lourmarin
La Motte-d'Aigues
St-Martin de-la-Brasque
Grambois
Corbières
D973
Puget
Lauris
Beaumont-de-Pertuis
Cadenet
Ansouis
N96
La Tour d'Aigues
Charleval
Abbaye de Silvacane
La Roque-d'Anthéron
Villelaure
Mirabeau
D973
Pertuis
La Bastidonne
Cazan
St-Paul-lès-Durance
St-Estève-Janson
Rognes
Chaîne de la Trévaresse
Lambesc
D543
15
Peyrolles-en-Provence
N96
Meyrargues
Jouques
4
St-Cannat
N7
Venelles
14
A51
Rians
N96
13
Puyricard
E712
12
605
La Tête du Marquis
Eguilles
Coudoux
Vauvenargues
185
E80 A8
Aix-en-Provence
Montagne Ste-Victoire
Ventabren
Le Tholonet
Puyloubier
29
Velaux
5
30
31
Beaurecueil
Pourrières
Les Milles
A7
Châteauneuf-le-Rouge
N7
32
28
Chaîne de Vitrolles
N8
Meyreuil
4
Rognac
Le Petit Arbois
32
Rousset
33
E80 A8
Pourcieux
3
Fuveau
A52
Calas
Vitrolles
880
Olympe
Peynier
Trets
Gardanne
D543
A51
Bouc-Bel-Air
Cabriès
Gréasque
29
Cité Biver
Belcodène
192
Simiane-Collongue
Mimet
St-Savournin
30
Les Pennes-Mirabeau
St-Victoret-Pas-des-Lanciers
N8
670
Pilon du Roi
Les Peyrets
Chaîne de l'Etoile
La Bouilladisse
Cadolive
N560
31
N368
A55
E712
33
590
Grande Etoile
l'Estaque
32
Nans-les-Pins
Le Rove
Château-Gombert
Huveaune
Le Logis-Neuf
Roquevaire
6
A7
Ensuès-la-Redonne
Plan-de-Cuques
Plan-d'Aups
994
St-Pilon
Rade de Marseille
Allauch
710
Croix de Garlaban
749
Tête de Roussargue
Massif de la Sainte
MARSEILLE
La Valentine
Les Camoins
Gémenos
Aubagne
2
Île Ratonneau
N8
N8
Île Pomègues
Carnoux-en-Provence
Roquefort-la-Bédoule
D559
Cap Croisette
Massif de Marseilleveyre
432
Le Brulat
Île Tiboulen
Les Goudes
Cassis
A50
Ceyreste
Île Maire
10
11
Cap Morgiou
Cap Canaille
La Cadière-d'Azur
Île de Jarre
Île Calseraigne
Les Calanques
St-Cyr-sur-Mer
Congloué
La Ciotat
Les Lecques
D559
Île de Riou
Île Verte
Bandol
Île de Bendor
1
Île des Embiez
D
E
F

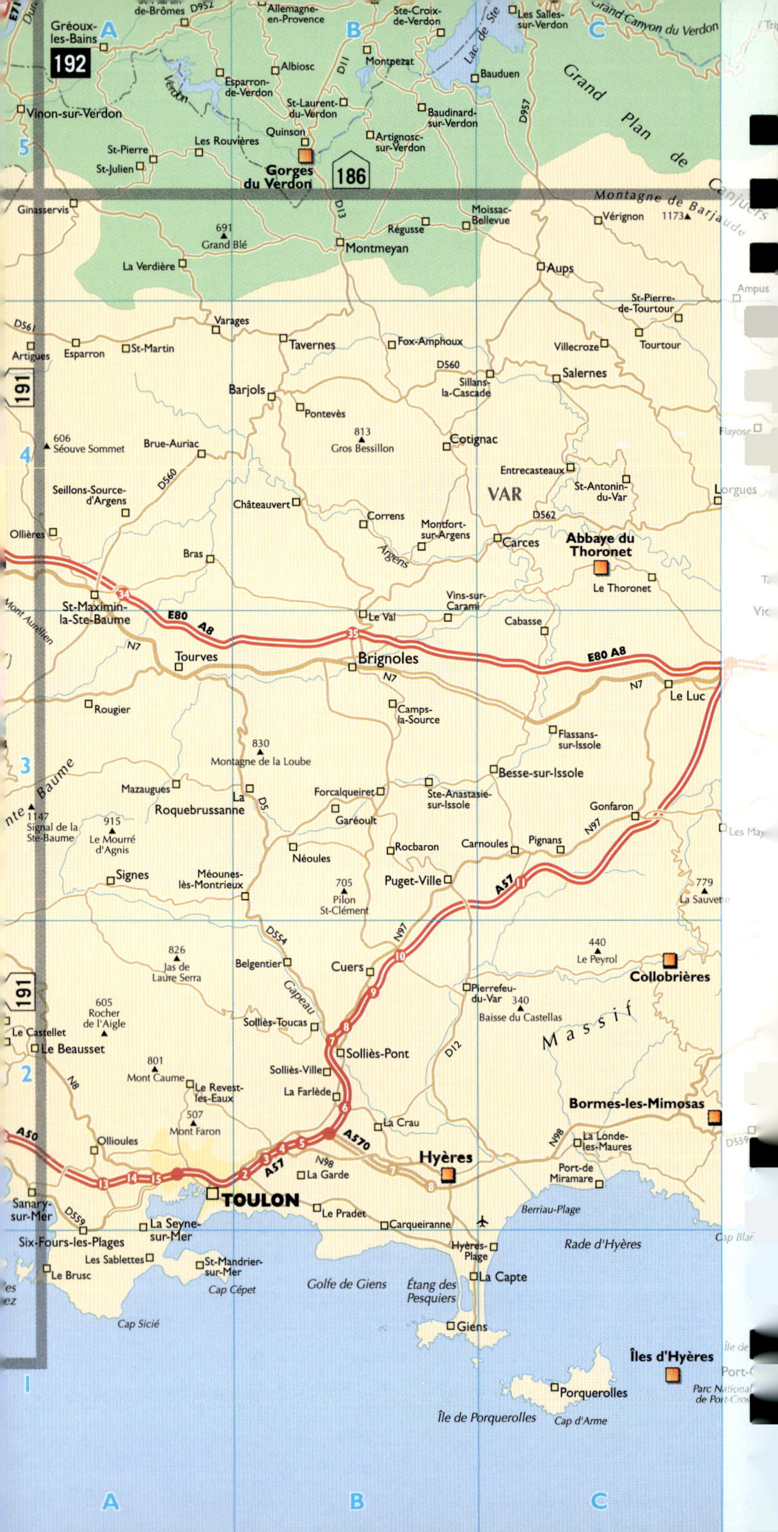

Gréoux-les-Bains
192
Allemagne-en-Provence
Ste-Croix-de-Verdon
Les Salles-sur-Verdon
Grand Canyon du Verdon
Albiosc
Montpezat
Bauduen
Esparron-de-Verdon
St-Laurent-du-Verdon
Baudinard-sur-Verdon
Vinon-sur-Verdon
Quinson
Artignosc-sur-Verdon
Grand Plan de Canjuers
Les Rouvières
St-Pierre
St-Julien
Gorges du Verdon
186
Montagne de Barjaude
Ginasservis
Moissac-Bellevue
Vérignon
1173
691
Grand Blé
Régusse
Montmeyan
La Verdière
Aups
Ampus
St-Pierre-de-Tourtour
Varages
Artigues
Esparron
St-Martin
Tavernes
Fox-Amphoux
Villecroze
Tourtour
D560
Sillans-la-Cascade
Salernes
191
Barjols
Pontevès
813
Gros Bessillon
Cotignac
606
Séouve Sommet
Brue-Auriac
Entrecasteaux
Seillons-Source-d'Argens
Châteauvert
VAR
St-Antonin-du-Var
Lorgues
Correns
D562
Ollières
Montfort-sur-Argens
Carces
Abbaye du Thoronet
Bras
Argens
Le Thoronet
St-Maximin-la-Ste-Baume
E80
A8
Vins-sur-Caramy
Le Val
Cabasse
N7
Tourves
Brignoles
E80 A8
Le Luc
Rougier
Camps-la-Source
Flassans-sur-Issole
830
Montagne de la Loube
Besse-sur-Issole
Mazaugues
La Roquebrussanne
Forcalqueiret
Ste-Anastasie-sur-Issole
Gonfaron
1147
Signal de la Ste-Baume
915
Le Mourré d'Agnis
Garéoult
N97
Les Mayons
Néoules
Rocbaron
Carnoules
Pignans
Signes
Méounes-lès-Montrieux
705
Pilon St-Clément
Puget-Ville
A57
779
La Sauvette
440
Le Peyrol
D554
826
Jas de Laure Serra
Belgentier
Cuers
Collobrières
Gapeau
Pierrefeu-du-Var
340
Baisse du Castellas
605
Rocher de l'Aigle
Solliès-Toucas
Massif
Le Castellet
Le Beausset
Solliès-Pont
D12
801
Mont Caume
Solliès-Ville
Le Revest-les-Eaux
La Farlède
Bormes-les-Mimosas
N8
507
Mont Faron
La Crau
A50
Ollioules
A570
La Londe-les-Maures
D559
N98
Hyères
Port-de-Miramar
La Garde
Sanary-sur-Mer
TOULON
Le Pradet
Berriau-Plage
La Seyne-sur-Mer
Carqueiranne
Six-Fours-les-Plages
Hyères-Plage
Rade d'Hyères
Cap Blanc
Les Sablettes
St-Mandrier-sur-Mer
Le Brusc
Cap Cépet
Golfe de Giens
Étang des Pesquiers
La Capte
Cap Sicié
Giens
Îles d'Hyères
Porquerolles
Parc National de Port-Cros
Île de Porquerolles
Cap d'Arme
A
B
C

Trigance
Brenon
La Martre
Montagne de l'Audibergue
1642
Caussols
193
Bargeme
La Bastide
La Roque-Esclapon
Comps-sur-Artuby
Mons
St-Vallier-de-Thiey
N85
Magagn
187
Cabris
Spéracèdes
Canjuers
D955
St-Cézaire-sur-Siagne
Le Tignet
Peymeinade
188
Seillans
Callian
Fayence
Montauroux
Siagne
Auribeau
Montferrat
Bargemon
Ampus
Châteaudouble
Claviers
Tanneron
Pégo
Callas
D562
Lac de St-Cassien
Rebouillon
Figanières
Massif du Tanneron
Draguignan
Bagnols-en-Forêt
Flayosc
N7
Théoule-sur-Mer
618
Mont Vinaigre
Miramar
La Motte
Le Trayas
Lorgues
496
Pic de l'Ours
Le Muy
E80 A8
Massif de l'Esterel
Les-Arcs-sur-Argens
Corniche de l'Esterel
Puget-sur-Argens
Valescure
Taradeau
Agay
Argens
Anthéor
Fréjus
St-Raphaël
Vidauban
N98
Le Dramont
Cap du Dramont
A8
Golfe de Fréjus
St-Aygulf
Aille
D25
N98
Les Issambres
D558
Maures
Plan-de-la-Tour
Val d'Esquières
La Garde-Freinet
Ste-Maxime
Les Mayons
636
Roches Blanches
Golfe de St-Tropez
N98
Beauvallon
Pointe de Rabiou
Port-Grimaud
Cap de St-Tropez
Grimaud
N98A
St-Tropez
Plage des Salins
Cogolin
Plage de Tahiti
Gassin
Plage de Pampelonne
Ramatuelle
La Croix-Valmer
Cap Camarat
N98
528
Les Pradels
D559
Plage de l'Escalet
Baie de Cavalaire
Le Rayol-Candel-sur-Mer
Cavalaire-sur-Mer
Cap Cartaya
Plage de la Briande
Cap Ladier
Cavalière
Corniche des Maures
D559
Le Lavandou
Cap Nègre
Baie du Gaou
Plage de la Faviere
Côte d'Azur
Cap Bénat
Cap Blanc
Île du Levant
Grand-Avis
Île de Bagaud
Port-Cros
Pointe Maupertuis
Île de Port-Cros
D
E
F
5
4
3
2
1

194
A
B
C
5
4
3
2
1
Bagnols-sur-Cèze
Orsan
N580
St-Marcel-de Carceiret
Seynes
La Bruguière
St-Laurent-la-Vernède
Cavillarques
N86
Laudun
Tresques
Fontarèches
St-Pons-la-Calm
Connaux
Belvézet
Le Pin
St-Paul-les-Fonts
Euzet
GARD
Gaujac
St-Jean-de-Ceyrargues
Masmolène
St-Victor-la-Coste
La Capelle-et-Masmolène
Baron
Foissac
Montaren-et-St-Médiers
Serviers-et-Labaume
St-Hippolyte-de-Montaigu
Pouzilhac
D981
N106
Ners
Massanes
Cruviers
Uzès
Valliguières
184
Boucoiran
Brignon
Garrigues
Arpaillargues-et-Aureillac
St-Maximin
St-Hilaire-d'Ozilhan
Lédignan
Moussac
Bourdic
Sauzet
Vers-Pont-du-Gard
E15 A9
Aigremont
D981
St-Geniès-de-Malgoires
Collias
Remoulins
Estézargues
Montignargues
Gard ou Gardon
Pont du Gard
Domazan
Montagnac
La Calmette
Fournès
Moulézan
St-Bauzély
Sernhac
Théziers
Fons
204
Pic de Guerre
Montmirat
Gajan
Aramon
St-Mamert-du-Gard
Parignargues
Les Fontilles
Meynes
Montfrin
D2
D999
N106
N86
Marguerittes
Vallabrègues
Combas
Montpezat
NÎMES
Comps
Redessan
D999
St-Côme-et-Maruéjols
Clarensac
Caveirac
Vistre
Rodilhan
Jonquières-St-Vincent
Manduel
St-Dionisy
Langlade
Beaucaire
Taras
Caissargues
Bouillargues
Calvisson
E15 A9
Aujargues
Nages-et-Solorgues
Milhaud
N113
D38
Boissières
Garons
Congénies
Bernis
Aubord
Bellegarde
Aubais
Aigues-Vives
Uchaud
Rhône
N570
Vestric-et-Candiac
Mus
Vergèze
Générac
N113
Fontv
Codognan
Gallargues-le-Montueux
Beauvoisin
Abb
N113
Fourques
Lunel
Aimargues
Vauvert
GARD
St-Gilles
Arles
Le Cailar
N572
Saliers
Marsillargues
N572
St-Just
St-Laurent-d'Aigouze
Étang de Grey
Étang de Scamandre
St-Nazaire-de-Pézan
Vidourle
D979
Rhône à Sète
Étang du Charnier
Petit Rhône
La Camargue
D58
Aigues-Mortes
Étang du Lairan
Parc Naturel Régional de Camargue
Le Boucanet
Étang de la Ville
Étang de Vaccarès
Le Grau-du-Roi
Étang des Fourneaux
Étang des Caitives
Étang de Consecanière
Étang du Repaus
D570
190
Port Camargue
Étang du Roi
Étang du Cabri
Étang de Gines
Parc Natu Régiona de Car
Étang d'Icard
Stes-Maries-de-la-Mer
Golfe de Beauduc
Golfe du Lion

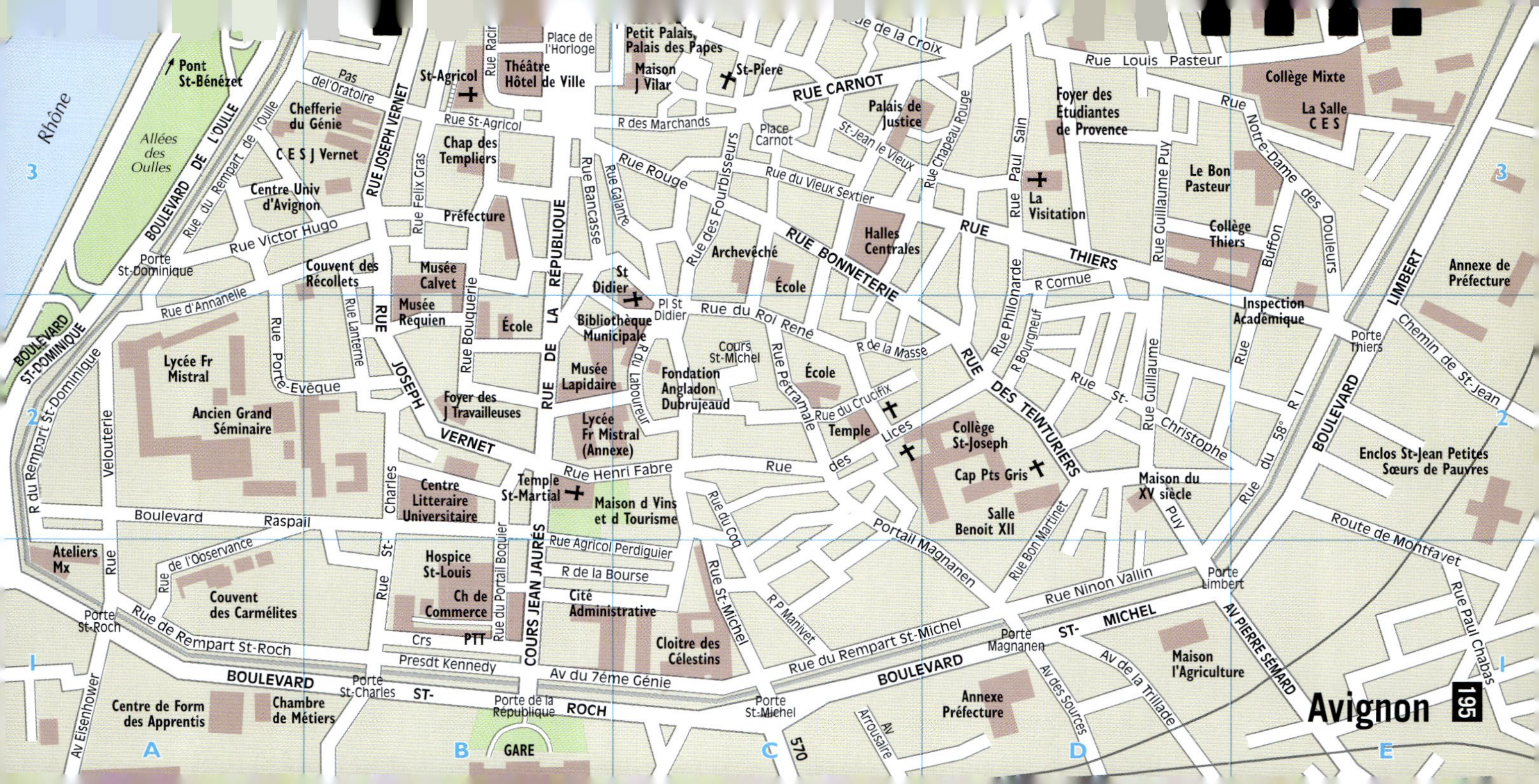
Avignon
195
Pont St-Bénézet
Rhône
Allées des Oulles
BOULEVARD DE L'OULLE
Rue du Rempart de l'Oulle
Pas de l'Oratoire
Chefferie du Génie
C E S J Vernet
Centre Univ d'Avignon
Rue Victor Hugo
Porte St-Dominique
BOULEVARD ST-DOMINIQUE
R du Rempart St-Dominique
Rue d'Annanelle
Lycée Fr Mistral
Ancien Grand Séminaire
Rue Porte-Evêque
Rue Lanterne
Couvent des Récollets
RUE JOSEPH VERNET
St-Agricol
Rue St-Agricol
Rue Racine
Théâtre Hôtel de Ville
Place de l'Horloge
Petit Palais, Palais des Papes
Maison J Vilar
St-Pierre
R des Marchands
Chap des Templiers
Rue Felix Gras
Préfecture
Musée Calvet
Musée Requien
Rue Bouquerie
École
RUE DE LA RÉPUBLIQUE
Rue Bancasse
Rue Galante
Rue Rouge
St Didier
Pl St Didier
Bibliothèque Municipale
R du Laboureur
Musée Lapidaire
Lycée Fr Mistral (Annexe)
Foyer des J Travailleuses
RUE JOSEPH VERNET
Velouterie
Boulevard Raspail
Rue St-Charles
Centre Litteraire Universitaire
Temple St-Martial
Maison d Vins et d Tourisme
Rue Henri Fabre
Ateliers Mx
Rue de l'Observance
Couvent des Carmélites
Porte St-Roch
Rue de Rempart St-Roch
Hospice St-Louis
Ch de Commerce
Rue du Portail Boquier
PTT
Crs Presdt Kennedy
COURS JEAN JAURÈS
Rue Agricol Perdiguier
R de la Bourse
Cité Administrative
Cloitre des Célestins
Av du 7ème Génie
BOULEVARD ST-ROCH
Porte St-Charles
Porte de la République
GARE
Centre de Form des Apprentis
Chambre de Métiers
Av Eisenhower
RUE CARNOT
Rue de la Croix
Palais de Justice
Place Carnot
St-Jean le Vieux
Rue Chapeau Rouge
Rue du Vieux Sextier
Rue des Fourbisseurs
Archevêché
École
RUE BONNETERIE
Halles Centrales
Rue du Roi René
Cours St-Michel
Fondation Angladon Dubrujeaud
Rue Pétramale
École
Rue du Crucifix
Temple
R de la Masse
Rue des Lices
Collège St-Joseph
Cap Pts Gris
Salle Benoit XII
Portail Magnanen
Rue du Coq
Rue St-Michel
R P Manivet
Rue du Rempart St-Michel
Porte St-Michel
570
Av Arrousaire
Annexe Préfecture
Av des Sources
Porte Magnanen
BOULEVARD ST-MICHEL
Av de la Trillade
Maison l'Agriculture
AV PIERRE SÉMARD
Rue Paul Chabas
Rue Ninon Vallin
Rue Bon Martinet
Porte Limbert
Route de Montfavet
RUE DES TEINTURIERS
R Bourgneuf
Rue Philonarde
R Cornue
RUE THIERS
Rue Paul Saïn
La Visitation
Foyer des Etudiantes de Provence
Rue Louis Pasteur
Rue Guillaume Puy
Le Bon Pasteur
Collège Thiers
Rue Buffon
Rue Notre-Dame des Douleurs
Collège Mixte
La Salle C E S
Inspection Académique
Rue St-Christophe
Rue Guillaume Puy
Maison du XV siècle
Rue du 58° R I
BOULEVARD LIMBERT
Porte Thiers
Chemin de St-Jean
Annexe de Préfecture
Enclos St-Jean Petites Sœurs de Pauvres
A
B
C
D
E
1
2
3

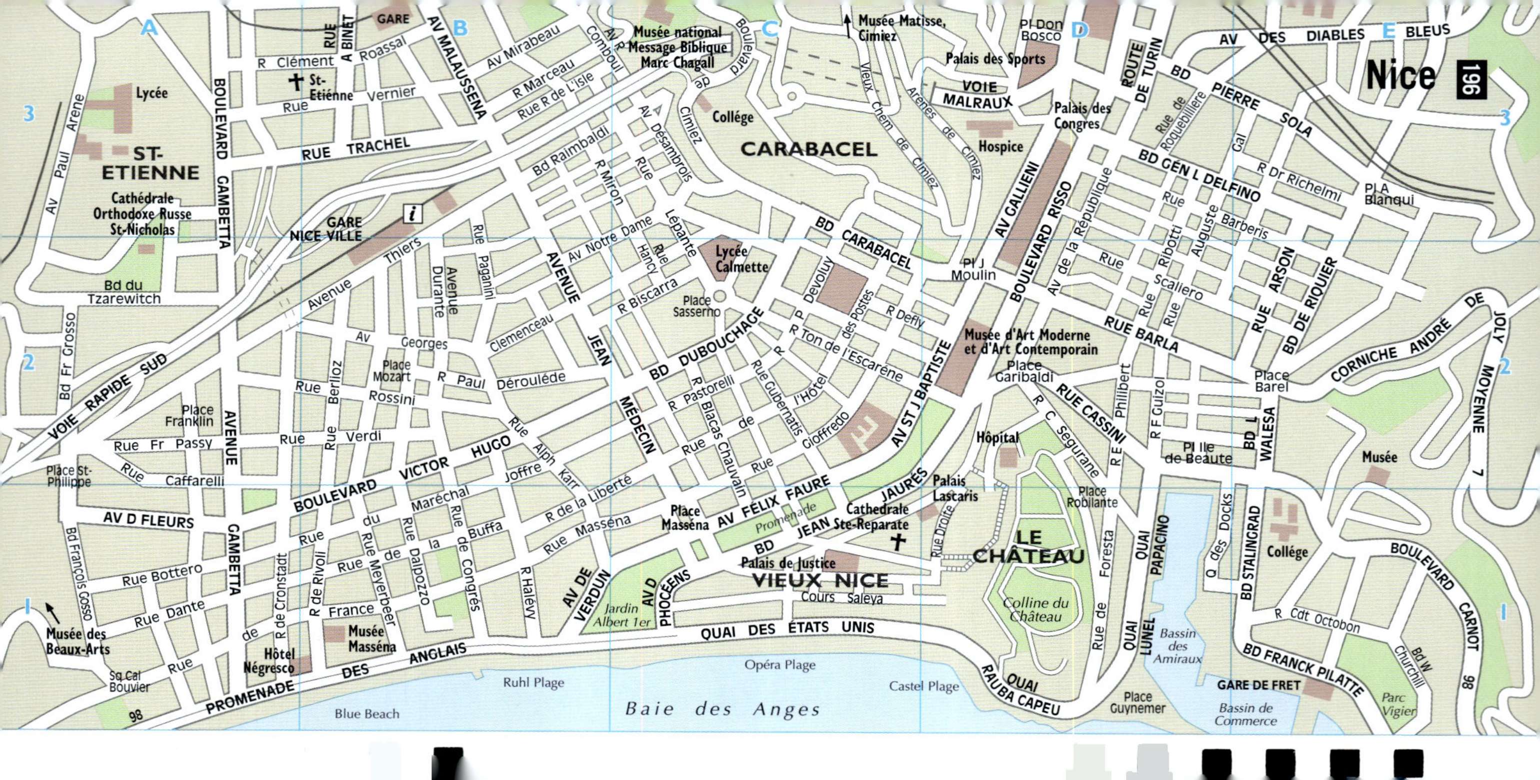
Nice
VIEUX NICE
LE CHÂTEAU
CARABACEL
ST-ETIENNE
Baie des Anges
Colline du Château
Musée Matisse, Cimiez
Musée national Message Biblique Marc Chagall
Musée d'Art Moderne et d'Art Contemporain
Musée Masséna
Musée des Beaux-Arts
Musée
Palais des Sports
Palais des Congres
Palais Lascaris
Palais de Justice
Cathedrale Ste-Reparate
Cathédrale Orthodoxe Russe St-Nicholas
Hôtel Négresco
Hôpital
Hospice
Lycée Calmette
Lycée
Collège
GARE NICE VILLE
GARE
GARE DE FRET
Bassin de Commerce
Bassin des Amiraux
Jardin Albert 1er
Parc Vigier
Promenade
Castel Plage
Opéra Plage
Ruhl Plage
Blue Beach
PROMENADE DES ANGLAIS
QUAI DES ÉTATS UNIS
QUAI RAUBA CAPEU
QUAI LUNEL
QUAI PAPACINO
BD FRANCK PILATTE
BD STALINGRAD
BOULEVARD CARNOT
Bd W Churchill
MOYENNE CORNICHE ANDRE DE JOLY
BD DE RIQUIER
RUE ARSON
BD L WALESA
RUE BARLA
RUE CASSINI
BOULEVARD RISSO
AV GALLIENI
AV ST J BAPTISTE
BD JEAN JAURÉS
AV FELIX FAURE
BD DUBOUCHAGE
BD CARABACEL
AVENUE JEAN MÉDECIN
BOULEVARD VICTOR HUGO
BOULEVARD GAMBETTA
AVENUE GAMBETTA
AV MALAUSSENA
RUE TRACHEL
VOIE RAPIDE SUD
AV D FLEURS
BD GEN L DELFINO
BD PIERRE SOLA
ROUTE DE TURIN
AV DES DIABLES BLEUS
VOIE MALRAUX
Boulevard de Cimiez
Arènes de Cimiez
Vieux Chem de Cimiez
Place Masséna
Place Garibaldi
Place Barel
Place Robilante
Place Sasserno
Place Mozart
Place Franklin
Place Guynemer
Place St-Philippe
Pl J Moulin
Pl Don Bosco
Pl Ile de Beaute
Pl A Blanqui
Cours Saleya
Rue Droite
Rue de Foresta
R C Segurane
R F Guizot
R E Philibert
Av de la République
Av Désambrois
Av Notre Dame
Rue Lépante
Rue Hancy
R Biscarra
R Pastorelli
Rue Blacas
Rue de Chauvain
Rue Gubernatis
R Gioffredo
R P Devoluy
R de l'Hôtel des Postes
R Ton de l'Escarène
R Defly
R Miron
Bd Raimbaldi
Av R Comboul
Av Mirabeau
R Marceau
Rue R de L'isle
Roassal
R Clément
Rue Vernier
RUE A BINET
St-Étienne
R Halévy
R de la Liberté
Rue Masséna
Rue Alph Karr
Rue Paganini
Avenue Durante
Av Georges Clemenceau
R Paul Déroulède
Rue Rossini
Rue Verdi
Rue Berlioz
Rue de la Buffa
Rue Maréchal Joffre
Rue de Congrès
Rue Dalpozzo
Rue Meyerbeer
Rue de France
R de Rivoli
R de Cronstadt
Avenue Thiers
Rue Fr Passy
Rue Caffarelli
Rue Bottero
Rue Dante
Bd François Gosso
Sq Cal Bouvier
Bd du Tzarewitch
Av Paul Arene
Bd Fr Grosso
Q des Docks
R Cdt Octobon
R Dr Richelmi
Rue de Roquebilliere
Cal
Rue Auguste Barberis
Rue Ribotti
Rue Scaliero
AV D PHOCÉENS
AV DE VERDUN
98
7
1
2
3
A
B
C
D
E

Monaco
MONTE-CARLO
LA CONDAMINE
MONACO-VILLE
FONTVIEILLE
Port de Monaco
Port de Fontvieille
Casino
Salle Garnier
Complexe des Spélugues
Centre de Congrès Auditorium
Forum Grimaldi
Jardins Larvotto
Jardin Japonais
Sporting Club d'Eté
Sporting Club d'Hiver
Place du Casino
Jardins du Casino
C C le Métropole
C C les A Lumières
Radio Monte-Carlo
Église Ste-Dévote
Place Ste Dévote
St-Charles
O T
Théâtre Princesse Grace
Douanes Capitainerie
Automobile Club
Stade Nautique Rainier III
Centre Admin
Bibliothèque
Square Gastaud
Théâtre des Variétés
Gare SNCF
Place d'Armes
Palais Princier
Jardin Animalier
Centre d'Acclim Zoologique
Place du Palais
Palais de Justice
Musée
Cathédrale
Mairie
Lycée
Ministère d'Etat
Place de la Visitation
Chapelle de la Visitation
Musée Océanographique
Jardins St-Martin
Pointe St-Martin
Pointe de la Poudrière
Théâtre du Port Antoine
Yacht Club
Pointe Sainte-Barbe
Place du Campanin
Parc Paysager de Fontvieille
C C de Fontvieille
Place du Canton
Église St-Martin
Jardin Exotique
Parc Princesse Antoinette
Pompiers
Square Lamarcq
École Primaire Jean Jaurès
Stade des Moneghetti
Boulevard du Larvotto
Boulevard des Moulins
Boulevard Princesse Charlotte
Av St-Michel
Avenue St-Michel
Rue Bellevue
Rue Bel Respiro
Boulevard de Suisse
Avenue de la Costa
Avenue Princesse Alice
Avenue de Monte Carlo
Avenue des Spélugues
Av de la Madone
Al des Boulingrins
Avenue Princesse Grace
Avenue de Grande-Bretagne
Avenue des Citronniers
Avenue de l'Hermitage
Avenue Dunant
Avenue d'Ostende
Avenue J F Kennedy
Quai des Etats-Unis
Boulevard Albert 1er
Quai Albert 1er
Rue Grimaldi
Rue Bretelle
Boulevard Rainier III
Boulevard Auréglia
Rue Aug Vento
Boulevard du Jardin Exotique
Boulevard de Belgique
Rue Bosio
Rue Jaurès
Rue J Bouin
Rue P Curie
R D Castillon
R H Labande
Avenue Hector Otto
Avenue Crovetto Frères
Av Prince P D Monaco
Rue d l Turbie
Rue Princesse Florestine
Rue S Reymond
Rue Princesse Caroline
Rue de Millo
Rue Saige
Avenue du Port
Boulevard Charles III
Avenue Prince Héréditaire Albert
Quai Antoine 1er
Avenue de la Quarantaine
Avenue de la Porte Neuve
Rue des Remparts
Rue Emile de Loth
Avenue St-Martin
Avenue Albert 1er
Quai des Sanbarbani
Av des Papalins
San Remo
Nice, Antibes, Cannes
N
A
B
C
D
E
1
2
3

Marseille

Marseille
AVENUES
LES GRANDS CARMES
LE PANIER
HÔTEL DE VILLE
BELSUNCE
THIERS
QUARTIER DE L'ARSENAL
CONCEPTION
BAILLE
NOTRE-DAME DUMONT
PREFECTURE
LE PHARO
Vieux Port
Bassin de la Grande Joliette
GARE MARITIME INTERNATIONALE
Cathédrale la Major
Fort St-Jean
Chateau d'If
Port de Plaisance
Port de la Réserve
Bas Fort St-Nicolas
Rowing Club
Jardin du Pharo
Institut Pasteur
Fort d'Entrecasteaux
Fort St-Nicolas
Caserne d'Aurelle
Théâtre National de Marseille la Criée
Musée du Albrechit
Lycée Technologique du Rempart
Basilique Notre-Dame de la Garde
Institut des Sourds Muets et Aveugles
Jardin P Puget
Église St-Philippe Notre-Dame de Lourdes
Banque de France
Préfecture des Boudes-du-Rhone
Hôpital M Levy
Couvent du Refuge
Hôpital de la Conception
École de Méd
École d'Ingénieurs
Place Jean Jaurès
Notre-Dame du Mont Cours Julien
Bibliothèque Collège et Lycée Thiers
Théâtre du Gymnase
Université de Droit d'Economie et des Sciences d'Art Marseille
Eglise des Réformés St-Vincent de Paul
Musée d'Histoire
Musée de la Mode
Palais de la Bours
Vieux-Port Hôtel de Ville
Opéra Municipal
Musée Cantini
Lycée
Palais de Justice
Collège Anatole France
Théâtre Grec
Musée des Docks Romains
Hôpital de l'Hôtel Dieu
La Vieille Charité
Hôtel de la Marine
Hôtel de Région
Cocbert Hotel de la Région
Les Carmes
Quai du Port
Quai de Rive Neuve
La Canebière
Cours Belsunce
Rue de la République
Tunnel St-Laurent
Tunnel Prado Carénage
Boulevard Charles Livon
Boulevard de la Corderie
Cours Pierre Puget
Rue Paradis
Rue de Rome
Cours Lieutaud
Boulevard Baille
Boulevard de la Libération
Bd National
Bd Garibaldi
Bd Dugommier
Bd d'Athènes
Av Pasteur
Av Robert Schuman
Quai de la Joliette

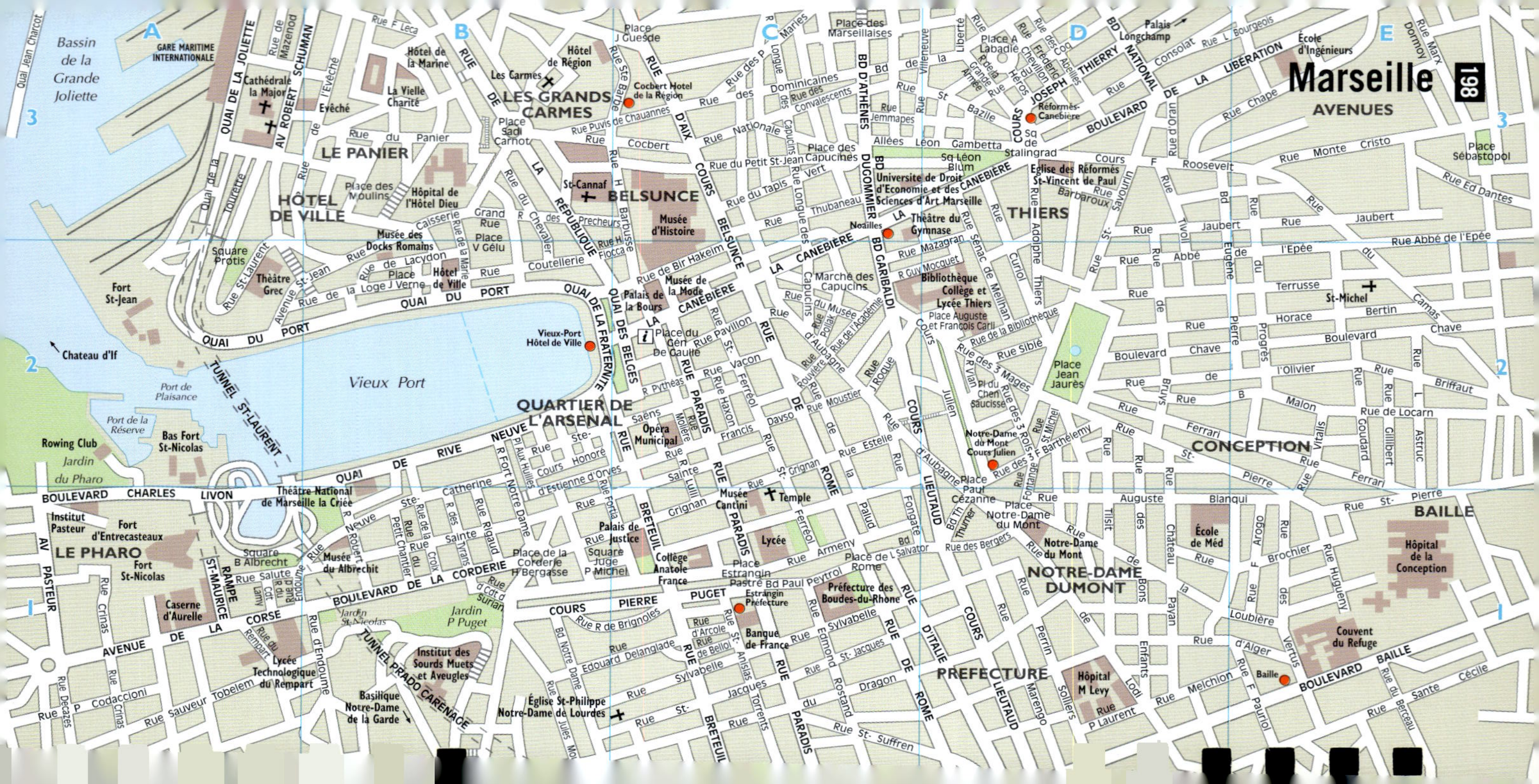

STREET INDEX

Avignon

58° R I, Rue du 195 E2
7éme Génie, Avenue du 195 B1
Agricol Perdiguier, Rue 195 B1
Annanelle, Rue d' 195 A2
Arrousaire, Avenue 195 C1
Bancasse, Rue 195 B3
Bon Martinet, Rue 195 D1
Bonneterie, Rue 195 C3
Bouquerie, Rue 195 B2
Bourgneuf, Rue 195 D2
Bourse, Rue de la 195 B1
Buffon, Rue 195 E2
Carnot, Place 195 C3
Carnot, Rue 195 C3
Chapeau Rouge, Rue 195 D3
Coq, Rue du 195 C2
Cornue, Rue 195 D3
Croix, Rue de la 195 C3
Crucifix, Rue du 195 C2
Eisenhower, Avenue 195 A1
Felix Gras, Rue 195 B3
Fourbisseurs, Rue des 195 C3
Galante, Rue 195 C3
Guillaume Puy, Rue 195 D2
Henri Fabre, Rue 195 B2
l'Horloge, Place de 195 B3
Jean Jaures, Cours 195 B1
Joseph Vernet, Rue195 B3
Laboureur, Rue du 195 C2
Lanterne, Rue 195 B2
Lices, Rue des 195 C2
Limbert, Boulevard 195 E2
Louis Pasteur, Rue 195 D3
Marchands, Rue des 195 C3
Masse, Rue de la 195 C2
Moliére, Rue 195 B3
Montfavet, Route de 195 E2
Ninon Vallin, Rue 195 D1
Notre-Dame des Douleurs, Rue 195 E3
l'Observance, Rue de 195 A1
Oratoire, Pas del' 195 B3
l'Oulle, Boulevard de 195 A3
Paul Chabas, Rue 195 E1
Paul Sain, Rue 195 D3
Pétramale, Rue 195 C2
Philonarde, Rue 195 D2
Pierre Sémard, Avenue 195 E1
P Manivet, Rue 195 C1
Portail Boquier, Rue du 195 B1
Portail Magnanen, Rue 195 C2
Porte-Evêque, Rue 195 A2
Presdt Kennedy, Cours 195 B1
Racine, Rue 195 B3
Raspail, Boulevard 195 A2
Rempart de l'Oulle, Rue du 195 A3
Rempart St-Dominique, Rue du 195 A2
Rempart St-Michel, Rue du 195 C1
Rempart St-Roch, Rue de 195 A1
République, Rue de la 195 B2
Roi René, Rue du 195 C2
Rouge, Rue 195 C3
St-Agricol, Rue 195 B3
St-Charles, Rue 195 B1
St-Christophe, Rue 195 D2
St-Didier, Place 195 C2
St-Dominique, Boulevard 195 A2
St-Jean, Chemin de 195 E2
St-Jean le Vieux 195 C3
St-Michel, Boulevard 195 C1
St-Michel, Cours 195 C2
St-Michel, Rue 195 C1
St-Roch, Boulevard 195 A1
Sources, Avenue des 195 D1
Teinturiers, Rue des 195 D2
Thiers, Rue 195 D3
Trillade, Avenue de la 195 D1
Velouterie, Rue 195 A1
Victor Hugo, Rue 195 A3
Vieux Sextier, Rue du 195 C3

Marseille

3 F Barthélemy, Rue des 198 D2
3 Mages, Rue des 198 D2
3 Rois, Rue des 198 D2
Abbé de l'Epée, Rue 198 D2
Abeilles, Rue des 198 D3
l'Académie, Rue de 198 C2
Adolphe Thiers, Rue 198 D3
Aix, Rue d' 198 C3
A Labadié, Place 198 D3
Alger, Rue d' 198 D1
Arcole, Rue d' 198 C1
Armeny, Rue 198 C1
Athènes, Boulevard d' 198 C3
Aubagne, Rue d' 198 C2
Auguste et François Carli, Place 198 D2
Baille, Boulevard 198 E1
B Albrecht, Square 198 A1
Barbaroux, Rue 198 D3
Belges, Quai des 198 C2
Belloi, Rue de 198 C1
Belsunce, Cours 198 C3
Berceau, Rue du 198 E1
Bergers, Rue des 198 D1
Bibliothèque, Rue de la 198 D2
Bir Hakeim, Rue de 198 C2
Blanqui, Rue Auguste 198 D1
B Malon, Rue 198 D2
Bons Enfants, Rue des 198 D2
Breteuil, Rue 198 C2
Briffaut, Rue 198 E2
Brochier, Rue 198 D1
Bruys, Rue de 198 D2
Caisserie, Rue 198 B2
Camas, Rue du 198 E3
Capucines, Place des 198 C3
Cdt d Surian, Rue d' 198 B1
Cdt Lamy, Rue du 198 A1
Chape, Rue 198 E3
Charcot, Quai Jean 198 A3
Charles Livon, Boulevard 198 A1
Château Payan, Rue 198 D2
Chave, Boulevard 198 D2
Chen Saucisse, Place du 198 D2
Chevalier, Rue du 198 B3
Cocbert, Rue 198 B3
Codaccioni, Rue P 198 A1
Consolat, Rue 198 D3
Convalescents, Rue des 198 C3
Coq, Rue du 198 D3
Corderie, Boulevard de la 198 B1
Corderie H Bergasse, Place de la 198 B1
Corse, Avenue de la 198 A1
Coutellerie, Rue 198 B2
Crinas, Rue 198 A1
Croix, Rue de la 198 B1
Curiol, Rue 198 D3
Decazes, Rue 198 A1
Dominicaines, Rue des 198 C3
Dragon, Rue du 198 C1
Dugommier, Boulevard 198 C3
Ed Dantes, Rue 198 E3
Edmond Rostand, Rue 198 C1
Edouard Delanglade, Rue 198 C1
Endoume, Rue d' 198 B1
Estelie, Rue 198 C2
Estrangin Pastré, Place 198 C1
Eugène Pierre, Boulevard 198 D2
l'Evêché, Rue de 198 B3
F Arogo, Rue 198 E1
Ferrari, Rue 198 D2
F Leca, Rue 198 B3
Fongate, Rue 198 C2
Fontange, Rue 198 D2
Fortia, Rue 198 B1
Fort Notre Dame, Rue 198 B2
F Pauriol, Rue 198 E1
Francis Davso, Rue 198 C2
Fraternite, Quai de la 198 B2
Fréderic Chevillon, Rue 198 D3
F Roosevelt, Cours 198 D3
Garibaldi, Boulevard 198 C2
Gén De Gaulle, Place du 198 C2
Gillibert, Rue 198 E2
Goudard, Rue 198 E2
Grande Armée, Rue de la 198 D3
Grand Rue 198 B3
Grignan, Rue 198 B1
Guy Mocquet, Rue 198 C2
Haxon, Rue 198 C2
H Barbusse, Rue 198 C3
Héros, Rue 198 D3
H Fiocca, Rue 198 B2
Honoré d'Estienne d'Orves, Cours 198 B2
Horace Bertin, Rue 198 D2
Hugueny, Rue 198 E1
Huilles, Place aux 198 B2
Italie, Rue d' 198 C1
Jaubert, Rue 198 D3
Jean Jaurès, Place 198 D2
Jemmapes, Rue 198 C3
J Guesde, Place 198 C3
Joliette, Quai de la 198 A3
Joseph Thierry, Cours 198 D3
J Roque, Rue 198 C2
Juge P Michel, Square 198 B1
Jules Moulet, Rue 198 B1
Julien, Cours 198 D2
J Verne, Place 198 B2
La Canebière 198 C2
Lacydon, Rue de 198 B2
L Astruc, Rue 198 E2
L Bourgeois, Rue 198 D3
Léon Blum, Sq 198 D3
Léon Gambetta, Allées 198 C3
Libération, Boulevard de la 198 D3
Liberté, Boulevard de la 198 C3
Lieutaud, Cours 198 C2
Locarn, Rue de 198 E2
Lodi, Rue de 198 D1
Loge, Rue de la 198 B2
L'Olivier, Rue de 198 D2
Longue des Capucins, Rue 198 C3
Loubière, Rue de la 198 D1
L Salvator, Boulevard 198 C1
Lulli, Rue 198 C2
Marengo, Rue 198 D1
Marie, Rue de la 198 B3
Marseillaises, Place des 198 C3
Marx Dormoy, Rue 198 E3
Mazagran, Rue 198 C2
Mazenod, Rue de 198 A3
Melchion, Rue 198 D1
Molière, Rue 198 C2
Monte Cristo, Rue 198 E3
Moulins, Place des 198 B3
Moustier, Rue 198 C2
Musée, Rue du 198 C2
National, Boulevard 198 D3
Nationale, Rue 198 C3
Neuve Ste-Catherine, Rue 198 B1
Notre Dame, Boulevard 198 B1
Notre-Dame du Mont, Place 198 D1
Oran, Rue d' 198 D3
Palud, Rue de la 198 C2
Panier, Rue du 198 B3
Paradis, Rue 198 C2
Pasteur, Avenue 198 A1
Paul Cézanne, Place 198 D2
Paul Peytrol, Boulevard 198 C1
Pavillon, Rue 198 C2
Perrin Solliers, Rue 198 D1
Petit Chantier, Rue du 198 B1
Petit St-Jean, Rue du 198 C3
Pierre Puget, Cours 198 B1
P Laurent, Rue 198 D1
P Maries, Rue des 198 C3
Pollak, Rue 198 C2
Port, Quai du 198 B2
Precheurs, Rue des 198 B3
Progrès, Rue du 198 E3
Protis, Square 198 A2
Puvis de Chauannes, Rue 198 B3
R de Brignoles, Rue 198 B1
Rempart, Rue du 198 A1
République, Rue de la 198 B3
Rigaud, Rue 198 B1
Rive Neuve, Quai de 198 B2
Robert, Rue 198 B1
Robert Schuman, Avenue 198 A3
Rome, Place de 198 C1
Rome, Rue de 198 C2
Rouvière, Rue 198 C2
Sadi Carnot, Place 198 B3
St-Anislas Torrents, Rue 198 C1
St Bazile, Rue 198 C3
Ste Barbe, Rue 198 C3
Sainte, Rue 198 B1
Ste-Saëns, Rue 198 B2
St-Ferréol, Rue 198 C2
St-Jacques, Rue 198 C1
St-Jean, Avenue 198 A2

St-Laurent, Rue 198 A2
St-Maurice, Rampe 198 A1
St Michel, Rue 198 D2
St-Pierre, Rue 198 D2
St-Savourin, Rue 198 D2
St-Suffren, Rue 198 C1
Salute, Rue 198 A1
Sante Cécile, Rue 198 E1
Sauveur Tobelem, Rue 198 A1
Sébastopol, Place 198 E3
Sénac de Meilhan, Rue 198 D3
Sibié, Rue 198 D2
Stalingrad, Sq de 198 D3
Sylvabelle, Rue 198 C1
Tapis Vert, Rue du 198 C3
Terrusse, Rue 198 D2
Th Thurner, Boulevard 198 D1
Thubaneau, Rue 198 C3
Tilsit, Rue 198 D2
Tivoli, Rue 198 D3
Tourette, Quai de la 198 A3
Tunnel Prado Carénage 198 B1
Tunnel St-Laurent 198 A2
Tyrans, Rue des 198 B1
Vacon R Pythéas, Rue 198 C2
Vertus, Rue des 198 E1
V Gélu, Place 198 B3
Vian, Rue 198 D2
Villeneuve, Rue 198 C3
Vitalis, Rue 198 E2

Monaco

Albert 1er, Boulevard 182 B2
Albert 1er, Quai 182 B2
Alsace, Avenue d' 182 B4
Anciens, Boulevard des 183 D5
Antoine 1er, Quai 182 B2
Armes, Place d' 182 A2
Aug Vento, Rue 182 A3
Belgique, Boulevard de 182 A3
Bellevue, Rue 182 C4
Bel Respiro, Rue 182 C4
Bosio, Rue 182 A3
Boulingrins, Al des 183 D3
Bretelle Auréglia, Rue 182 A3
Bretelle du Centre 182 B5
Canton, Place du 182 A2
Carnier, Avenue du 183 D4
Casino, Place du 183 D3
C Blanc, Avenue 183 D4
Charles III, Boulevard 182 A2
Ch de l'Usine Electrique 182 B4
Chemin de la Bordina 182 B5
Chemin de la Turbie 182 A5
Citronniers, Avenue des 183 E4
Combattants d'Afrique du Nord 183 D5
Costa, Avenue de la 182 C3
Crém du Riviera Langevin, Rue de la 182 C5
Crovetto Frères, Avenue 182 A3
D Castillon, Rue 182 A4
Emile de Loth, Rue 182 B1
Etats-Unis, Quai des 182 C3
France, Boulevard de 183 D4
Gastaud, Square 182 B2
Gaulle, Avenue de 183 D4
Grande-Bretagne, Avenue de 183 E4
Grimaldi, Rue 182 B3
Guynemer, Boulevard 183 E5
Hector Otto, Avenue 182 A3
Hermitage, Avenue de l' 182 C3
H Labande, Rue 182 A3
I Turbie, Rue d 182 A2
Italie, Boulevard d' 183 E4
Jardin Exotique, Boulevard du 182 A3
Jaurès, Rue 182 A4
J Bouin, Rue 182 A4
J F Kennedy, Avenue 182 C3
Lacets, Boulevard 183 F5
Lamarcq, Square 182 B4
Larvotto, Boulevard du 183 E3
Libération, Place de la 183 D5
Lucioles, Rue des 182 C5
Madone, Avenue de la 183 D4
Maréchal Foch, Avenue du 182 C4
Martys de la Rèsistance, Rue des 182 B4
Millo, Rue de 182 A2
Monte Carlo, Avenue de 183 D3
Moulins, Boulevard des 183 D4
Moulins, Place des 183 E4
Moyenne Corniche, Route de la 182 C5
Orchidèes, Rue des 183 F5
Ostende, Avenue d' 182 C3
Palais, Place du 182 A2
Pasteur, Rue 182 B4
Paul Doumer, Avenue 182 A4
P Curie, Rue 182 A4
Port, Avenue du 182 A2
Porte Neuve, Avenue de la 182 B2
Prince P D Monaco, Avenue 182 A3
Princesse Alice, Avenue 183 D3
Princesse Caroline, Rue 182 A2
Princesse Charlotte, Boulevard 182 C4
Princesse Florestine, Rue 182 A2
Princesse Grace, Avenue 183 E3
Prof, Avenue de 182 C4
Quarantaine, Avenue de la 182 B2
Rainier III, Boulevard 182 A3
Raynal, Place Rue 183 E5
Remparts, Rue des 182 B2
République, Boulevard de la 183 D4
Saige, Rue 182 B2
Ste-Cecile, Avenue 182 C4
Ste Dévote, Place 182 B3
St-Martin, Avenue 182 B1
St-Michel, Avenue 182 C4
St-Michel, Avenue 183 D4
Sanbarbani, Quai des 182 A1
Serres, Route des 183 E5
Source, Place de la 182 C4
Spélugues, Avenue des 183 D3
S Reymond, Rue 182 B3
Suisse Dunant, Boulevard de 182 C3
Turbie, Boulevard de la 183 E5
Verdun, Avenue de 183 E5
Victor Hugo, Rue 182 A4
Villaine, Avenue de 182 C4
Visitation, Place de la 182 B1

Nice

A Blanqui, Place 196 E3
Alph Karr, Rue 196 B2
André de Joly Moyenne 7, Corniche 196 E2
Anglais, Promenade des 196 A1
Arson, Rue 196 E2
Auguste Gal, Rue 196 D2
Barberis, Rue 196 D3
Barel, Place 196 E2
Barla, Rue 196 D2
Beaute, Place Ile de 196 D2
Berlioz, Rue 196 B2
Binet, Rue a 196 B3
Biscarra, Rue 196 C2
Blacas Chauvain, Rue 196 C2
Bottero, Rue 196 A1
Buffa, Rue de la 196 B1
Caffarelli, Rue 196 A2
Cal Bouvier, Sq 196 A1
Carabacel, Boulevard 196 C3
Carnot 98, Boulevard 196 E1
Cassini, Rue 196 D2
Cdt Octobon, Rue 196 E1
Chem de Cimiez, Vieux 196 C3
Cimiez, Arenes de 196 C3
Cimiez, Boulevard de 196 C3
Clément Roassal, Rue 196 A3
Congrés, Rue de 196 B1
Cronstadt, Rue de 196 A1
C Segurane, Rue 196 D2
Dalpozzo, Rue 196 B1
Dante, Rue 196 A1
Defly, Rue 196 C2
Désambrois, Avenue 196 C3
Diables Bleus, Avenue des 196 E3
Docks, Quai des 196 D1
Don Bosco, Place 196 D3
Droite, Rue 196 D1
Dr Richelmi, Rue 196 E3
Dubouchage, Boulevard 196 C2
Durante, Avenue 196 B2
E Philibert, Rue 196 D2
Etats Unis, Quai des 196 C1
Félix Faure, Avenue196 C1
Fleurs, Avenue d' 196 A1
F Guizol, Rue 196 D2
Foresta, Rue de 196 D1
France, Rue de 196 A1
Franck Pilatte, Boulevard 196 E1
François Gosso, Boulevard196 A1
Franklin, Place 196 A2
Fr Grosso, Boulevard 196 A2
Gallieni, Avenue 196 D3
Gambetta, Avenue 196 A2
Gambetta, Boulevard 196 A3
Garibaldi, Place 196 D2
Gén L Delfino, Boulevard 196 D3
Georges Clemenceau, Avenue 196 B2
Gioffredo, Rue 196 C2
Gubernatis, Rue 196 C2
Guynemer, Place 196 D1
Fr Passy, Rue 196 A2
Halévy, Rue 196 B1
Hancy, Rue 196 C2
Jean Jaurés, Boulevard 196 C1
Jean Médeci, Avenue 196 B2
J Moulin, Place 196 D2
Lépante, Rue 196 C3
L'Hôtel des Postes, Rue de 196 C2
Liberté, Rue de la 196 B1
L'isle, Rue R de 196 B3
Lunel, Quai 196 D1
L Walesa, Boulevard 196 E2
Malaussena, Avenue 196 B3
Malraux, Voie 196 D3
Marceau, Rue 196 B3
Maréchal Joffre, Rue du 196 B1
Massena, Place 196 C1
Masséna, Rue 196 B1
Meyerbeer, Rue 196 B1
Mirabeau, Avenue 196 B3
Miron, Rue 196 B3
Mozart, Place 196 B2
Notre Dame, Avenue 196 B2
Paganini, Rue 196 B2
Papacino, Quai 196 D1
Pastorelli, Rue 196 C2
Paul Arene, Avenue 196 A3
Paul Déroulède, Rue 196 B2
P Devoluy, Rue196 C2
Phocéens, Avenue d' 196 C1
Pierre Sola, Boulevard 196 D3
Raimbaldi, Boulevard 196 B3
Rapide Sud, Voie 196 A2
Rauba Capeu, Quai 196 D1
R Comboul, Avenue 196 B3
République, Avenue de la 196 D2
Ribotti, Rue 196 D2
Riquier, Boulevard de 196 E2
Risso, Boulevard 196 D2
Rivoli, Rue de 196 B1
Robilante, Place 196 D1
Roquebilliere, Rue de 196 D3
Rossini, Rue 196 B2
St J Baptiste, Avenue 196 C2
St-Philippe, Place 196 A2
Saleya, Cours 196 C1
Sasserno, Place 196 C2
Scaliero, Rue 196 D2
Stalingrad, Boulevard 196 E1
Thiers, Avenue 196 B2
Ton de l'Escaréne, Rue 196 C2
Trachel, Rue 196 B3
Turin, Route de 196 D3
Tzarewitch, Boulevard du 196 A2
Victor Hugo, Boulevard 196 B1
Verdi, Rue 196 B2
Verdun, Avenue de 196 B1
Vernier, Rue 196 B3
W Churchill, Boulevard 196 E1

Abbaye de Montmajour 126–127
Abbaye de Sénanque 15, 150–151
Abbaye de Silvacane 103–104
Abbaye de St-Pons 105
Abbaye du Thoronet 80
accommodation 29–30
Alpes-Maritimes 58–59
bed-and-breakfast 29
Camargue area 130–131
camping 30
hotels 29
Marseille area 106–107
restaurants with rooms 20
self-catering 30
Var and Haute-Provence 84–85
Vaucluse 159–160
youth hostels 30
aerial tours 22, 62, 164
Aigues-Mortes 112, 126
Aiguines 174
air travel 24, 25, 177
Aix-en-Provence 10, 22, 28, 33, 90, 100–101, 109, 110, 166
Atelier Paul-Cézanne 10, 101
Cathédrale St-Sauveur 100
Musée Granet 101
Albaron 168
alcohol licensing laws 33
Alpes-Maritimes 35–62
accommodation 58–59
Antibes 55, 62
Biot 16, 55–56, 61
Cagnes-sur-Mer 56, 57
Cannes 22, 55, 62
children's activities 57
Corniches 44–47
eating out 59–60
entertainment 62
Fondation Maeght 51
Grasse 54, 57, 61
map 36–37
Menton 57
Monaco 48–50
Nice 8, 22, 33, 40–43, 61, 62
Parc National du Mercantour 13, 52–53
shopping 61
three-day itinerary 38–39
Vence 54
Villa Ephrussi de Rothschild 46, 56–57
Alyscamps 119–120
amusement park 80
Anatole Jakovsky International Museum of Modern Art 42
Ansouis 153, 154
Antibes 55, 62
Château Grimaldi 11, 55
Marineland 22, 57
Musée Picasso 11, 55
Apt 152, 154, 163
Arc de Triomphe 144, 145
architecture 15–17
Les Arènes, Arles 119, 121
Les Arènes, Nîmes 122, 123
Arles 8, 10, 15, 22, 28, 112, 119–121, 133, 134
Alyscamps 119–120
Les Arènes 119, 121
Cathédral St-Trophime 120–121
Fondation Van Gogh 121
Musée de l'Arles Antique 121
Muséon Arlaten 8, 121
Théâtre Antique 119
artists 9–11
Asian Arts Museum 42
Atelier Paul-Cézanne 10, 101
ATM cash dispensers 177
Aubagne 105, 109
Little World of Marcel Pagnol 7–8
Avignon 28, 33, 136, 140–143, 163, 164
Fondation Angladon Dubrujeaud 143
Musée Calvet 141, 142
Palais des Papes 141, 142, 143
Petit Palais 141, 143
Pont St-Bénézet 141–142
Villeneuve-lès-Avignon 142

banks 178
Barrage de Bimont 99, 166
beaches 22, 71
Beaulieu-sur-Mer 46
Villa Grecque Kérylos 46
Beaumes-de-Venise 158
bed-and-breakfast 29
Biot 16, 55–56, 61
Musée national Fernand Léger 56
Verrerie de Biot 16, 56, 61
boat trips 22, 97, 125, 134
Bonnieux 153, 154
bories 15, 150, 151
Bormes-les-Mimosas 79, 87
Bouches du Rhône 112
bouillabaisse 21
bowling 62, 110, 164
bullfighting 8, 122
buses
local 27–28
long-distance 27

café-bars 22, 33
Cagnes-sur-Mer 56, 57
Musée Renoir 9, 56
Calanques 12–13, 97
Camargue 8, 13, 22, 28, 116–118
tour 168–169
Camargue area 111–134
Abbaye de Montmajour 126–127
accommodation 130–131
Aigues-Mortes 112, 126
Arles 8, 10, 15, 22, 112, 119–121, 133, 134
children's activities 129
eating out 131–132
entertainment 134
Glanum 129
Les Baux-de-Provence 127–128
map 112–113
Nîmes 112, 122, 123
Pont du Gard 112, 122–123
shopping 133
Stes-Maries-de-la-Mer 124–125, 133
St-Rémy-de-Provence 128–129, 133, 134
Tarascon 129
three-day itinerary 114–115
camping 30
Camus, Albert 153
Cannes 22, 28, 55, 62
canoeing and kayaking 22, 34, 88
Cap de St-Tropez 71, 80

Cap Ferrat 46
Villa Ephrussi de Rothschild 46, 56–57
car rental 26
Carrée d'Art 122, 123
Casino (Monte-Carlo) 33, 49, 50, 62
casinos 33, 62, 110
Cassis 22, 97, 104–105
Castellane 172
Cathédrale des Images 128
Cavaillon 155
Musée Archéologique 155
cave complexes 22, 97, 128
Centre d'Art Présence Van Gogh 129
Centre d'Information La Capelière 117
ceramics 16, 81, 105, 109
Cézanne, Paul 10, 90, 98, 101
Chagall, Marc 43, 51, 54
Chaîne des Alpilles 13
Chaîne de l'Estaque 102
Chapelle du Rosaire 11, 54
Chapelle St-Pierre 47
Chartreuse de la Verne 79
Château de la Barben 103, 104
Château de Gordes 150, 151
Château d'If 94, 96
Château de Tarascon 129
Châteauneuf-du-Pape 144–145
Musée Père Anselme 144, 145
children 180
children's activities 22
Alpes-Maritimes 57
Camargue area 129
Marseille area 104
Var and Haute-Provence 80
Vaucluse 158
climate and seasons 176
climbing 34
clothing sizes 178
clubs 33
Cocteau, Jean 47, 57
Collobrières 79, 87
concessions 180
consulates and embassies 180
Corniches 44–47
Corniche de l'Esterel 12, 64, 77
Corniche Inférieure 44–45, 47
Corniche Sublime 75, 76
Grande Corniche 44
Moyenne Corniche 44
Côte d'Azur 12
credit and debit cards 32, 177
crime 179
La Croix de Provence 99
culture 6–8
currency 177
cycling 34, 164

Daudet, Alphonse 8
dental services 180
Dentelles de Montmirail 158
Digne-les-Bains 81–82, 87, 88
disabilities, travellers with 180
diving and snorkelling 73, 88, 97, 110
drinking water 180
driving
car rental 26
documents 26, 176
in Provence 26–27
regulations 26–27
to Provence 24
drugs and medicines 180
Ducasse, Alain 20, 21

eating out
Alpes-Maritimes 59–60
Camargue area 131–132
Marseille area 107–108
Var and Haute-Provence 85–86
Vaucluse 161–162
electricity 179
emergencies 179
En Vau 97
entertainment 33–34
Alpes-Maritimes 62
Camargue area 134
Marseille area 110
Var and Haute-Provence 88
Vaucluse 164
Entrevaux 82–83
Ermitage St-Pierre 127
Espace Van Gogh 120
Étang de Vaccarès 117, 168–169
Eurotunnel 24
Èze 22, 45, 61
Jardin Exotique 45

Ferrières 102
ferries 24, 177
festivals and events 8, 33
Alpes-Maritimes 56, 57, 62
Camargue area 129
Marseille area 101
Var and Haute-Provence 69, 78, 79, 82
Vaucluse 143, 144–145, 146, 149, 156
fishing 34
flora and fauna 13, 53, 116, 117, 123, 134
Fondation Angladon Dubrujeaud 143
Fondation Maeght 51
Fondation Van Gogh 121
Fontaine-de-Vaucluse 156–157
Le Monde Souterrain de Norbert Casteret 158
Moulin à Papier Vallis Clausa 157
Musée Pétrarque 157
Fontvieille 8
food and drink 31
drinking water 180
menu reader 182
Provençal cuisine 8, 19–21, 31
shopping for 32, 61, 109, 133, 163
wines 14, 31, 144–145, 158
see also eating out
football 34, 110
foreign exchange 177
Fréjus 77

***garrigue* 13, 123**
Gassin 78, 87
Gauguin, Paul 10, 120
Gémenos 105
Giens Peninsula 72
gifts and souvenirs 32, 87, 109, 133, 163
Gigondas 158
Giono, Jean 7
Glanum 129
glass-blowing 16, 56, 61
go-karting 57, 110
golf 34, 88

Gordes 22, 150–151
Abbaye de Sénanque 150–151
Château de Gordes 150, 151
Museum of Pol Mara 150
Village des Bories 150, 151
Gorges du Verdon 13, 22, 64, 74–76
drive with walks 172–174
Grace, Princess 49
Grasse 54, 57, 61
Gréoux-les-Bains 88
Grimaud 22, 78–79
Grottes de St-Cézaire 22
gypsies 124

hang-gliding 22
Haut-de-Cagnes 9
health 176, 180
helicopter rides 22
hilltop village 22, 45–46, 51, 78–79, 152
horse racing 34
horse-back riding 22, 34, 134
hot-air ballooning 164
hotels 29
see also accommodation
Hyères-les-Palmiers 72
Jardins Olbius-Riquier 72

ice-skating 62, 164
Îles d'Hyères 22, 73
insurance 26, 176, 180

Jardin Exotique, Èze 45
Jardin Exotique, Monaco 49, 50
Jardins Olbius-Riquier 72
Jonquières 102
Juan-les-Pins 22

La Palud-sur-Verdon 173–174
La Turbie 45
Trophée des Alpes 45
Lac du Bimont 99
Lac de Ste-Croix 74, 174
Lacoste 153
Lacroix, Christian 8, 119, 133
landscapes 12–13
language
menu reader 182
Provençal 6–7, 8
useful phrases 181
lavender 82
Léger, Fernand 56
Les Baux-de-Provence 127–128
Val d'Enfer 128
Ville Morte 127
Levant 73
L'Îsle 102
L'Îsle-sur-la-Sorgue 22, 163
Lourmarin 153
Lubéron 13, 136, 152–154
Luna Park 80

Maison Carrée 122, 123
Maison de Nostradamus 102, 103
Maison du Parc Naturel du Lubéron 152, 154
Manosque 7
Marineland 22, 57
marionette theatre 22, 110
markets 22, 32, 61, 87, 109, 155, 163
Marseille 22, 33, 90, 94–96, 109, 110
airport 25
Cathédrale de la Major 95
Château d'If 94, 96
Musée des Beaux-Arts 95
Musée Cantini 96
Musée des Docks Romains 95, 96
Musée d'Histoire de Marseille 95, 96
Musée d'Histoire Naturelle 95
Notre-Dame de la Garde 94
Palais Longchamp 95, 96
La Vieille Charité 95
Vieux Port 94
zoo 95
Marseille area 89–110
Abbaye de Silvacane 103–104
accommodation 106–107
Aix-en-Provence 10, 22, 33, 90, 100–101, 109, 110
Aubagne 7–8, 105, 109
Calanques 12–13, 97
Cassis 22, 97, 104–105
Château de la Barben 103, 104
children's activities 104
eating out 107–108
entertainment 110
Gémenos 105
map 90–91
Martigues 102
Mont Ste-Victoire 10, 90, 98–99
Salon-de-Provence 102–103
shopping 109
two-day itinerary 92–93
Martel, Édouard-Alfred 75
Martigues 102
mas and *bastide* 16–17
Massif de l'Esterel 77
Matisse, Henri 11, 43, 54
Mayle, Peter 17, 19, 136, 153, 154
medical treatment 180
Méjanes 168
Ménerbes 153
Menton 57
Musée Jean-Cocteau 57
Musée de la Préhistoire Régional 57
Palais Carnolès 57
Mistral, Frédéric 6, 7, 8, 121
Monaco 48–50
Casino 33, 49, 50, 62
La Condamine 49
Fontvieille 49, 57
Jardin Exotique 49, 50
Monaco-Ville 48–49
Monte-Carlo 48, 49
Musée Napoléon 49
Musée National 57
Musee Océanographique 22, 49, 50, 57
Palais Princier 49, 50
Princess Grace Rose Garden 49
Le Monde Souterrain de Norbert Casteret 158
money 177
Mont Ste-Victoire 10, 90, 98–99
Mont Ventoux 22, 157–158
Monte-Carlo 33, 48, 49
motor racing 34, 50
Mougins 11
Moulin à Papier Vallis Clausa 157
Moustiers-Ste-Marie 16, 22, 80–81, 87, 174

Musée de l'Annonciade 68, 69, 71
Musée Archéologique 155
Musée Archéologique de Cimiez 42, 43
Musée de l'Arles et de la Provence Antique 121
Musée de l'Armes et d'Histoire Militaire 103
Musée d'Art Moderne et d'Art Contemporain (MAMAC) 10, 43
Musée Baroncelli 125
Musée des Beaux-Arts 95
Musée Calvet 141, 142
Musée Cantini 96
Musée des Docks Romains 95, 96
Musée Granet 101
Musée Matisse 11, 43
Musée d'Histoire de Marseille 95, 96
Musée d'Histoire Naturelle 95
Musée Jean-Cocteau 57
Musée Napoléon 49
Musée national Fernand Léger 56
Musée national Message Biblique Marc Chagall 43
Musée National, Monaco 57
Musee Océanographique 22, 49, 50, 57
Musée Père Anselme 144, 145
Musée Pétrarque 157
Musée Picasso 11, 55
Musée de la Préhistoire des Gorges du Verdon 76
Musée de la Préhistoire Régional 57
Musée Renoir 9, 56
Musée Souleïado 16, 129
Musée Ziem 102
Muséon Arlaten 8, 121
Museum of Pol Mara 150
museum/monument opening hours 178
music and dance 33

national holidays 178
Nice 8, 22, 33, 40–43, 61, 62
  airport 24
  Anatole Jakovsky International Museum of Modern Art 42
  Asian Arts Museum 42
  Cathédrale Orthodoxe Russe St-Nicolas 42, 43
  Cimiez 42
  Colline du Château 41
  Hôtel Négresco 41
  Musée Archéologique de Cimiez 42, 43
  Musée d'Art Moderne et d'Art Contemporain (MAMAC) 10, 43
  Musée Matisse 11, 43
  Musée national Message Biblique Marc Chagall 43
  promenade des Anglais 41
  Roman sites 42
  Vieux Nice 42
nightlife 33
Nîmes 112, 122, 123
  airport 25
  Les Arènes 122, 123
  Carrée d'Art 122, 123
  Maison Carrée 122, 123
Nostradamus 90, 102, 103, 128

ochre industry 17, 156
opening hours 32, 178
Oppède-le-Vieux 153, 154
Orange 33, 146–147, 164
  Arc de Triomphe 144, 145
  Colline St-Eutrope 147
  Municipal Museum 147
  Théâtre Antique 146, 147

Pagnol, Marcel 7, 90, 105
Palais Longchamp 95, 96
Palais des Papes 141, 142, 143
Palais Princier 49, 50
Parc National du Mercantour 13, 52–53
Parc Naturel Régional du Lubéron 13, 152
Parc Ornithologique du Pont de Gau 117, 118
Parc Régional de Quayras 13
passports and visas 176
pastis 14
perfume factories 45, 54, 61
personal safety 179
pétanque 18
Petit Palais 141, 143
Petrarch 157
Peynier 167
pharmacies 178, 180
Picasso, Pablo 11, 55, 166
police 179
Pont du Gard 112, 122–123
Pont St-Bénézet 141–142
Porquerolles 73
Port-Cros 73
Port-Miou 97
Port-Pin 97
post offices 178, 179
Pourrières 99
Princess Grace Rose Garden 49
Provençal language 6–7, 8
public transport 26–28

Ramatuelle 78
Renoir, Pierre Auguste 9, 56
restaurants 20, 21, 31
  see also eating out
Riviera 12, 36
Rognes 22
Roquebrune-Cap Martin 46–47
Rougiers 166
Roussillon 17, 155–156, 158, 163
Route des Crêtes 75, 173
sailing 34
Salin-de-Giraud 169
Salon-de-Provence 102–103
  Maison de Nostradamus 102, 103
  Musée de l'Armes et d'Histoire Militaire 103
santons 105, 109, 129, 158
Séguret 158
senior citizens 180
Sentier des Ocres 17, 156
Serre-Chevalier 22
shopping 32, 178
  Alpes-Maritimes 61
  Camargue area 133
  Marseille area 109
  Var and Haute-Provence 87
  Vaucluse 163
skiing 22
spas 81–82, 88, 134
sports and activities 18, 22, 34, 62, 88, 110, 134, 164

St-Jean-Cap Ferrat 46
Stes-Maries-de-la-Mer
124–125, 133
Musée Baroncelli 125
St-Maximin-la-Ste-Baume
166
St-Paul-de-Mausole 129
St-Paul-de-Vence 22, 51
Auberge de la Colombe
d'Or 51
Fondation Maeght 51
St-Raphaël 22, 77
St-Rémy-de-Provence
128–129, 133, 134
Centre d'Art Présence
Van Gogh 129
St-Paul-de-Mausole 129
St-Tropez 22, 64, 68–71,
87
beaches 71
La Citadelle 69–70
Église St-Tropez 69
Musée de l'Annonciade
68, 69, 71
students/young travellers
180
sun safety 180

Tarascon 129
Château de Tarascon
129
Musée Souleïado 16,
129
taxis 28
telephones 179
Tende 52
Théâtre Antique, Arles
119
Théâtre Antique, Orange
146, 147
time differences 177,
178
tipping 31, 179
toilets 180
Toulon 25
tourist information
176–177
train services 24–25, 27,
177
travellers' cheques 177
Trets 167
Trigance 75, 174
Trophée des Alpes 45

Vacqueyras 158
Vaison-la-Romaine
148–149
Cathédrale Notre-Dame
de Nazareth 149, 170
medieval quarter 149
Pont Romain 170
Roman sites 148, 149,
171
walk 170–171
Val d'Enfer 128
Vallauris 11, 16
Vallée de Fontanalbe 53
Vallée des Merveilles 53
Van Gogh, Vincent 10,
120, 128–129
Var and Haute-Provence
63–88
Abbaye du Thoronet 80
accommodation 84–85
Bormes-les-Mimosas 79,
87
children's activities 80
Collobrières 79, 87
Corniche de l'Esterel
12, 64, 77
Digne-les-Bains 81–82,
87, 88
eating out 85–86
entertainment 88
Entrevaux 82–83
Gorges du Verdon 13,
22, 64, 74–76
Grimaud 22, 78–79
Hyères and Îles
d'Hyères 22, 72–73
map 64–65
Moustiers-Ste-Marie
80–81, 87
Ramatuelle 78
shopping 87
St-Tropez 22, 64,
68–71, 87
three-day itinerary
66–67
Vaucluse 135–164
Abbaye de Sénanque
150–151
accommodation
159–160
Avignon 33, 136,
140–143, 163, 164
Cavaillon 155
Châteauneuf-du-Pape
144–145
children's activities 158
Dentelles de Montmirail
158
eating out 161–162
entertainment 164
Fontaine-de-Vaucluse
156–157, 158
four-day itinerary
138–139
Gordes 22, 150–151
Lubéron 13, 136,
152–154
map 136–137
Mont Ventoux 22,
157–158
Orange 33, 146–147,
164
Roussillon 155–156,
158, 163
shopping 163
Vaison-la-Romaine
148–149
Vauvenargues 99, 166
Vence 54
Chapelle du Rosaire 11,
54
Villa Ephrussi de
Rothschild 46, 56–57
Villa Grecque Kérylos 46
Village des Bories 150,
151
Village des Tortues 80
Villefranche-sur-Mer
45–46
Chapelle St-Pierre 47
Villeneuve-lès-Avignon
142

walking and hiking trails
34
walks and tours
Camargue 168–169
Gorges du Verdon
172–174
heart of Provence
166–167
Vaison-la-Romaine
170–171
websites 176
windsurfing 34
wines 14, 31, 144–145,
158

youth hostels 30

Ziem, Felix 102
zoos 57, 95, 103, 104

Picture Credits

The Automobile Association would like to thank the following photographers, companies and picture libraries for their assistance in the preparation of this book.

Abbreviations for the picture credits are as follows - (t) top; (b) bottom; (c) centre; (l) left; (r) right; (AA) AA World Travel Library.

2(i) AA/C Sawyer; 2(ii) AA/A Baker; 2(iii) AA/C Sawyer; 2(iv) AA/C Sawyer; 2(v) AA/C Sawyer; 3(i) AA/B Smith 3(ii) AA/R Moore; 3(iii) AA/C Sawyer; 3(iv) AA/A Baker; 5 AA/C Sawyer; 6/7c AA/ R Strange; 6/7b Renn-Films/A2/RA12/The Kobal Collection; 7t AA/A Baker; 7c R Strange; 8b/g AA/C Sawyer; 8t AA/A Baker; 8b AA/C Sawyer; 9 Bridgestone Museum of Art, Tokyo, Japan/Giraudon/ Bridgeman Art Library, London; 10t AA/R Moore; 10/11 Musee d'Orsay, Paris, France/Bridgeman Art Library, London; 11c R Strange; 11b Private Collection/ Bridgeman Art Library, London; 12t AA/C Sawyer; 12c AA/C Sawyer; 12b AA/C Sawyer; 13t AA/C Sawyer; 13c AA/C Sawyer; 13b AA/R Moore; 14b/g AA/R Strange; 14t AA/C Sawyer; 14c AA/R Strange; 14b AA/R Strange; 15t AA/C Sawyer; 15c AA/R Strange; 15b AA/C Sawyer; 16b AA/A Baker; 16/17t AA/R Strange; 16/17c AA/R Moore; 17b AA/A Baker; 18t AA/C Sawyer; 18ct AA/C Sawyer; 18cl AA/C Sawyer; 18cr AA/C Sawyer; 19 AA/C Sawyer; 20/21t AA/C Sawyer; 20bl AA/C Sawyer; 20/21c AA/C Sawyer; 21c AA/C Sawyer; 21b AA/R Victor; 22 AA/C Sawyer; 23 AA/A Baker; 35 AA/C Sawyer; 36 AA/N Ray; 37 AA/D Ireland; 38 AA/C Sawyer; 39c AA/C Sawyer; 39b AA/C Sawyer; 40 AA/C Sawyer; 41c AA/C Sawyer; 41b AA/ R Moore; 42t AA/C Sawyer; 42c AA/C Sawyer; 43t AA/C Sawyer; 43c AA/C Sawyer; 43b AA/C Sawyer; 44 AA/A Baker; 45t AA/R Strange; 45c AA/R Strange; 46/47 AA/R Moore; 48 AA/C Sawyer; 48/9 AA/C Sawyer; 49t AA/A Baker; 49b AA/R Strange; 50 AA/A Baker; 51 AA/C Sawyer; 52 AA/C Sawyer; 53l AA/C Sawyer; 53r AA/C Sawyer; 54 AA/R Strange; 55l AA/C Sawyer; 55r AA/C Sawyer; 56/57 AA/C Sawyer; 63 AA/C Sawyer; 64 AA/C Sawyer; 66 B Hall; 67t AA/C Sawyer; 67c AA/B Smith; 68 AA/C Sawyer; 69l AA/C Sawyer; 69r AA/C Sawyer; 70/71 AA/C Sawyer; 71c AA/C Sawyer; 71b AA/C Sawyer; 72 AA/A Baker; 73 AA/A Baker; 74/75 AA/C Sawyer; 76 AA/C Sawyer; 77 B Hall; 78 AA/R Strange; 79 AA/C Sawyer; 80 AA/A Baker; 81tl AA/B Smith; 81b AA/C Sawyer; 82/3 AA/B Smith; 83 AA/R Moore; 89 AA/C Sawyer; 90 AA/C Sawyer; 92 AA/C Sawyer; 93c AA/C Sawyer; 93b AA/C Sawyer; 94 AA/C Sawyer; 95c AA/A Baker; 95b AA/A Baker; 96 AA/A Baker; 97 AA/C Sawyer; 98/99 AA/C Sawyer; 99 Pushkin Museum, Moscow, Russia/Giraudon/Bridgeman Art Library, London; 100 AA/C Sawyer; 100/1 AA/C Sawyer; 101l AA/R Strange; 101r AA/R Strange; 102t AA/A Baker; 102b AA/R Strange; 103 AA/A Baker; 104 AA/C Sawyer; 104/5 AA/B Smith; 105 AA/C Sawyer; 111 AA/B Smith; 112c AA/C Sawyer; 112b AA/R Strange; 113 AA/C Sawyer; 114c AA/A Baker; 114b AA/C Sawyer; 115t AA/R Strange; 115b AA/C Sawyer; 116 AA/R Strange; 116/7 AA/R Strange; 117t AA/R Strange; 117c AA/C Sawyer; 117b AA/C Sawyer; 118t AA/C Sawyer; 118c AA/C Sawyer; 119 AA/R Strange; 120t AA/A Baker; 120c AA/R Strange; 121 AA/C Sawyer; 122/3/b/g AA/B Smith; 122 AA/B Smith; 124/5 AA/R Moore; 125t AA/A Baker; 125b AA/C Sawyer; 126 AA/R Strange; 127cl AA/A Baker; 127tr AA/R Moore; 128 AA/R Strange; 128/9 AA/R Strange; 135 AA/R Moore; 136t AA/A Baker; 136b AA/C Sawyer; 137 AA/C Sawyer; 138 AA/A Baker; 139t AA/R Strange; 139c AA/A Baker; 140 AA/R Strange; 141t AA/C Sawyer; 141b AA/A Baker; 142/3 AA/A Baker; 144 AA/C Sawyer; 145t AA/A Baker; 145cl AA/A Baker; 145cr AA/C Sawyer; 146t AA/C Sawyer; 146b AA/C Sawyer; 147 AA/A Baker; 148 AA/A Baker; 149t AA/C Sawyer; 149c AA/T Oliver; 150 AA/A Baker; 150/1 AA/A Baker; 151 AA/C Sawyer; 152t AA/R Strange; 152b AA/R Strange; 153t AA/A Baker; 153b AA/T Oliver; 154t AA/C Sawyer; 154c AA/C Sawyer; 155 AA/A Baker; 156t AA/A Baker; 156b AA/R Strange; 157 AA/A Baker; 158 AA/R Strange; 165 AA/C Sawyer; 169 AA/C Sawyer; 170 AA/R Strange; 171 AA/R Strange; 174 AA/R Strange; 175 AA/A Baker; 179t AA/C Sawyer; 179cl AA/M Jourdan; 179cr AA/C Sawyer.

Every effort has been made to trace the copyright holders, and we apologise in advance for any accidental errors. We would be happy to apply the correction in the following edition of this publication.

SPIRAL GUIDE

Questionnaire

Dear Traveller
Your comments, opinions and recommendations are very important to us. Please help us to improve our travel guides by taking a few minutes to complete this simple questionnaire.

You do not need a stamp (unless posted outside the UK). If you do not want to remove this page from your guide, then photocopy it or write your answers on a plain sheet of paper.

***Send to:* The Editor, Spiral Guides, AA World Travel Guides,FREEPOST SCE 4598, Basingstoke RG21 4GY.**

Your recommendations...

Please state the establishment name, location and your reasons for recommending it.

____

____

____

____

If we use your recommendation in the next edition of the guide we will send you a free AA Spiral Guide of your choice.

About this guide...

Which title did you buy? ____________________

Where did you buy it? ____________________

When? m m / y y

Why did you choose an AA Spiral Guide?

____

____

____

Did this guide meet your expectations?
Please give your reasons.

Exceeded ☐ Met all ☐ Met most ☐

Fell below ☐

____

____

____

____

Were there any aspects of this guide that you particularly liked or thought could have been done better?

____

____

____

About you...

Name (Mr/Mrs/Ms) ____________________

Address ____________________

____

Postcode ____________________

Daytime tel nos ____________________

Please *only* give us your mobile number if you wish to hear from us about other products and services from the AA and partners by text or mms.

Which age group are you in?

Under 25 ☐ 25–34 ☐ 35–44 ☐ 45–54 ☐

55–64 ☐ 65+ ☐

How many trips do you make a year?

Less than one ☐ One ☐ Two ☐

Three or more ☐

Are you an AA member? Yes ☐ No ☐

About your trip...

When did you book? m m / y y

When did you travel? m m / y y

How long did you stay? ____________________

Did you buy any other travel guides for your trip?

☐ Yes ☐ No

If yes, which ones? ____________________

The information we hold about you will be used to provide the products and services requested and for identification, account administration, analysis, and fraud/loss prevention purposes. More details about how that information is used is in our privacy statement, which you'll find under the heading "Personal Information" in out terms and conditions and on our website: www.theAA.com. Copies are also available from us by post, by contacting the Data Protection Officer at AA, Fanum House, Basing View, Basingstoke, Hampshire, RG21 4EA.

We may want to contact you about pther products and services provided by us, or our partners (by mail, telephone) but please tick the box if you DO NOT wish to hear about such products and services from us by mail or telephone.

☐

Marseille Transport Map

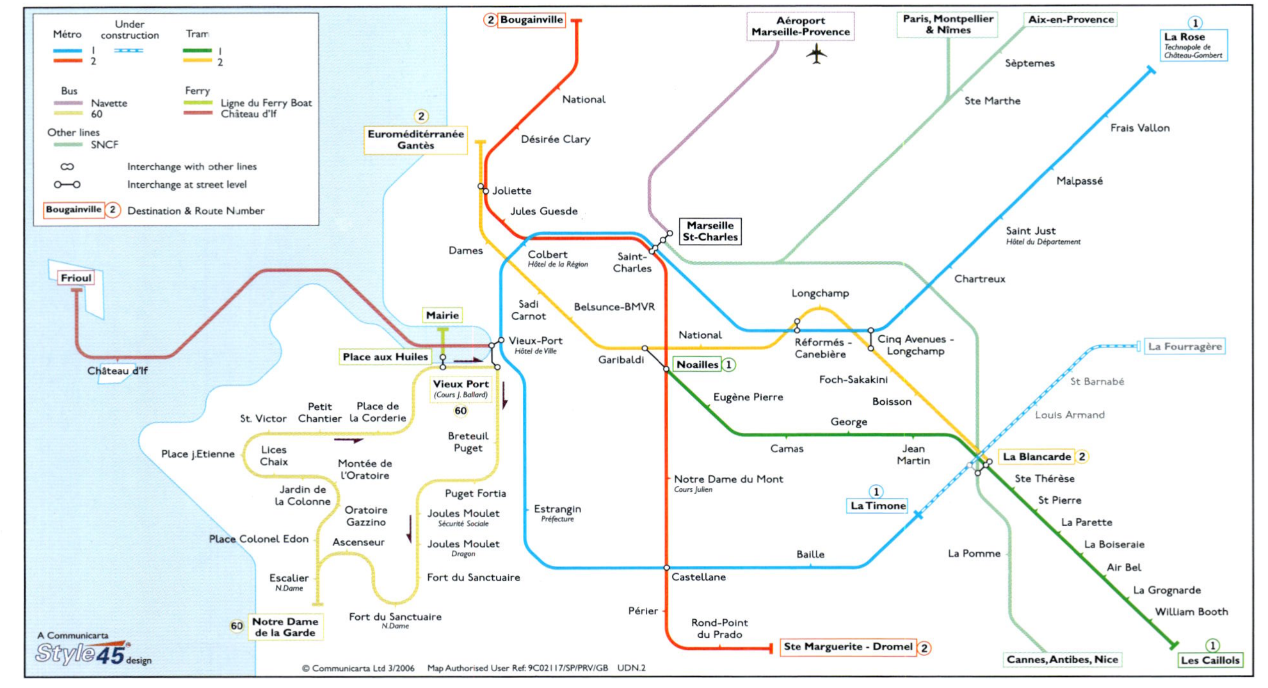